DATA PROCESSING:
The Fundamentals

DATA PROCESSING:
The Fundamentals

WILSON T. PRICE

Merritt College, Oakland, California

HOLT, RINEHART AND WINSTON

New York   Chicago   San Francisco   Philadelphia
Montreal   Toronto   London   Sydney   Tokyo
Mexico City   Rio de Janeiro   Madrid

Photographs used on section-opening pages and repeated in the frontispiece were supplied through the courtesy of the following corporations: Burroughs Corporation (p. 24 *bottom*); International Business Machines Corporation (p. 72 *top* and p. 104 *top*); Digital Equipment Corporation and Dysan Corporation (p. 104 *bottom*); Northern Telecom Systems Corporation (p. 138 *bottom*). Cover photographs are courtesy of International Business Machines Corporation.

Library of Congress Cataloging in Publication Data
Price, Wilson T.
    Data Processing, the fundamentals.

    Includes index.
    1. Electronic data processing.   I. Title.
QA76.P6686   001.64   81-23753
ISBN 0-03-059744-7   AACR2

Printed in the United States of America
          3   039   9 8 7 6 5 4

CBS COLLEGE PUBLISHING
Holt, Rinehart and Winston
The Dryden Press
Saunders College Publishing

Preface for the Instructor

The data processing instructor of today has a wide variety of excellent, comprehensive books from which to select when teaching an introductory course. However, in many instances, these books (some of which are virtually encyclopedias) are simply too much. For instance, a short course that serves as a brief orientation and simply hits the highlights does not require a massive, comprehensive book. Neither does a course in which a primary emphasis is placed on programming and the introductory text is used in conjunction with a beginning programming book. These and a host of other situations are best served by a book that extracts the introductory items of most significance to the beginning student. *Data Processing: The Fundamentals* is such a book. The emphasis is on eliminating bulk quantity while preserving important concepts and maintaining the highest quality.

A major effort has been made to provide the instructor maximum flexibility in adjusting use of the book to best serve the student audience. The book is divided into five basic sections. The first section describes principles of data processing through the use of a hypothetical small grocery business that grows into a large company. Many concepts of business data processing, including terminology, are introduced via a relatively "hardware independent" approach. This section lays the foundation and serves as a springboard to the rest of the text.

Even though this book is a condensed and highly concentrated introduction, there remains considerable flexibility regarding the use of Sections 2 through 5. For example, a course might be designed in which minimal emphasis is placed on computer hardware. In such a situation, it would be quite practical to omit Section 2 (Computers and Computer Hardware) entirely with little loss of continuity. However, as a rule, some discussion of at least various categories of computers is usually valuable. The point is, this book is designed with versatility in mind.

To enhance its usability, each section opens with a statement of objectives and a vocabulary list and closes with a summary and some relevant exercises. Included within the sections at appropriate places are topical exercises of the "jog the memory" category. Answers to these exercises are at the end of the section. The instructor should emphasize to the students the value of using these aids—their lives will be much easier.

Wilson T. Price

Preface for the Student

To say that the computer has had a broad and significant impact on our lives would be an understatement at the least. Microcomputers are currently available for $2000 or less which have computing powers in excess of large-scale machines costing a million or more dollars 25 years ago. If progress in transportation had proceeded at the same pace as that in computing, a round-the-world airline flight would take 24 minutes and the average automobile would get 550 miles per gallon. Indeed, high-speed computational devices have been a primary factor in rapidly changing techniques used in many areas. For instance, with the computational and information manipulation capabilities of the computer, the office clerk sees many of the office procedures significantly change, the accountant must adjust to dramatically changing accounting techniques, the business manager must learn to use highly sophisticated market forecasting tools, the engineer must become reoriented to a whole new set of ground rules in problem solving, and most importantly, the average individual must adjust to the manner in which computers affect his or her life. As a result, it seems important that every college student gain a basic knowledge about how this powerful tool affects our lives in so many ways and about how we can make it best serve our needs.

To facilitate the learning process, each section of this book includes a number of built-in aids. The section openings include a set of learning objectives and a vocabulary list. Study these and you will gain an insight as to what is coming. Included within are exercises which are essentially "minute tests" to give you a feel of whether or not you caught the significant points of the preceding section. It is intended that each of these exercises be completed and checked before proceeding with pages which follow. (Answers are given at the end of the section.)

The computer field is a vast and broad one and is rapidly changing. Most professionals in the field find it exciting and very challenging. Every effort has been made to reflect some of this excitement in this book and to design it so that it is easy and interesting for you to use. I hope that it meets this objective.

Wilson T. Price

Acknowledgments

The first recognition must go to my students who have in so many ways contributed, directly and indirectly, to the formulation of this book.

Numerous colleagues have offered advice and suggestions, many of which are incorporated in this book. I would like to express particular thanks to Frank Kushner, Towson State University and George Miller, North Seattle Community College for the careful analysis of this project. Furthermore, I owe thanks to Brete Harrison, Senior Editor, Holt, Rinehart and Winston who first urged me to take on this project.

To each of them, my sincerest thanks.

Contents

Section 3   Computer Software and Programming

Section 4   Advanced Software Systems

Section 5   System Design and Development

DATA PROCESSING:
The Fundamentals

1

Basic Concepts of Business Data Processing

OBJECTIVES

The purpose of this section is to help you discover data processing concepts that are common to business. The vehicle for this is a hypothetical grocery business that evolves into a modern, automated supermarket. Through this example with its overall data processing problems and applications you will gain an insight into the following.

- The importance of efficient data handling and processing systems in business
- The need to analyze and carefully define systems for handling paperwork and processing
- Operations that are basic to business data processing, whether performed manually, mechanically, or with computers
- The overall concept of a system as the means and procedures by which an organization does a job
- Principles of files, records, and fields
- The concept of master-transaction processing
- Principles of records and files relative to the computer
- The routing and handling of paperwork and data within a business organization.
- The need for reports in the business operation
- Basic notions behind system design and analysis

Key terminology important in this section includes:

data collection	online
field	output
file	record
input	sort
Master Record	source document
master-detail processing	system
merge	Transaction Record
offline	Universal Product Code (UPC)

Introduction to PQR

BASIC CONCEPTS   Whenever the average person hears the words "data processing," the word "computer," or even IBM, immediately comes to mind. We must not be saddled with that misconception. Our ancestors were processing data long before computers or the International Business Machines Corporation came into being. To operate virtually any business, records must be maintained and data processed. The information handling and processing functions that are vital to the existence of virtually every business can be grouped as follows:

- *Input.*   Information must be entered into the processing system. For example, an order for goods must be written on an order form and then entered into the system.
- *Processing.*   Once entered into a system the data must be processed. For instance, a sales order must be filled, a customer billed, accounts updated, and so on.
- *Storage.*   The results of processing must be stored for later use.
- *Output.*   The results of processing must be printed or otherwise recorded. For example, an end-of-the month summary and billing for each customer of a department store must be printed.
- *Retrieval.*   Stored data must be readily accessible when it is needed.

It is important to note that the preceding operations make no reference to the computer. However, they are very significant since they are basic to the processing of data whether they are accomplished by the simplest of manual methods or through use of the computer.

THE NATURE OF BUSINESS   To gain a better insight into the principles of data processing, let us consider a hypothetical wholesale grocery company. The PQR Wholesale Grocery Company was founded during the early 1930s. Although the founder knew the grocery business well, his background in accounting and bookkeeping was very limited. As a result his desk became buried in paperwork and his business began to flounder. One evening he sat down at his desk to ponder his problems and try to come up with some ideas. The results of his efforts are shown in Figure 1-1. It was quite clear that help was needed and so he hired a consulting company that specialized in such matters. The consultant, working with the founder, grouped the data processing functions of PQR as shown in Figure 1-2. Here we can see that the data processing operation can indeed become significant. The paperwork tasks include:

1. Incoming goods
    - Purchase order processing
    - Verification of receipt of goods
    - Accounts payable (money owed to suppliers)

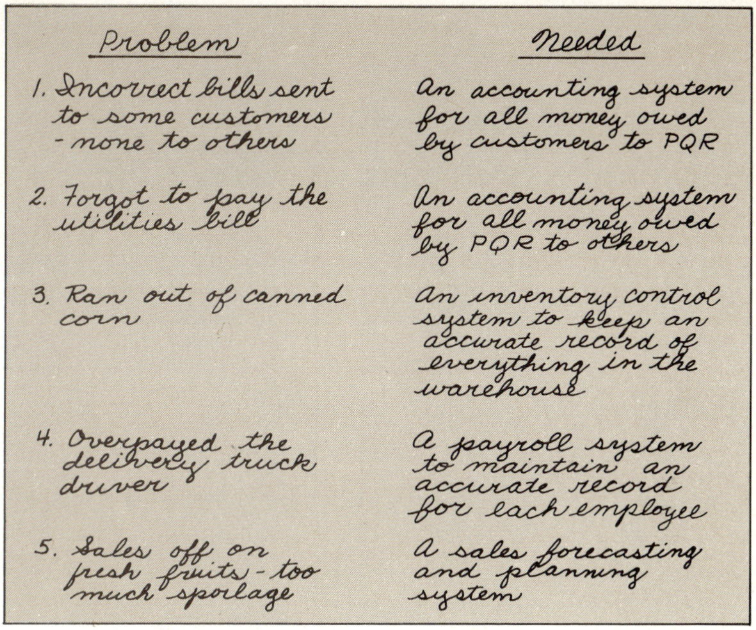

**Figure 1-1
Problems and
solutions.**

Problem	Needed
1. Incorrect bills sent to some customers - none to others	An accounting system for all money owed by customers to PQR
2. Forgot to pay the utilities bill	An accounting system for all money owed by PQR to others
3. Ran out of canned corn	An inventory control system to keep an accurate record of everything in the warehouse
4. Overpayed the delivery truck driver	A payroll system to maintain an accurate record for each employee
5. Sales off on fresh fruits - too much spoilage	A sales forecasting and planning system

2. Internal processing
   • Inventory control of goods
3. Sale of goods to customers
   • Order handling and filling
   • Delivery
   • Accounts receivable (money owed to the company)
   • Collections
4. Institutional functions
   • Company payroll
   • Cost and price studies
   • Operating analysis

It is important to recognize that various segments of a data processing system are closely related and must not be considered independently of each other. For example:

• Sales projections are partially based on past sales.
• Purchasing is based on sales projections and existing inventory.
• Current inventories are based on purchases and sales.
• Billing and collecting are based on orders shipped.
• Payroll is based on all phases of the operation.
• And so on.

Task | Data Processing

Purchase | Purchase order issued

Receive | Match with purchase order | Update inventory information | Pay for goods received

Control | Maintain inventory records | Cost studies to reduce costs

Serve | Sales studies to provide selection

Sell | Order processing | Billing | Collecting

Institutional processing | Payroll | Operating analyses

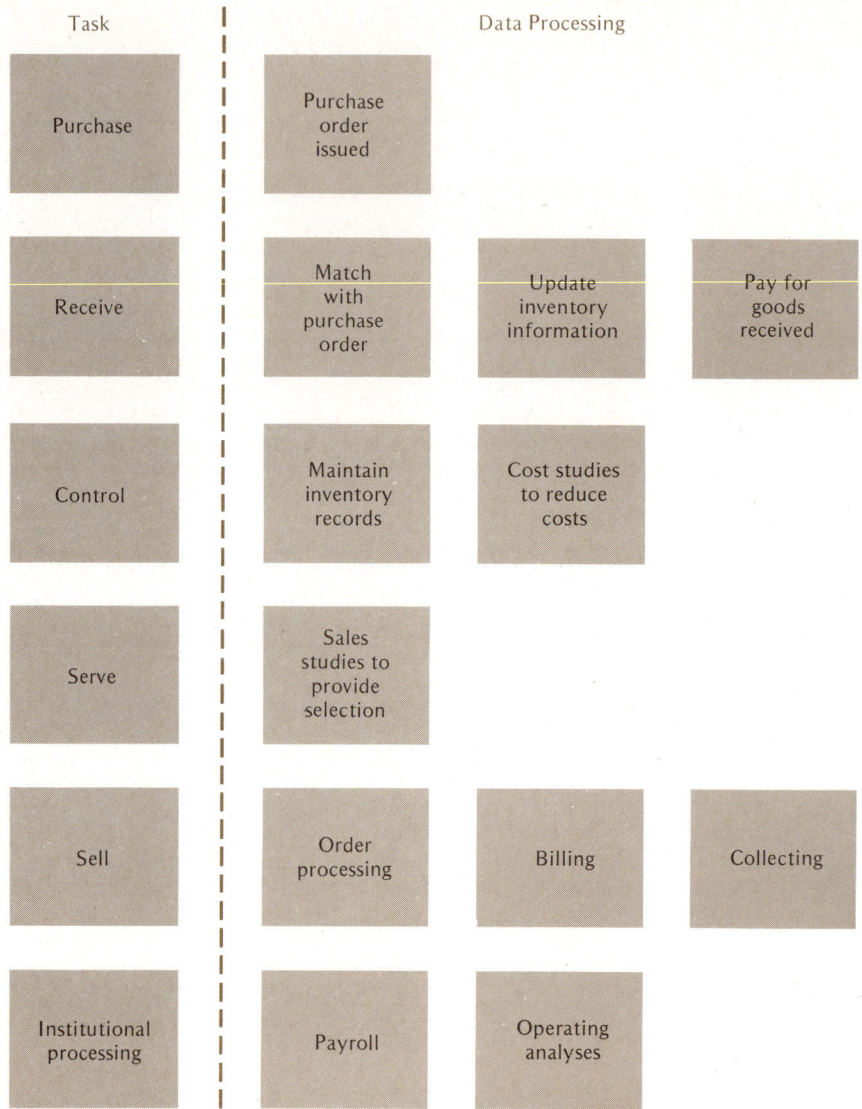

**Figure 1-2
Data processing
functions at PQR.**

Each portion of the system influences and is influenced by each other portion of the system.

The degree of success, or the failure, of any company depends to a large extent on the overall efficiency of its data processing systems. These systems may be simple, manual procedures for a very small company or they may be highly complex and involve the use of sophisticated computers in the case of a large corporation. However, the need for a well-planned system is as crucial to the well being of a small company as it is for a large corporation.

EXERCISE

1.1   Comment on the observation that "in any business, data processing operations are always carried out by the computer department."

The Customer Accounting System

With these thoughts in mind, let us turn our attention to one phase of the PQR data processing need—the *customer accounting system*. To keep things simple for this first example, it is assumed that the customer receives the goods at the time the order is placed or when the goods are delivered by PQR. Each customer maintains an account with PQR and is billed at the end of the month. Briefly, the customer accounting system involves maintaining customer account records for customer purchases and payments as follows:

- As each purchase is made the charges and other information are recorded.
- As each payment is received a receipt is prepared and recorded.
- At the end of the month each customer account is brought up to date by adding new charges and subtracting payments.
- When the account records are updated, a bill is prepared and mailed to each customer.

A broad simplification of this overall processing, illustrated in Figure 1-3, gives us an insight into the system. Basic to the system are the following data components.

Periodic input to the system:
- *Sales Order Records*
- *Payment Received Records*

Permanent information requiring periodic updating:
- *Customer Master Records*

These concepts are illustrated and described in Figures 1-4, 1-5, 1-6, and 1-7.

EXERCISE

1.2   What is the difference between the Payment Received Record and the monthly sales file?

Data Processing Aspects of This Case Study

BASIC TERMINOLOGY   Before proceeding further with this case study, let us review the data processing concepts introduced by this example. The function of this system is to

Monthly transactions

Sales Order Records
(Charges)

Bakery Goods 72.22

Produce   125.38

Canned Corn 55.75

Payment Received Records
(Credits)

Returns   58.12

Payment   228.18

Customer
record

JOHNSON GROCERY

Balance
due   182.80

Old balance	182.80
+Charges	253.35
	436.15
—Credits	286.30
Updated balance	149.85

Updated
customer
record

JOHNSON GROCERY

Balance
due   149.85

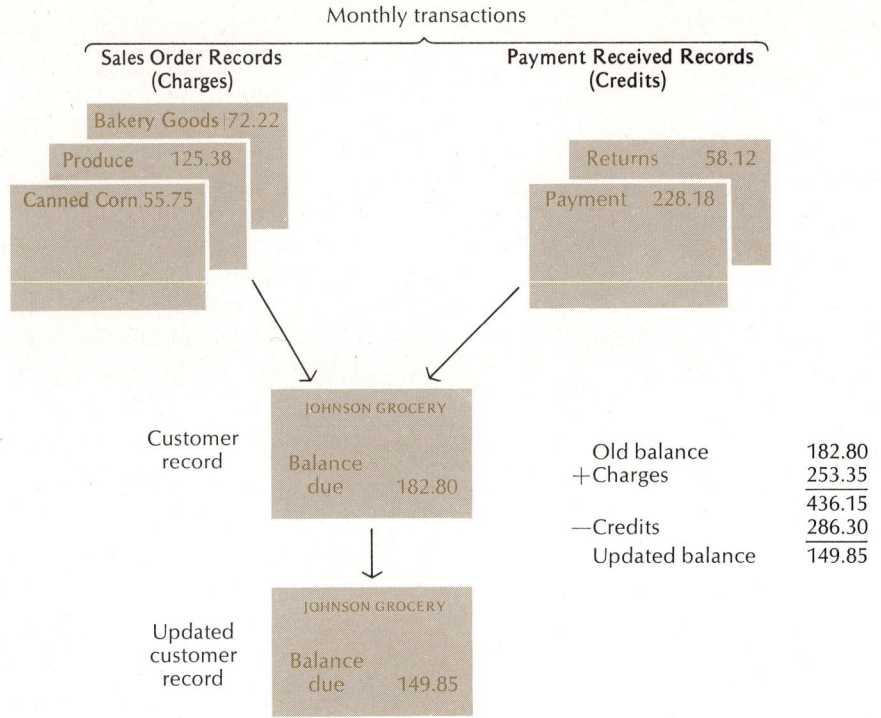

Figure 1-3
Updating a customer
account.

- Maintain a record of customer purchases and payments
- Prepare management reports summarizing sales
- Periodically update customer accounts
- Prepare customer billings

In general, the term *system* may be defined as

System   The method or means by which an organization or individual accomplishes a task or set of tasks required by the organization.

A person employed in data processing continually encounters systems. For example, all employees are quite concerned about their periodic paychecks, which are one of the end results of a *payroll* system. At first consideration, calculating take-home pay might appear to be a simple job, but it often involves one of the more complex systems in the operation of the average company. This complexity is usually caused by the many intricate deductions that are withheld, either at the employee's request or as required by the government. The actual printing of the check is a very small part of the operation. We should note that a payroll system can be manual for a very small company, or it can be highly automated for a large corporation.

Fundamental to PQR's customer accounting system is the *data base,* * that is, the basic set of information around which processing revolves. For PQR this is, of course, the Customer Master File consisting of the customer records. In a real-life situation these records would contain far more information on the customer than is shown in the simplified example. From the data base a broad set of reports can be prepared, such as those covering accounts that are past due and the sales patterns of various customers. Obviously, the broader the data base (that is, the more information contained in the customer record), the more versatile and useful it is to the management and employees of PQR.

The terms *file* and *record* are often confusing to the beginning data processing student. As we have seen, the Customer Master Record is a set of

Database as a single word is defined in Section 4.

Figure 1-4 Input to the system: sales order data.

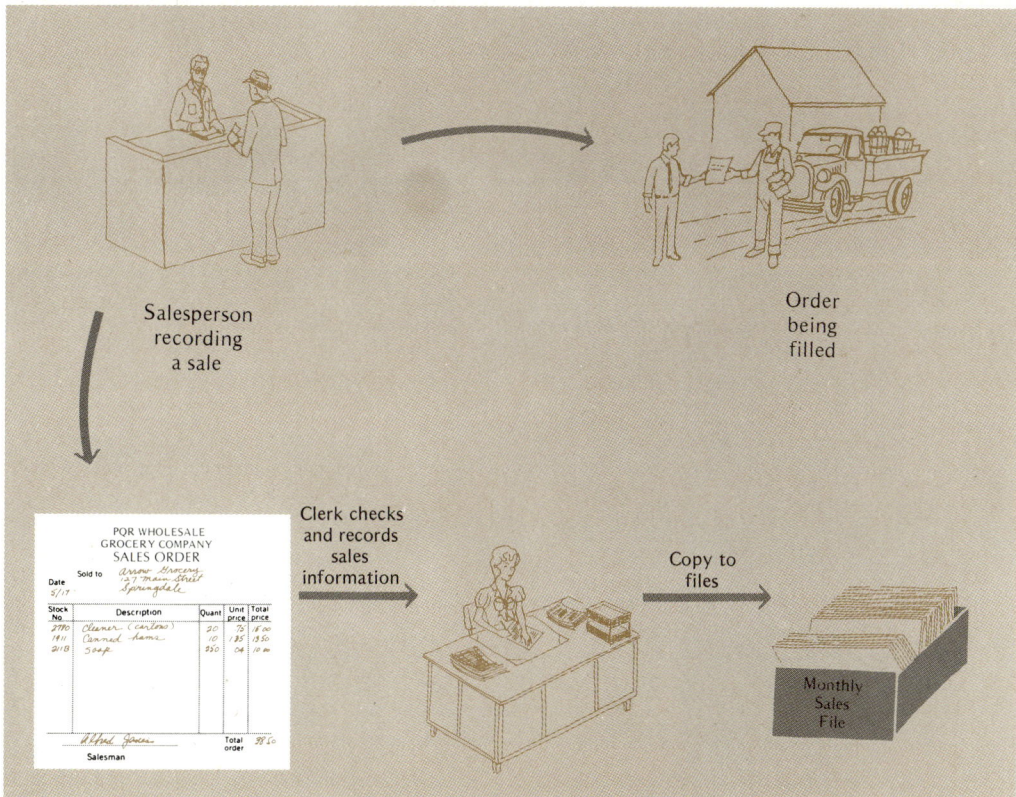

As each office copy of the Sales Order Form is received, it is transmitted to a clerk who checks the entries and records sales information. The Sales Order Form is then placed in a file drawer labeled *Monthly Sales File,* where it remains until the end of the month.

information describing a customer account. In general a record is defined as follows:

Record A group of related facts or *fields* of information treated as a unit.

Field A basic unit of information.

Thus the Master Record consists of the customer name *field,* the address *field,* and so on. The Payroll Record for the employees of a business firm would contain all fields relating to them for payroll processing, such as name, Social Security number, and pay rate. Similarly, each *Transaction Record (detail record)* in the PQR system includes data on one particular transaction, which may be a purchase or a payment. As we have seen, the collection of Master Records form the Master File, the Payment Records form the Payment File, and so on. In general we can think of a file as

Figure 1-5 Input to the system: payment received data.

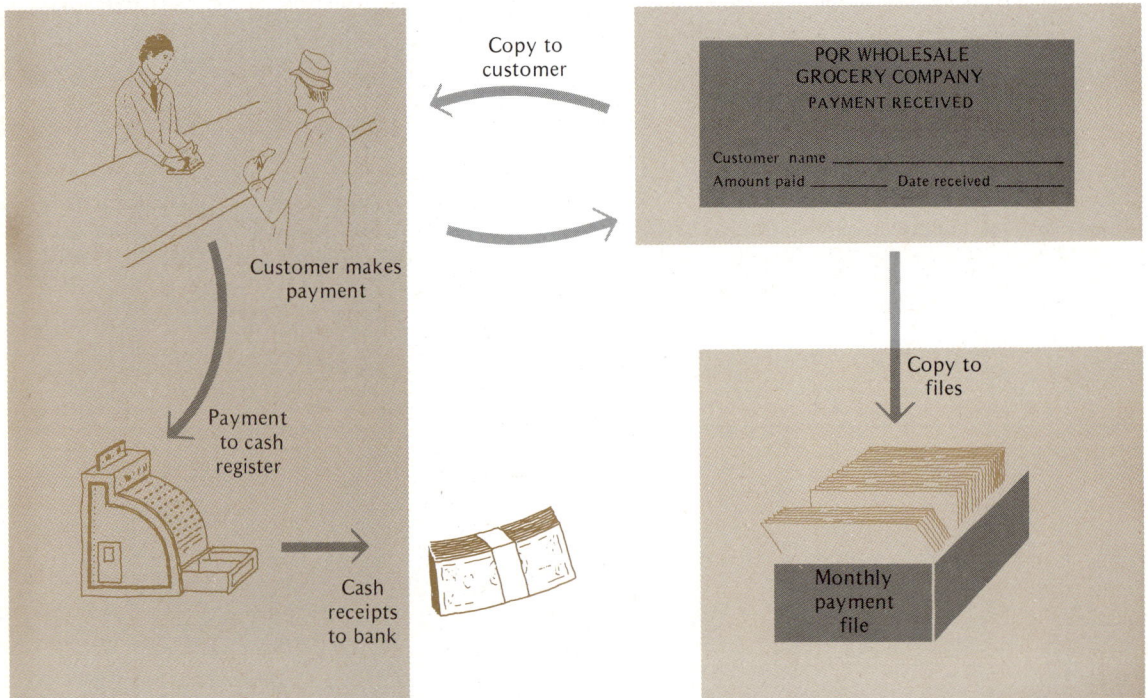

As each payment is received, a clerk fills out a Payment Received Form and places the money in the cash register. There it remains until the end of the day, when it is taken to the bank. One copy of each Payment Received Record is given to the customer; the other is placed in a file drawer labeled *Monthly Payment File,* where it remains until the end of the month.

File   The organized collection of all the records of a given type.

Thus we see the following relationships:

A COLLECTION OF RELATED **FIELDS** FORMS A **RECORD.**

A COLLECTION OF **RECORDS** FORMS A **FILE.**

The data base for our accounting system is the Customer Master File; the system itself consists of a basic procedure through which the end objective, that of maintaining customer records and preparing required reports, is achieved. This procedure illustrates the basic principles of data processing (whether manual or automated), namely, the *gathering, processing, storing,* and *transmitting* of information.

DATA COLLECTION AND RECORDING   As the name implies, data collection is the gathering of the original information to be entered into the system. In the PQR system this occurred each time a salesperson wrote out a sales order or a payment receipt. Needless to say,

Figure 1-6   Customer Master Record and File.

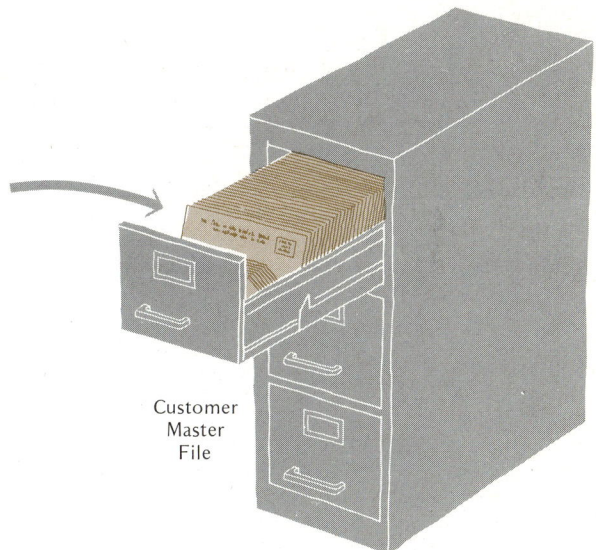

PQR WHOLESALE GROCERY COMPANY		CUSTOMER MASTER RECORD	
Name *Arrow Grocery*			
Address *127 Main St. Springdale*			
Discount Group *2A*		Credit Limit *$1000.00*	
Closing date	Purchases	Payments	Balance
1/31	150.50	25.50	125.00
2/28	42.50	50.00	117.50
3/31	—	117.50	0.00
4/30	73.54	—	73.54

Customer Master File

For each customer of PQR, a *Customer Master Record* is maintained. The master record includes the company name, address, and other general data, as well as a monthly summary of transactions for that company. A master record is prepared for each new customer desiring an account with PQR. At the end of each month this record is updated by entering the summary of the monthly transactions (described in a later section of this section).

All of the Customer Master Records are stored in a file cabinet in alphabetic order. This file, called the *Customer Master File.* Note that the Customer Master File is simply a collection of all Customer Master Records arranged in a useful and logical order. The file does *not* contribute any additional information above and beyond that contained in the individual records.

Figure 1-7.   Account updating procedure.

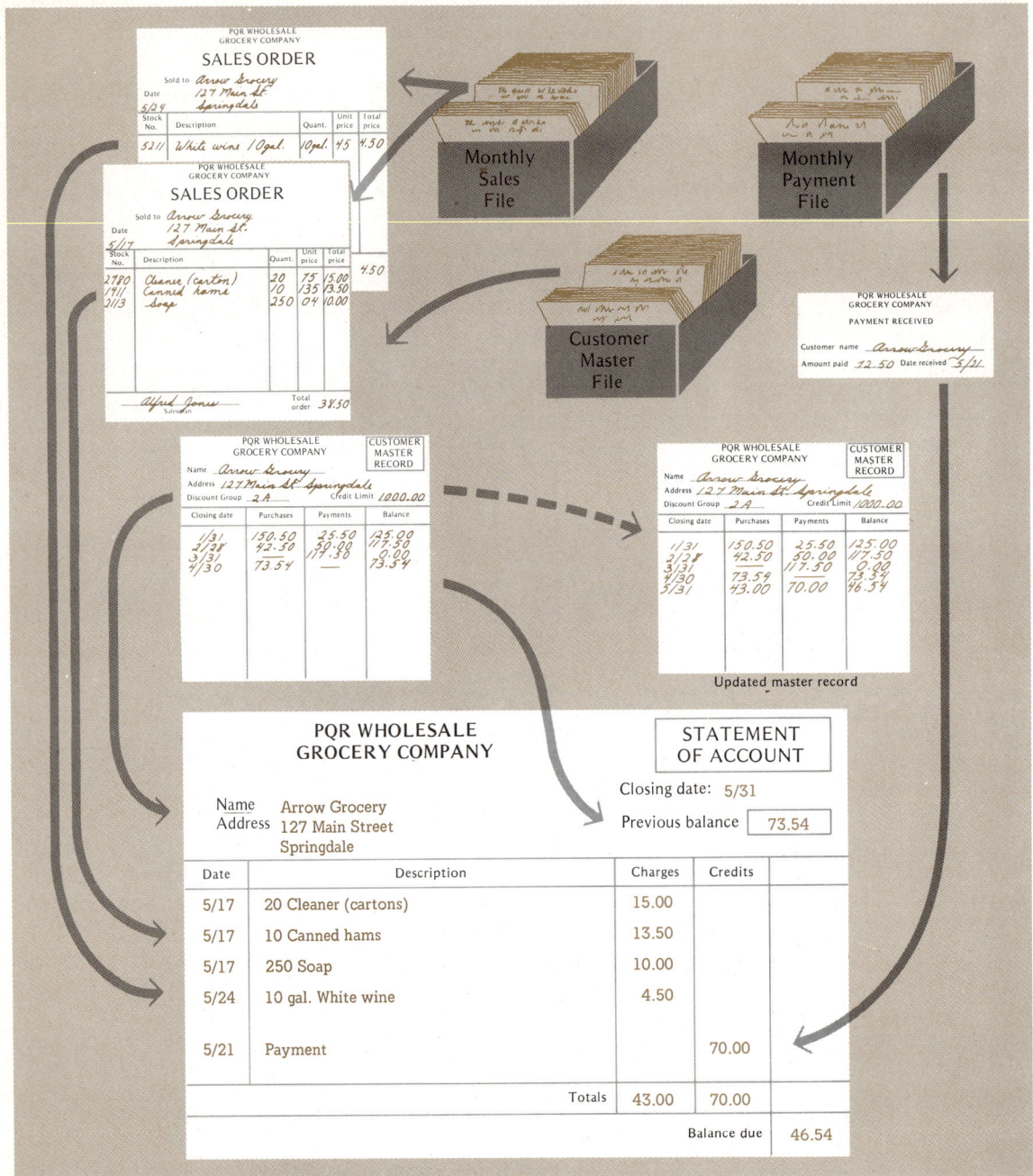

At the end of the month each customer account is updated using the data stored in the Monthly Payment File, the Monthly Sales File, and the Customer Master File. At this time a customer *Statement of Account* is prepared and mailed to the customer. We can see that master data from the Master File is *merged* with transaction data from the Payment and Sales Files to update the account and prepare the Statement of Account. The updated Master Record is also shown.

as each record is written it is then checked to verify that all entries are correct. In each case the original information is recorded on a *source document* and then entered into the system.

SORTING A number of processing operations are performed on the data within this system. Prior to performing the account updating, the records in each Payment and Sales File are arranged in alphabetic sequence. In data processing this is commonly call *sorting,* which simply means to place data in some type of order. This order may be alphabetic, as is the case in this system, or it could be numeric, based on customer number (not used in this simple illustration). In numerical sorting records can be sorted into an ascending sequence in which the smallest number would be first, with progressively larger numbers following; for example, 25, 33, 59, 82, 128 is an ascending sequence. Occasionally a descending sequence, which is just the opposite, is used; for example, 128, 82, 59, 33, 25 is a descending sequence.

MERGING The operation of bringing two or more sets of data together for processing purposes is illustrated in Figures 1-3 and 1-7, in which the Transaction Record information is combined with the Master Record to update the Master Record. This process is commonly referred to as *merging.*

CALCULATING AND SUMMARIZING At the end of each month it is necessary to perform mathematical operations in order to bring each customer's record up to date. This involves calculating total charges and total credits as illustrated in Figure 1-7 for Arrow Grocery. In referring to the Statement of Account we see that the information is recorded in two forms: the *detailed* information, which includes item descriptions and dates; and the monthly *summaries,* which are results of the calculations. As we can see, the updated Customer Master Record includes only the monthly summaries.

REPORT GENERATION The information retained in the Master File (or any other data file, for that matter) is of little value if it cannot be retrieved. In the example, Statement of Account reports are prepared from the data files at the end of each month. Note that this type of report contains detailed information in the form of the items purchased and the payments received. The preparation of other reports would be a simple matter; for example, the clerk might be instructed to prepare a report consisting of the customers' names and their account balances for all customers whose balances exceed their credit limit.

MASTER-DETAIL PROCESSING This process of bringing together two or more files (or *merging,* in a broad sense of the word) to perform updating is commonly referred to as *master-detail processing* (or *master-transaction* processing), and is the most common type of task encountered in business data processing. In this example the Customer Master File is the *master file* and the Monthly Sales File and Monthly Payment File are the *detail files.* Information recorded on detail records is used to update the corresponding master record and produce an updated master record and billing statement. The sequence of operations is then (1) sort the detail file(s) and the master file (if it is not already in proper sequence), (2) get the next set of detail records and their corresponding master record, (3) update the master, and (4) repeat steps 2 and 3 until the processing is complete.

EXERCISES

1.3   What is the difference between a record and a data base?

1.4   Define, either by description or examples, the following terms: field, record, file, system, merge, and summarize.

Computerized Data Processing

THE NATURE OF INVENTIONS   As the years progressed PQR grew and expanded its operations into the retail supermarket area. With this growth came increasingly complex data processing needs. As technology evolved, the company kept abreast by using the latest automated data processing equipment available. In this respect it has been observed that there are two types of inventions. First, there are those inventions that allow us to do things that would otherwise be impossible. For instance, we could stand and flap our arms all day long and never fly. However, the airplane allows us to do the "impossible." Second, there are those inventions that improve our ability to do things of which we are already capable. For example, we can dig a hole by hand—but a shovel makes the task much easier. If the hole is to be large, then a backhoe is even better. But we pay a price for these better ways. A backhoe is far more complex to design and requires much more skill to operate than a shovel.

The computer is one of those inventions that allows us to do a better job of something which we can already do. The automated supermarket that PQR opened during the 1970s was designed around the use of the computer. Its design and manufacture involve very sophisticated techniques. The programming required to make it do the job had to be precise and detailed. Systems and procedures of the business had to conform to the manner in which the computer was programmed. Even the computer operator and the clerk who entered information into the machine required special training.

RECORDS AND FILES IN THE COMPUTER   In dealing with computers a common notion is that "the computer does it all." However, even with the modern computer the record-file concept (described for the manual system) is still important. In fact, with the versatility of the modern computer and its huge storage capacities, record and file handling are an important facet of data processing. Even the relatively small and inexpensive business microcomputers available today provide file processing capabilities that were available only on very large machines 20 years ago. The concept of records and files on magnetic storage media such as tape and disk is discussed on a later section.

The computerized version of PQR's system now involves extensive use of magnetic-disk storage. This medium, as we shall learn, provides a very large storage capacity and nearly instant access to any and all of the data stored. Furthermore, the versatility of disk storage makes it possible to integrate and coordinate various systems more fully.

For the present we shall focus our attention on cornflakes—a staple item in any grocery store. Within the computer data base we would find an inventory record for every product in the store, including our venerable cornflakes. This concept is illustrated in Figure 1-8. Here we see that the record includes the item stock number, the unit price, the number of pieces on hand, and other information. Now let us consider what takes place when we stop at PQR and purchase a box of cornflakes.

THE AUTOMATED CHECKSTAND The key to automating supermarket operations is the encoding of machine-readable information on each item in the store. This is done through use of the *Universal Product Code,* or *UPC,* an example of which is shown here.

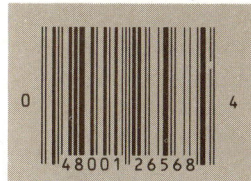

Each food manufacturer—for example, General Mills—is assigned a unique 5-digit code (the left portion of the UPC). The manufacturer then assigns a unique 5-digit code (the right portion of the UPC) to each product in the product line, such as our box of cornflakes. Stored within the computer for this item (stock number) is such information as item description and price (see Figure 1-8).

Basic elements of the automated supermarket are

- Encoded information on each product item (the UPC)
- An electronic scanning device for reading that encoded information

**Figure 1-8
Example data in an
inventory record.**

- Linking of the scanning device to an electronic cash register (a UPC scanner and electronic cash register are shown in Figure 1-9)
- Linking of one or more cash registers to a computer

Figure 1-10 illustrates what happens when the clerk passes the UPC symbol on the cornflakes over the scanner unit.

- The coded information from the UPC symbol is read by the sensing unit and transmitted to the computer.
- The computer searches its inventory file for the proper record as keyed on the UPC inventory number, 81200 in this case.
- Upon finding the record, pricing and descriptive information is returned to the cash register and recorded on the register slip.

We should note that this file is commonly called an *online* file since it is always ready and available to the computer—as opposed to an *offline* file such as a deck of punched cards stored in a file cabinet, which is not automatically available.

As each transaction is transmitted to the computer the customers see nothing more than the price rung up on the register. However, the transaction information is instantly recorded within the online data file, and, referring to

**Figure 1-9
The Sweda UPC
scanner linked to a
cash register.
(*Courtesy Sweda
International.*)**

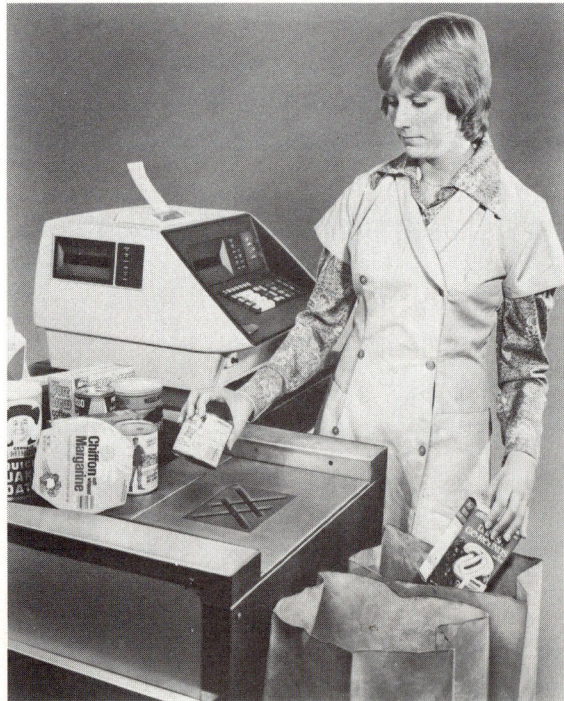

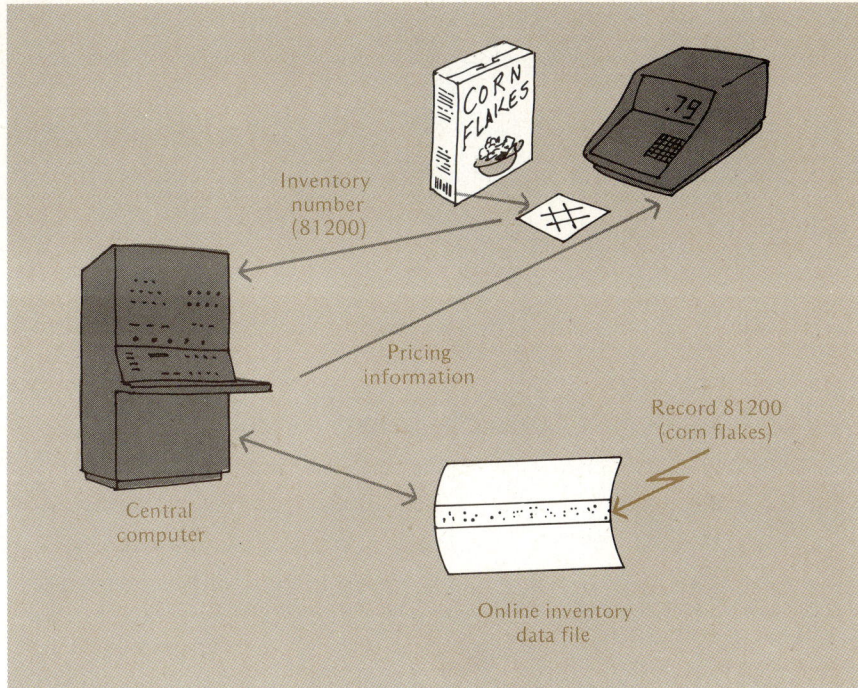

**Figure 1-10
Direct assessing of
information in
a data file.**

Figure 1-8, the stock on hand will be decreased from 501 to 500. The same will occur for each item that we and the other customers purchase. Obviously, at the end of the day all inventory figures will be complete and will accurately reflect the stock in the store. We might logically conclude, therefore, that the store manager could run down the list of all items in the inventory and place orders for those that are at low stock levels. But wait, why should the manager do this? Why not take advantage of the computerized information system and have the computer do it automatically? As described in the following paragraph, this indeed is the way in which the problem is handled.

EXERCISE

1.5   How is pricing information stored in the UPC data encoded on each item in the store?

A Data Processing Cycle

**GENERATING
AN ORDER**   Let us consider once again the inventory *and other information* stored in the computer regarding our cornflakes. In Figure 1-11 we see, in addition to the stock number, description, and price, the following:

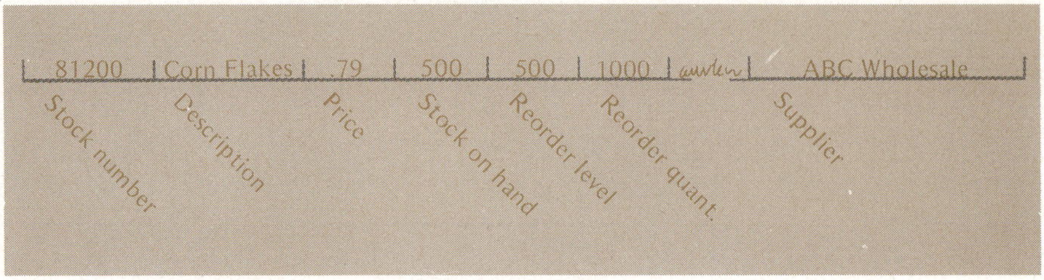

Figure 1-11
Example data in file.

- *Stock on hand.*   Number of boxes of cornflakes currently in stock.
- *Reorder level.*   Stock level at which more cornflakes must be ordered.
- *Reorder quantity.*   Number of boxes to be ordered when an order must be placed.
- *Supplier.*   The wholesaler from whom the cornflakes are to be purchased.

Now, at the end of each day a special processing run can be made. For every item that has dropped to the reorder level, a purchase order can be generated automatically. A copy will be mailed to the wholesaler (ABC Wholesale) and another copy retained in the files of PQR with further computer processing awaiting delivery of the ordered cornflakes (see Figure 1-12).

THE SEQUENCE Once this piece of paper leaves the supermarket it causes a chain of events
OF EVENTS to take place, both at ABC Wholesale and PQR Supermarket. The general sequence is as follows:

1. At ABC Wholesale
   - Enter the order into a computer sales order file and prepare order documents.
   - Assemble the order and ship it to PQR.
   - Prepare and send a bill based on the goods shipped.

Figure 1-12
Computer preparation
of purchase orders.

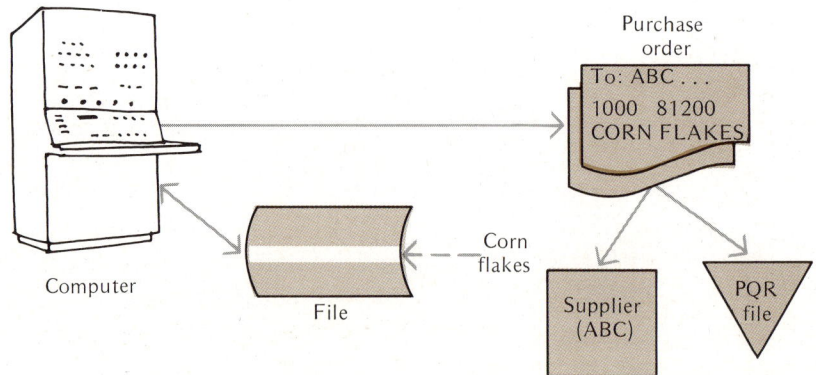

2. Back to PQR Supermarket
   • Receive the shipment of goods.
   • Verify the goods received against the original order.
   • Receive the bill, verify it against goods received, and then enter the billing information into the computer.
   • Issue a check.
3. Back to ABC Wholesale
   • Receive payment.
   • Enter into computer, credit the account of PQR.

Let us consider the steps of this process in more detail.

ORDER PROCESSING When the purchase order from the supermarket is received at the wholesaler, it becomes a source document to the ABC data processing system. Thus the first step is to enter it into the computer for automated handling. At the end of each day shipping orders are run and, for each sales order, a shipping order is produced consisting of the following copies:

1. *Order acknowledgement:* sent to the customer to verify the order.
2. *Office copy:* filed in the office for information purposes.
3. *Picking copy:* together with the packing slip, sent to shipping, where the order is prepared. When the order is filled, this document will serve as input to the computer system.
4. *Packing slip:* included with the merchandise shipped.

This process is illustrated in Figure 1-13.

Figure 1-13 Order processing at ABC Wholesaler.

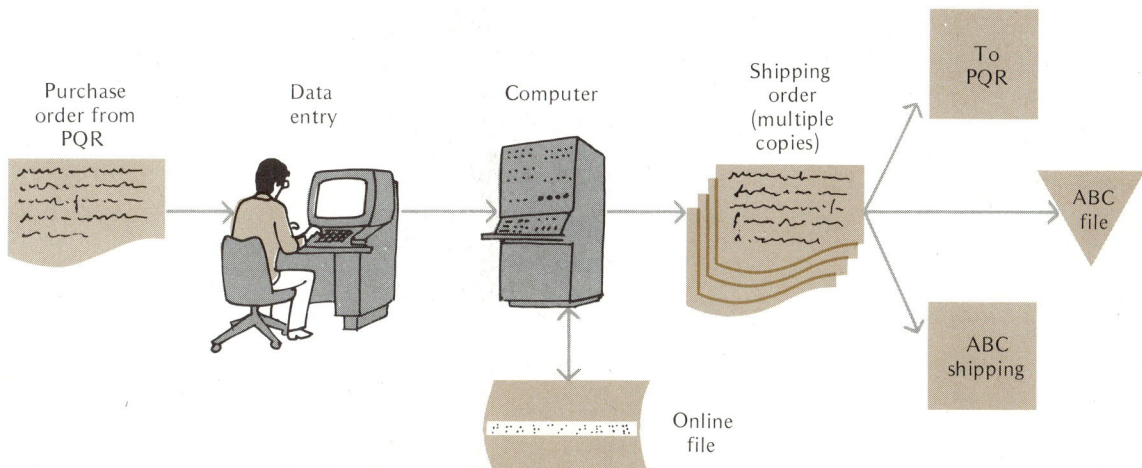

Using the order "picking" copy, the order is filled in the shipping department. If items are out of stock, a notation is made on both the picking copy and the shipping copy. The ordered goods, together with the packing slip, are shipped to the customer (PQR) and the picking slip is returned to the office. A continuation of this "flow" is illustrated in Figure 1-14.

INVOICING Upon receiving the processed picking slip from the warehouse, the shipping information is immediately entered into the computer. The original order record within the computer is brought up to date with regard to exactly what was shipped. At this point shipping charges, appropriate discounts, and other billing information can be entered. The computer now contains enough information to generate an invoice (a bill), which is mailed to the customer. This sequence of steps is illustrated in Figure 1-15.

Processing this invoice and getting it to the customer as quickly as possible are of primary importance. In most billing systems the customer has a certain period of time dating from the date of the invoice in which to pay. For example, a "NET 30" billing means that the billed amount is due within 30 days of the invoice date. If the accounting department is slow in processing the invoices, this free credit period is lengthened and the total amount owed ABC by its customers (the accounts receivable) becomes larger. The result: more working capital (money) is required to operate the company. For precisely this reason many businesses will grant a 2 percent discount if the bill is paid within 10 days. In the ABC system entry of the shipping information also causes some other actions to take place. If any goods are out of stock, a *backorder* relating to the PQR order is generated and stored within the computer. When the backordered goods are received and placed in inven-

Figure 1-14 Order preparation in the ABC warehouse.

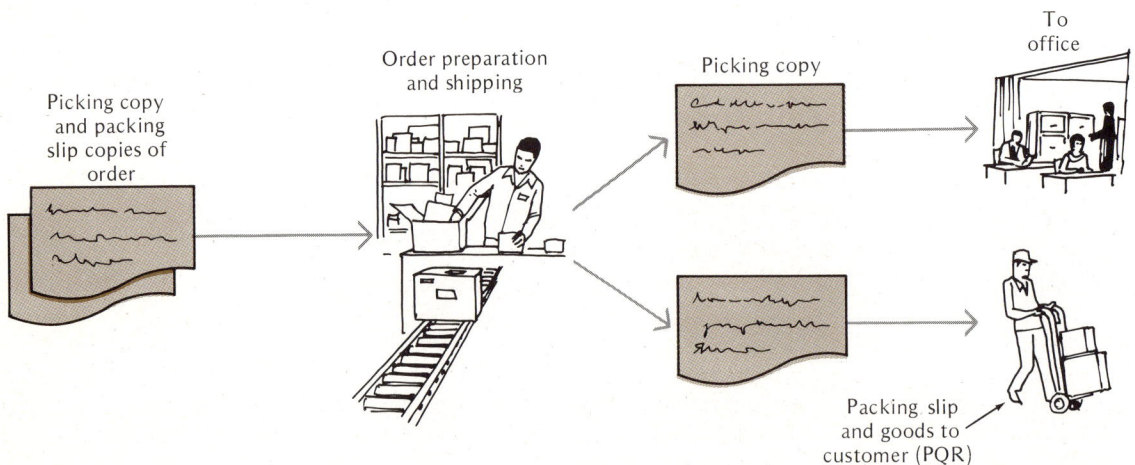

Figure 1-15 Preparing an invoice for merchandise shipped.

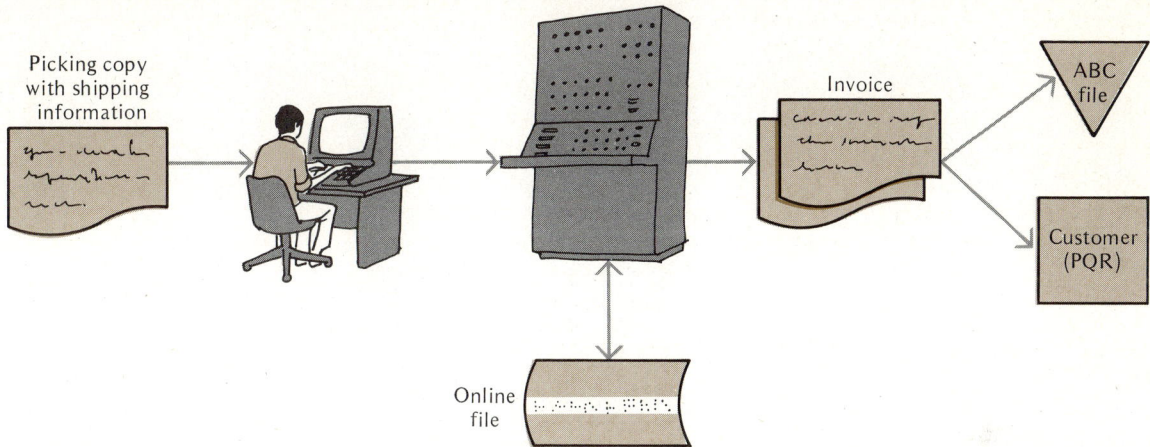

tory, a backorder form is generated automatically and the backordered goods sent to PQR, thus completing the original order.

RECEIVING THE ORDERED GOODS AT THE SUPERMARKET Upon arrival of the order at PQR's receiving department, the goods delivered are compared with the packing slip and any discrepancies are noted. The packing slip is then routed to the office and the information relating to goods received on the order is entered into the computer. When the invoice is received, that information will also be entered. At this point all files will be updated and this order will be listed as an account to be paid (an account payable). Periodically, computer runs will be made to print checks and a check will be issued to ABC Wholesale for the goods purchased. This sequence is illustrated in Figure 1-16.

PROCESSING THE PAYMENT Upon receipt of the payment ABC enters the payment received information into its computer. The customer (PQR) account is updated and the check is processed. As we might suspect, each processing operation will trigger other operations. For instance, depositing the check will involve another system completely. The check will proceed from ABC's bank to a central clearinghouse to PQR's bank. There it will be charged against the PQR account and returned to PQR, thus completing the cycle.

EXERCISES

1.6 What would be the consequence if the picking copy of the sales order were lost in the shipping department after the order had been filled?

1.7 Why is it important to process paperwork as quickly as possible after the order has been shipped?

Figure 1-16 Receiving ordered goods at PQR Supermarket.

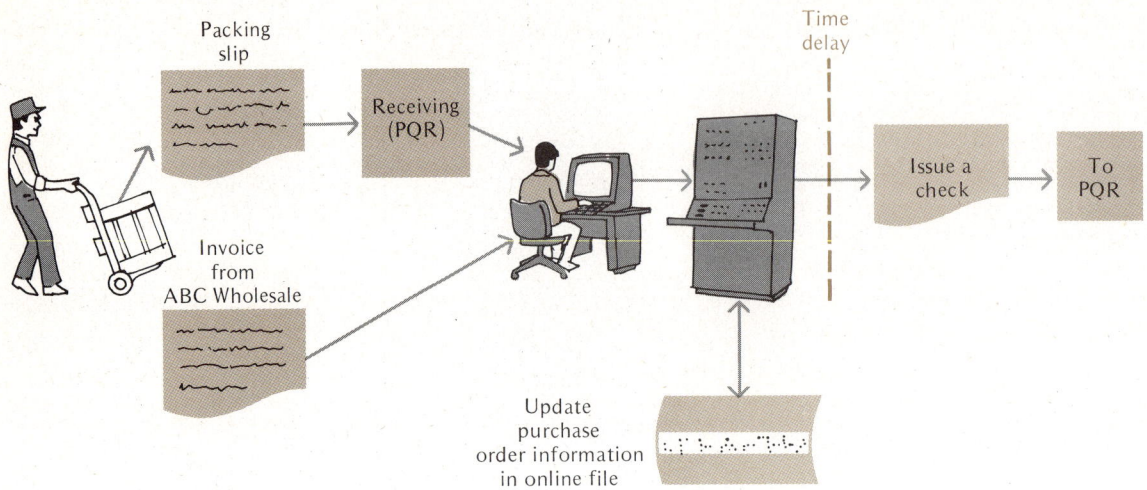

System Design

Flow of data into and out of the sales order system of ABC Wholesale is summarized in Figure 1-17. A well-organized system will minimize the need for manual paper shuffling. As a general rule timely and thorough reporting systems will allow a company to operate more efficiently and be more competitive in today's market. Indeed, the computer is a valuable tool for use in virtually all areas of business. However, for every quoted success story we can find a corresponding situation that is not nearly so happy. It is hardly sufficient merely to "buy a computer"; that is the easy part. Making the computer function in a useful and productive fashion is the difficult part—one that requires considerable planning and expense. The overall data processing functions must be carefully designed and interrelated. The results will be quite unsatisfactory if each component of the system is designed in a vacuum without due consideration for other parts of the system. As we have learned, the output of one portion of the system serves as the input of another portion. In planning and designing a system it is imperative to define and plan carefully the overall and detailed data flow within the system. This is commonly referred to as *systems design* and must be carried out with great care. The beginner might be inclined to feel that so much attention to such simple detail is a waste of time. After all, the steps in making a sale and processing the paperwork seem to be relatively simple. But for any real-life application there are many "packets" of data, each with its own destination, and many of them are related to others. Unless the overall system is carefully designed and planned, it will not function adequately. A data processing system is very much like a complex machine: each part must be in place, properly function-

Figure 1-17 Flow of data into and out of a computerized record.

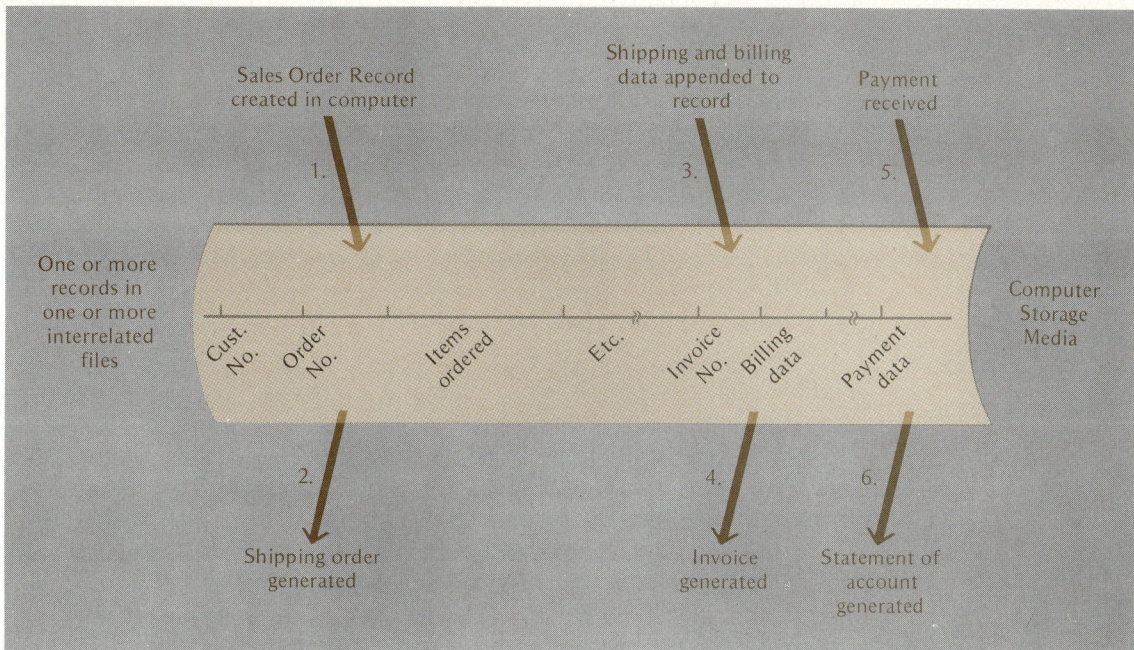

ing and carefully aligned (and well oiled), or the machine will not operate properly.

In Retrospect

The simple example of a manual customer accounting system illustrates many of the basic principles of data processing. It is important that we recognize the meaning of data processing and the fact that data processing does not necessarily mean "computer."

The basic operations illustrated by this example include

- Data recording
- Sorting
- Merging
- Calculating
- Summarizing
- Reporting

It is imperative to recognize that these functions exist in most data processing applications, whether manual or automated. The use of a computer in data processing is illustrated by the sales transaction system.

This section also illustrates the use of a computerized system via a sales transaction system. Here, the purchase of a box of cornflakes set in motion the following chain of events:

- An inventory record was updated.
- Because the item fell to its reorder level, a purchase order was issued.
- The purchase order was entered into the wholesaler's computer as a sales order.
- The order was processed and shipped by the wholesaler.
- An invoice was generated by the wholesaler and sent to the purchaser.
- Receipt of the goods by the purchaser was recorded and a check issued to the wholesaler.

The interrelationships among components of a data processing system become evident through this example.

Before a computer can be used successfully in a business organization, all aspects of the business must be analyzed. The files and procedures must be carefully designed. Often many data processing operations of a business (such as accounts payable and accounts receivable) appear to be quite independent of one another. Yet virtually *all* data processing operations of a business are interrelated to some extent. In designing a system these interrelationships must be taken into account.

ANSWERS TO PRECEDING EXERCISES

1.1   The computer is a tool that is commonly used to perform data processing functions. People were processing data long before the computer arrived on the scene. Even today, in most businesses some data is more conveniently processed by hand.

1.2   The Payment Received record, being a *record,* contains data on a single transaction (in this case, on a payment received). The Monthly Sales File, being a *file,* is a collection of *all* Payment Received records. It is not especially realistic to contrast one type of file with another type of record. A more realistic question would be: "What is the difference between a Payment Record and a Sales Record?" (They are both transactions, the first a credit and the second a debit.) Another meaningful and related question would be: "What is the difference between the Payment Record and the Payment File?"

1.3   *Record*—a collection of related fields of data that are treated as a basic unit of information; for example, the Customer Master Record. All records of a given type form a file.
       Data base—the collection of all data (that is, all files) around which a system is designed.

1.4   See the definitions in the text.

1.5   The UPC coding includes an inventory number, *not* pricing information. The inventory number is used by the computer to look up the price, which it has stored in its memory.

1.6 The shipping information will not be entered into the computer, an invoice will not be prepared, and the customer will not be billed.

1.7 Billing is based on the date of the invoice. The sooner the paperwork is completed and mailed, the sooner the company will be paid for goods shipped.

ADDITIONAL EXERCISES

1.8 The computer-printed shipping order includes the following four copies: order acknowledgment, office copy, picking copy, and packing slip. What would be the consequence of each of these being lost immediately after leaving the data processing department?

1.9 **Matching** Match each term in items (a) through (h) with the most appropriate description in 1 through 8.

a. Merge   e. Sort
b. System   f. Data collection
c. File   g. Summarize
d. Record   h. Field

1. Arrange a group of student grade reports in order on the basis of student numbers.
2. Part of a record.
3. The collection of all the procedures and data files used for customer accounting.
4. Bring two or more data sets together.
5. A clerk writes down an order on a Sales Order Form.
6. All sales and receipts for the day are added up for the day end report.
7. All of the Customer Master Records.
8. A Payment Received Form.

1.10 **True–False** Determine whether each of the following is true or false.

1. In a nutshell, the basic operations common to most data processing systems include data input, processing, storage, output, and retrieval.
2. The collection of all fields of a given type form a file.
3. The concept of a Customer Master Record as described for the PQR Market refers to a document containing master information on all customers of PQR.
4. The record-file concept is every bit as important with modern computer systems as it was with manual systems.
5. When a purchase order is received, it is entered into the computer; the computer can then immediately prepare an invoice.
6. The shipping copy of an order serves as the bill to the customer.
7. With a well-designed computer system, once an original order has been entered into the computer, no further manual data entry will be required relating to that order since everything will be automatic.
8. As a rule most individual operations in a business data processing system are relatively simple. However, the combination and interrelationships of these simple functions within a system can become very complex.

2

Computers and
Computer Hardware

OBJECTIVES

The evolution of the computer over the past 30 years has occurred at an astonishing rate. During recent years we have been swamped with the notion of computers in all areas. And more recently the microcomputer has become an important factor in both our business and our personal lives.

Although it is hardly necessary to understand the electronics of a computer to use one, it is useful to have a basic insight into what a computer is and how it works. From this section you will learn about the following important aspects of computers and computer hardware.

- Evolution of the computer
- The basic components of the computer, which are input and output, arithmetic/logic unit, control unit, storage, and auxiliary storage
- The central processing unit (CPU) of the computer
- Characteristics of the internal storage (memory) devices, core, semiconductor, and magnetic bubble
- Features of magnetic tape and magnetic disk as auxiliary storage devices
- Classification of computers by size: large-scale, medium-scale, and small machines
- Characteristics of mini- and microcomputers
- The small business computer and its impact on data processing for small companies

Key terminology important to this section includes:

arithmetic unit	magnetic disk
auxiliary storage	magnetic tape
bubble memory	microcomputer
control unit	microprocessor
digital computer	minicomputer
direct access device	output device
disk storage	random access memory
family of computers	read-only memory
input device	semiconductor memory
integrated circuit	software
logical operation	storage
magnetic core	

Evolution of Computing Devices

On June 14, 1951, the first commercial computer, known as Univac I, was delivered to the U.S. Census Bureau. (Univac is a contraction of *Universal Automatic Computer.*) Its capabilities were mind boggling at the time, and yet home microcomputers of today (a mere 30 years later) have more computing power. Our constant search for better computing machines makes a fascinating history. Highlights of this evolution are portrayed in Figure 2-1.

Logical Components of the Computer

COMPUTER LOGICAL STRUCTURE Two commonly encountered computer terms are hardware and software. *Hardware* refers to the physical components of the computer. This section of the book deals primarily with the hardware aspects of the modern *stored program digital computer.* (The meaning of the terms *program* and *digital* will become apparent as we progress.) Computer *software* refers to programs of instructions that make the hardware work for us. This topic is covered in Section 3.

Overall, the stored program computer consists of the following components:

- *Input/output.* These devices accept input data and deliver output reports.
- *Storage.* When a program is to be run, the instructions that make up that program are placed in computer storage. During the execution of the program current data to be operated upon is also held in storage.
- *Arithmetic unit.* This unit provides the capability for performing arithmetic and comparing operations.
- *Control unit.* This unit controls all operations carried out by the computer.

The relationship between these fundamental components is illustrated in Figure 2-2 (see p. 30). As we can see, the control unit, storage, and arithmetic unit make up what is usually called the *central processing unit* (CPU) of the computer. The age of microelectronics has resulted in astonishing developments in the computer field. The CPU of a small-scale computer of several years ago was commonly housed in a desk-size cabinet. In contrast, the entire CPU of a microcomputer occupies less than a square inch, as shown in the enlarged photograph of Figure 2-3 (see p. 31).

Let us consider each of these components in more detail.

INPUT/OUTPUT In order for computers to provide us with useful results, we must have a way to get data into them and get the results out. Means for communicating with computers have always posed a formidable problem to computer designers since all input/output devices involve some type of mechanical components and, in general, mechanical methods are relatively slow. Furthermore, different applications have very different needs. For instance, the supermarket checkout stand requires a device to read bar codes on grocery products whereas an airline office requires a typewriter-like terminal. These circumstances have contributed to the many and varied means used to get information into and out of the computer. An extensive discussion of input/output is included later in this section.

THE ARITHMETIC UNIT   The primary purpose of every digital computer is to perform computations with numbers. The *arithmetic/logic unit* of the computer contains the electronic switches and circuits necessary for such computations. They provide the capability to perform, directly or indirectly, the operations of addition, subtraction, multiplication, and division. It is in the area of computational speed that our capabilities have been most remarkably extended through the computer. For instance, if we were to consider the multiplication of two 5-digit numbers (for example, 52381 and 26552), typical times required to perform the operation manually and on relatively small computers would be as follows:

Method of Calculation	Approximate Speed
Human (manual calculation)	1 each 60 seconds
Burroughs E101 early wired panel computer (1954)	4 per second
IBM 1130 small scientific computer (1964)	600,000 per second
Digital Equipment Corporation PDP 11 minicomputer (1974)	1,000,000 per second
Cray-1 modern supercomputer	13,000,000 per second

In other words, a modern computer is capable of performing such operations at speeds in excess of 10 million per second. The computer has provided us with an increase in computational speed of over one *billion* times. This is truly an amazing accomplishment.

In addition to arithmetic, the arithmetic/logic unit performs *logical operations.* Herein lies the key to the versatility of the modern computer because logical operations provide "decision-making" capability. For example, in Section 1 we studied the notion of processing the master file, which had been sorted on the customer name. A program to process the file would probably include an instruction to *compare* the newly read master record with the previous one to ensure that the latest value is higher in the sequence. Similarly, if the application happened to be payroll, the hours worked for each

Figure 2-1 The evolution of machine-aided computation.

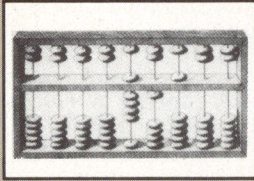

1. The abacus. One of the earliest developed computational devices, the abacus has been in continuous use for 2000–3000 years.

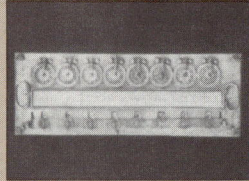

2. Pascal adding machine, 1642. The basic principles of this, the first true adding machine, are used in modern devices such as gas meters and odometers.

3. The Jacquard loom, 1801. Invented by Joseph Jacquard, this textile weaving loom operated under the automatic control of punched cards.

4. Replica of Charles Babbage's difference engine, 1812. This machine, involving the Pascal adding machine principle, was conceived to calculate logarithm tables.

5. Pasteboard card to control analytic engine, 1833. Before completing the difference engine, Babbage conceived the analytic engine, the mechanical equivalent of today's electronic computer.

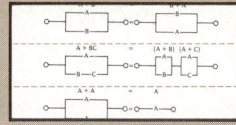

6. Boolean algebra, 1854. The theoretical work of George Boole forms the basis for design of electrical and electronic circuitry.

7. First punched card processing, 1890. Herman Hollerith developed the first system for processing data by automated machine (used by U.S. Census Bureau).

8. Punched card processing. By the 1920s, card processing equipment developed by Hollerith and others was widely used in business and government.

9. The ABC computer, 1942. John Atanasoff is generally credited with inventing the electronic computer at Iowa State College.

10. Mark I, 1944. The first fully automatic electromechanical computer was designed by Howard Aiken and built at Harvard University.

11. Eniac, 1946. The first electronic computer, designed by John Mauchly and J. Presper Eckert contained 18,000 vacuum tubes and weighed about 30 tons.

12. Univac I, 1951. The first commercially available electronic computer based on the principles developed by Mauchly and Eckert.

(Frames 7, 8, 10, 13, 14, 15, 17, *courtesy IBM Corporation;* 3 *courtesy Bettmann Archives;* 5 *courtesy Science Museum, London;* 9 *reprinted with permission of Datamation©, Copyright 1974 by Technical Publishing Company, Greenwich, Conn. 06830;* 11, 12 *courtesy Sperry Rand Corporation;* 16 *courtesy DEC Corporation;*

13. Punched card processing. Supply needs of World War II saw wide use of punched card equipment. During the 1950s, punched card equipment was the backbone of data processing.

14. First-generation computers, 1954. The IBM 650 proved to be a highly versatile machine. It set the trend for domination of the computer market by IBM.

15. Second-generation computers, 1959. Many companies introduced second-generation computers. However, by 1964, there were more IBM 1400 machines than all others put together.

16. The minicomputer 1964. The minicomputer had its beginning with the Digital Equipment Corporation PDP 8.

17. Third-generation computers, 1964. One of the important features of these machines (such as the IBM 360) was the wide availability of computer software, programs to "make the machine work."

18. Continued evolution, 1970. Machines such as the Honeywell 6000 brought continued improvement in size, speed, and versatility.

19. Supercomputers. Machines such as the Cray-1 are so large and powerful that large-scale machines are commonly used to feed jobs to them.

20. Computer kits, 1975. Microminiature circuits on chips developed in the early 1970s led to microcomputers. The first computer kit was the Altair 8800.

21. Microminiature electronics. The minature chip shown here contains all of the "thinking" parts of a computer. It has made possible the modern microcomputer.

22. Microcomputer, 1977. The Radio Shack TRS 80 is the most widely used microcomputer today. It has capacities exceeding those of Univac I (see frame 12).

23. Micrographics. Specialized minicomputers are used for a variety of operations. This one is designed as part of a microfilm processing system.

24. Magnuson M80, 1979. Can be obtained as a moderate-size machine and expanded to large-scale simply by plugging in more components.

18 *courtesy Honeywell Information Systems;* 19 *courtesy Cray Research;* 20 *courtesy MITS Corporation;* 21 *courtesy NCR Corporation;* 22 *courtesy Radio Shack Division of Tandy Corporation;* 23 *courtesy DalagraphiX, Incorporated;* 24 *courtesy Magnuson Systems, Incorporated.)*

Central Processing Unit (CPU)

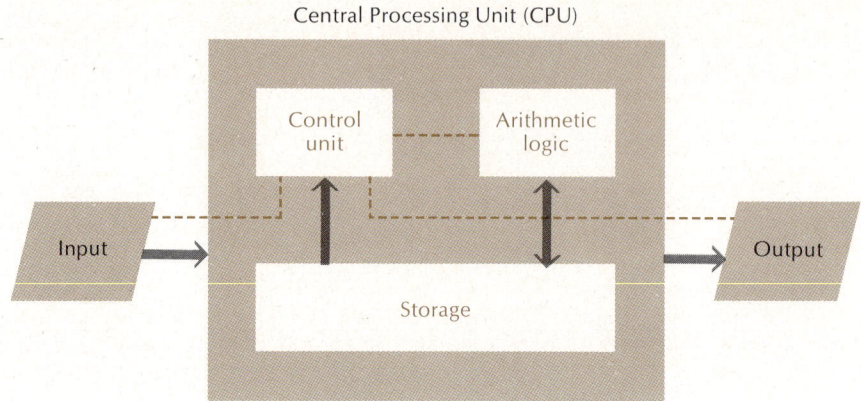

Figure 2-2
The logical structure
of a computer.

employee would likely be *compared* with 40 in order to determine overtime. In other words, a *logical operation* is simply a comparison of two quantities that produces a "yes" or "no" type of result. For instance:

"Is the value of total hours > 40?"
"Is the employee code = E?"
"Is employee number > previous employee number?"

Note that alphabetic fields as well as numeric fields can be compared. Once the comparison is made within the arithmetic/logic unit, other instructions can decide what to do on the basis of the result of the comparing operation. Interestingly, this simple comparing ability represents the extent of the computer's ability to make decisions. It is the well-conceived and often sophisticated programs *written by people* using this simple feature that make the computer appear almost human in its decision-making abilities.

EXERCISE
  2.1   What is a "logical operation"?

CONTROL UNIT The task of directing operations within the computer is the function of the automatic *control unit*. This portion of the computer can be considered analogous to a combination of traffic officer and automatic telephone switchboard. It obtains instructions from storage, interprets them, and makes certain that they are carried out as required. These functions require the opening and closing of appropriate circuits, starting and stopping of input/output devices, and, in general, directing the flow of information within the computer. Let us assume that we have placed a program of instructions in the storage and that the computer is about to perform the sequence: read a data record, perform some calculations, then print the results. The following would take place.

**Figure 2-3
The Intel MCS 48
Single Chip
Microcomputer sitting
on a daisy. (*Courtesy
of Intel Corporation*.)**

1. The control unit obtains from storage the instruction to read data and begins the reading process.
2. Under direction of the control unit, the data is read from the input device into storage.
3. The next instruction (for a calculation, in this case) is obtained from storage by the control unit.
4. Under direction of the control unit, the needed fields are transmitted from storage to the arithmetic/logic unit, where the calculation is performed. The results are transmitted back to storage from the arithmetic/logic unit.
5. Each calculation required in the program is performed as in steps 3 and 4.
6. Upon encountering a print statement the control unit transfers the desired quantities to the output device, which performs the required output operation.

Internal Storage

BINARY CONCEPTS Computer *storage,* the single component of computers that is probably the most glamorized, is often referred to as a *memory* analogous to the human memory. However, the popular representation can be misleading since the storage unit is better compared to a file cabinet, which is capable of storing information in an orderly fashion, than to human memory. To gain an insight into how information can be stored electronically, let us consider a simple coding method using electrical components that may be on or off.

In Figure 2-4 we see six rows, each consisting of four indicators. (These may be thought of as light bulbs, transisters, magnetic devices, or anything else that may be on–off, charged–uncharged, magnetized in either of two directions, or whatever.) By assigning the respective indicators in each row a place value (1, 2, 4, or 8), each column may represent one decimal digit. Since the indicators of each row can be set to yield any decimal digit (0 through 9), the collection of six rows can store any 6-digit decimal number.

This example illustrates a number of important concepts. The choice of 8, 4, 2, and 1 to represent positional values of the indicators was no random choice. These are the first four powers of two. Since the indicators may have either of two values (on or off) they are said to be *binary.* This leads to the relationship between the binary number system (which uses digits 0 and 1) and electronic circuits, which is basic to the design of computing devices. Using 0 to represent an indicator that is off and 1 to represent one that is on, the binary number equivalent of Figure 2-4 is shown in Figure 2-5. Although

Figure 2-4 A binary-coded storage device.

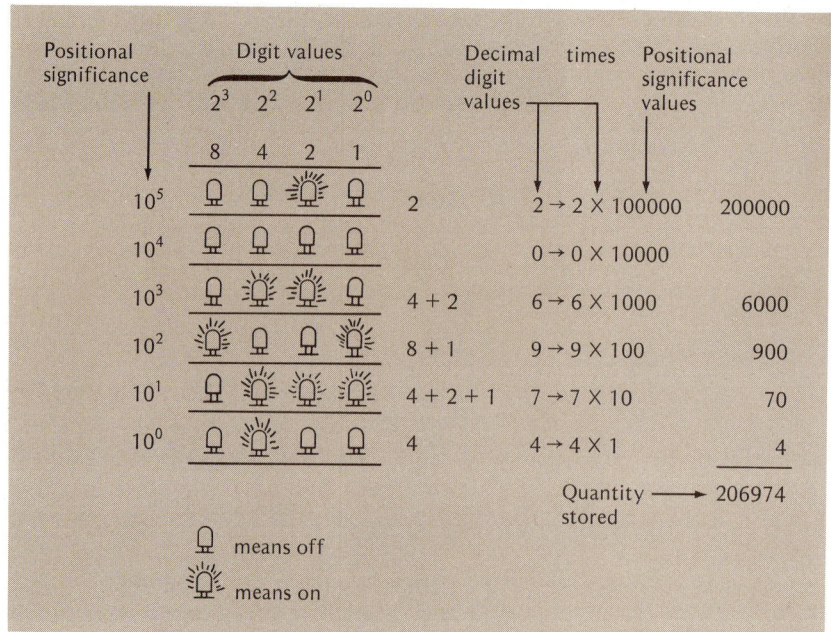

Positional significance	Digit values 2^3 2^2 2^1 2^0 / 8 4 2 1	Decimal digit values	Decimal times Positional significance values	Positional significance values
10^5	off off **on** off	2	$2 \rightarrow 2 \times 100000$	200000
10^4	off off off off		$0 \rightarrow 0 \times 10000$	
10^3	off **on** **on** off	4 + 2	$6 \rightarrow 6 \times 1000$	6000
10^2	**on** off off **on**	8 + 1	$9 \rightarrow 9 \times 100$	900
10^1	off **on** **on** **on**	4 + 2 + 1	$7 \rightarrow 7 \times 10$	70
10^0	off **on** off off	4	$4 \rightarrow 4 \times 1$	4

Quantity stored $\longrightarrow$ 206974

off means off
on means on

Positional significance →	2^3	2^2	2^1	2^0		
	8	4	2	1		
	0	0	1	0	$0 \times 8 + 0 \times 4 + 1 \times 2 + 0 \times 1 \rightarrow 2$	$\rightarrow 2$
	0	0	0	0	$0 \times 8 + 0 \times 4 + 0 \times 2 + 0 \times 1 \rightarrow 0$	$\rightarrow 0$
	0	1	1	0	$0 \times 8 + 1 \times 4 + 1 \times 2 + 0 \times 1 \rightarrow 4 + 2$	$\rightarrow 6$
	1	0	0	1	$1 \times 8 + 0 \times 4 + 0 \times 2 + 1 \times 1 \rightarrow 8 + 1$	$\rightarrow 9$
	0	1	1	1	$0 \times 8 + 1 \times 4 + 1 \times 2 + 1 \times 1 \rightarrow 4 + 2 + 1 \rightarrow 7$	
	0	1	0	0	$0 \times 8 + 1 \times 4 + 0 \times 2 + 0 \times 1 \rightarrow 4$	$\rightarrow 4$

**Figure 2-5
Binary numbers used
to represent decimal
quantities.**

binary number system concepts are not described in this book, this example illustrates the system's basic characteristics. Here we see place value associated with a 2-digit (base 2) system. (It should be noted that the binary system includes all of the properties and operations of our familiar base 10 system.) Since each position represents 1 binary digit it is commonly referred to as a *bit* (contraction of binary digit). The coding method illustrated by Figures 2-4 and 2-5 is called *binary coded decimal* because it uses 4 binary digits to represent 1 decimal digit. It forms the basis for one of two commonly used codes in modern computer design.

Within the computer a variety of methods are used to represent data. For example, a whole number might be stored in binary using 16, 32, or even more bits. This is commonly referred to as *integer* or *fixed-point* form. On the other hand, a number that includes a fractional part might be encoded in a binary floating-point format code, which is quite different from the simple binary integer form.

Obviously the storage of letters and special characters requires special coding techniques. Within the computer industry two character codes are commonly encountered: the *Extended Binary-Coded Decimal Interchange Code (EBCDIC)* and the *American Standard Code for Information Interchange (ASCII)*. EBCDIC, an 8-bit code, was introduced by IBM and is used by IBM and other companies that make IBM-compatible equipment. ASCII, a 7-bit code, is used by most other manufacturers. The binary codes for the letters, digits, and some of the special characters are shown in Figure 2-6.

THE STORAGE BYTE The illustration of Figure 2-4 uses 4 bits in a group to represent a single decimal digit. The internal storage of digital computers utilizes similar groupings of bits to form a basic unit storage. The most commonly encountered unit size is the *byte*, which consists of 8 bits. Depending upon the internal coding used, a byte can store one character (letter, digit, or special character), or 2 or more bytes can be used together to store numeric information in a variety of forms.

Figure 2-6   Partial character set for EBCDIC and ASCII.

Character	EBCDIC	ASCII	Character	EBCDIC	ASCII
Space	0100 0000	0100000	N	1101 0101	1001110
.	0100 1011	0101110	O	1101 0110	1001111
(	0100 1101	0101000	P	1101 0111	1010000
+	0100 1110	0101011	Q	1101 1000	1010001
&	0101 0000	0100110	R	1101 1001	1010010
*	0101 1100	0101010	S	1110 0010	1010011
)	0101 1101	0101001	T	1110 0011	1010100
#	0111 1011	0100011	U	1110 0100	1010101
@	0111 1100	1000000	V	1110 0101	1010110
=	0111 1110	0111101	W	1110 0110	1010111
			X	1110 0111	1011000
A	1100 0001	1000001	Y	1110 1000	1011001
B	1100 0010	1000010	Z	1110 1001	1011010
C	1100 0011	1000011			
D	1100 0100	1000100	0	1111 0000	0110000
E	1100 0101	1000101	1	1111 0001	0110001
F	1100 0110	1000110	2	1111 0010	0110010
G	1100 0111	1000111	3	1111 0011	0110011
H	1100 1000	1001000	4	1111 0100	0110100
I	1100 1001	1001001	5	1111 0101	0110101
J	1101 0001	1001010	6	1111 0110	0110110
K	1101 0010	1001011	7	1111 0111	0110111
L	1101 0011	1001100	8	1111 1000	0111000
M	1101 0100	1001101	9	1111 1001	0111001

Exercise

2.2   What is the difference between a byte and a bit?

CHARACTERISTICS OF INTERNAL STORAGE   While prices have *decreased,* the storage capacity and speed of digital computers have *increased* remarkably in the past 20 years (see Figure 2-7). Early computers had capacities equivalent to a few hundred to a few thousand bytes. Microcomputers are now commonly available with storage capacities of up to 64,000 bytes at a cost of $2000 or less. (The letter K is used in the computer field to represent the amount 1024. Thus a computer with 64K bytes of storage would have a capacity slightly larger than 64,000.) Some of the larger minicomputers have capacities of up to 2,000,000 bytes, a size found only in very large computers of 10 years ago. One of the important features of internal storage is that the contents of a given storage location can be changed easily. Furthermore, the storage unit is designed so that any

Figure 2-7 Changing characteristics of computers.

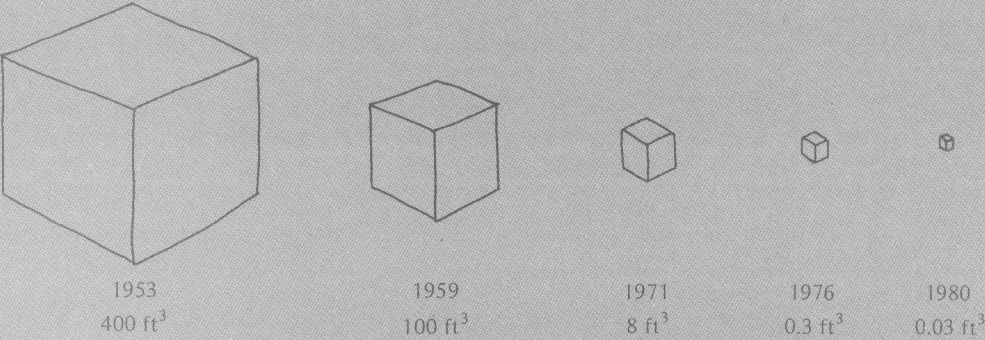

1953	1959	1971	1976	1980
400 ft^3	100 ft^3	8 ft^3	0.3 ft^3	0.03 ft^3

Space in cubic feet required for 1 million characters of internal storage

Since 1953, the physical space needed for one megabyte of storage has dropped from a cube measuring over 7 feet on a side to one measuring less than 4 inches.

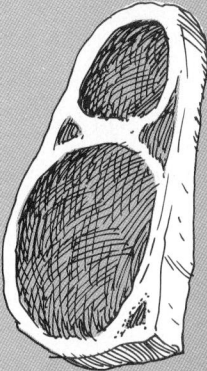

Twenty-five years ago it cost $1.26 to do 100,000 multiplications by computer. Today it costs less than a penny. If other costs had gone down the same, you would be able to buy a sirloin steak for about 9¢ per pound and an around-the-world airline trip for $3.

Built in 1946, the first fully electronic computer contained 18,000 vacuum tubes. The technology of today can pack that much computing power in a space the size of one of these tubes.

If technology and productivity in other industries had progressed at the same rate as computer technology, an around-the-world airline flight would take 24 minutes, and a standard size car would get 550 miles per gallon.

given area of storage can be accessed just as easily and quickly as any other. By comparison, the reader might consider "accessing" a particular piece of music on a tape cassette. Its accessibility will depend upon its placement on the tape. The easy-to-change and quick-to-access features are important characteristics. Because of the latter feature general-purpose internal storage is commonly referred to as *random access memory,* or simply *RAM.*

With the coming of microcomputer technology, there has also been a surge in the use of special internal storage, which is "factory loaded" and cannot be changed. For example, a computer manufacturer might build a sequence of coded instructions permanently into a storage unit. Such a program might be designed to perform certain commonly used operations. Storage units of this type are referred to as *read-only memory,* or simply ROM. It is possible to read or use the stored information but impossible to destroy it or otherwise *write* to the unit.

TYPES OF STORAGE In the short history of electronic computers many different devices have been used for internal storage of information. These include *mercury delay lines* and the *magnetic drum* on early computers. Until recently the *magnetic core* was by far the most commonly used device. Core storage design is based on the fact that a magnetic material in the form of a small circular ring can be magnetized in either of two directions (see Figure 2-8). Thus we have the basis for a binary system. Core memories were built by stringing thousands or even millions of cores on a mesh-like network of wires. The direction of magnetism, and thus the binary contents, can be controlled by passing electric currents through the wire network. One of the important features of core is that a storage unit would retain its stored information even if the electric power were turned off. Hence it is commonly referred to as *nonvolatile* storage.

Microelectronics and semiconductor technology allow the emplacement of thousands of electronic components on a tiny chip of silicon. These miniature circuits are commonly referred to as *integrated circuits,* or ICs. (As technology has progressed, it has been possible to put more and more circuits in a given space. Hence we hear the terms *large-scale integration,* LSI, and *very-large-scale integration,* VLSI.) During the mid-1960s integrated circuits were incorporated into computer design and by 1970 they began to be used for internal storage. *Semiconductor memory* is now used in computers ranging from the smallest microcomputers to the largest general-purpose machines. It offers the following advantages over the magnetic core:

- Smaller physical size
- Lower cost
- Lower power consumption (and less heat generation)
- Faster (access times measured in *billionths* of a second)

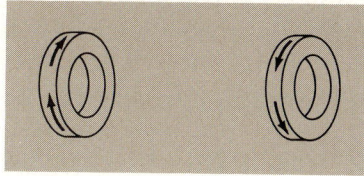

**Figure 2-8
Magnetic cores.**

As a consequence semiconductor memories have, by and large, replaced the magnetic core. However, one disadvantage of semiconductor memory is that it requires continuous power in order to retain the stored information. That is, if the power is turned off, the information is lost. In most cases this is no longer a problem but some applications do require continuous storage of data with or without power.

Like the magnetic core, semiconductor memory is composed of units of which each is capable of representing a 0 or 1 (a binary) state. In one commonly used technique the information is stored as an electric charge on a capacitor. If the capacitor is charged, it contains a 1; if uncharged, it contains a 0.

EXERCISE

2.3   How is binary information stored within a computer?

MAGNETIC BUBBLE MEMORY One of the important features of internal storage is its random access feature. That is, information from any given location (of the thousands or millions of locations) can be accessed just as quickly as any other location. For internal storage fast access is generally essential. There are many situations, however, in which superfast data access is not a necessity. For applications of this type much larger storage capacities can be achieved at a lower price. Whereas conventional semiconductor memories mean "bringing one or more conductors to each storage unit," other techniques involve "bringing the storage unit to the conductor." One such technique revolves around the principle that it is possible to cause microscopic magnetic domains or "bubbles" on the surface of certain magnetic materials (hence the term *magnetic bubble memory*). Furthermore, these bubbles (of which there can be millions per square inch) can be moved along the surface of the material by applying an external magnetic field.

The design of current bubble storage involves organizing the bubbles in a series of loops that move past special detection devices so that information can be read or written. Each loop operates somewhat like a continuously rotating merry-go-round. The larger the loop, the slower the access but the greater the storage capacity. An important characteristic of bubble memory is that it retains stored information if the power is turned off. Figure 2-9 shows a bubble memory capable of storing 1 million units of binary data.

Recently some companies which were very active in the development of bubble memory have abandoned this technology.

EXERCISE

2.4   What is the main advantage of regular semiconductor memory over bubble memory? Of bubble memory over semiconductor?

Auxiliary Storage

From an overall point of view, computer storage can be considered in two broad categories: internal and auxiliary. In a sense *internal storage* or *memory* might be considered the "working storage" portion. Any program to be run must be placed in internal storage from which it will be run and will control the computer. Similarly, data (from files or whatever) must be brought into internal

Figure 2-9
The Intel 7110 one megabit Bubble Memory. (*Courtesy of Intel Corporation.*)

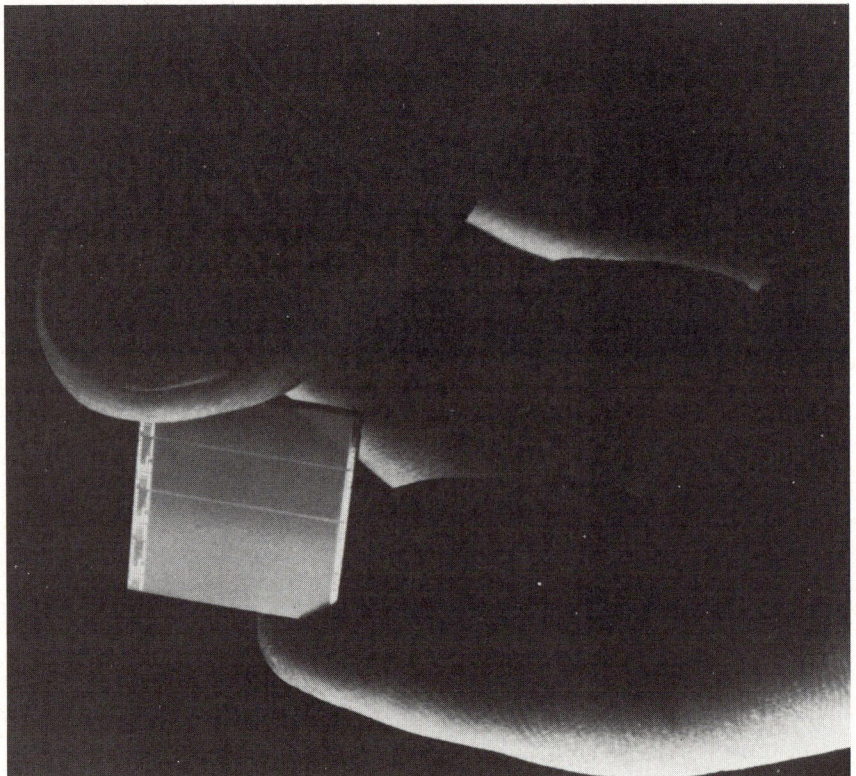

storage in order to be operated upon. On the other hand, data files and programs not currently in use are stored in *auxiliary storage* devices. Typically, the auxiliary storage capacity of a computer will be 10 to 100 times that of internal storage. For instance, a microcomputer with 64K bytes of internal storage might have an auxiliary storage capacity of ½ megabyte (½ million bytes).

The relationship between internal and auxiliary storage is somewhat analogous to the relationship between a desk top and a file cabinet, as illustrated in Figure 2-10. The primary advantage of auxiliary storage over internal storage is very high capacity at a relatively low cost. The disadvantage is that data must be transferred into internal storage for processing; this

Figure 2-10
Relationship between internal and auxiliary storage.

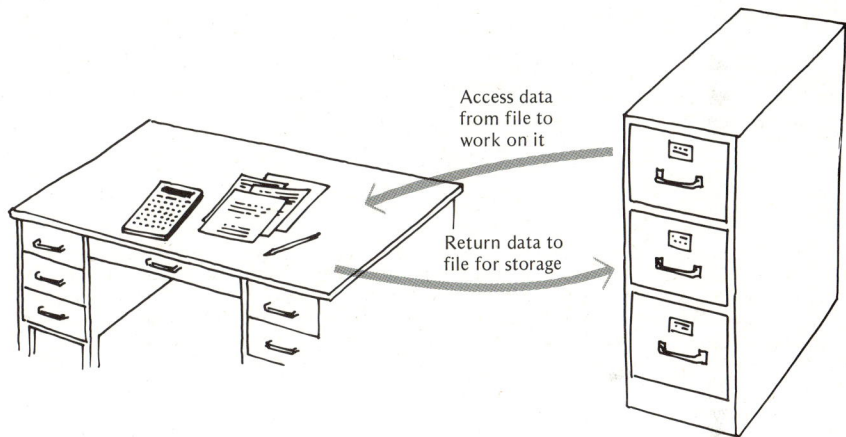

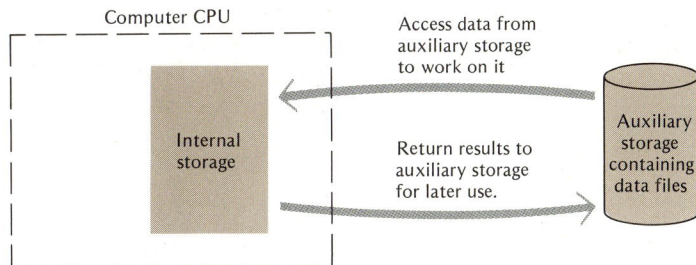

Access data
from file to
work on it

Return data to
file for storage

Computer CPU

Access data from
auxiliary storage
to work on it

Internal
storage

Return results to
auxiliary storage
for later use.

Auxiliary
storage
containing
data files

Note: It is *not* possible to work on the data while it is stored within the file cabinet (auxiliary storage).

The data must first be "accessed" from the file and brought to the "desk top" (internal storage).

Operations can then be performed on the data; for example, the inventory information for cornflakes might be brought up to date. Then the updated results can be returned to the file for storage.

accessing operation is very slow as compared with internal storage speeds.

The two most commonly encountered auxiliary storage devices are magnetic tape and magnetic disk. Both of these devices offer large storage capacities at relatively low prices. Tape is well suited to applications in which records of a file must be processed in the order in which they are recorded (sequential processing). Magnetic disk may be used with sequential processing or with processing in which records must be accessed in *random* order.

Magnetic Tape

BASIC CONCEPTS OF TAPE   Magnetic-tape units function in much the same manner as ordinary home tape recorders. That is, a tape drive machine is used to transport a magnetic-tape strip while the recording or reading of information takes place. The tape reel contains 2400 feet of half-inch-wide tape and has the capacity to store approximately 250,000 fully punched cards. A typical tape drive with a tape mounted in place is shown in Figure 2-11. The relatively low cost of storing vast quantities of information is a distinct advantage of magnetic tape. Its principal disadvantage, however, lies in the fact that records in a tape file must be in a particular sequence and must be processed in that sequence. In a sales accounting system records are processed sequentially, beginning with the lowest customer number and proceeding through the highest. This is an ideal tape application.

Although the tape consists of a uniform magnetic strip, it is (by virtue of the tape drive mechanism) effectively divided into lengthwise strips or *tracks*. Modern tape units are 9-track-tape units with the features illustrated in Figure

**Figure 2-11
Magnetic tape drive.**

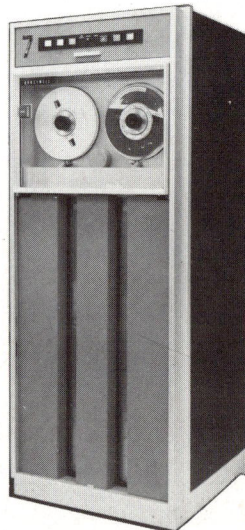

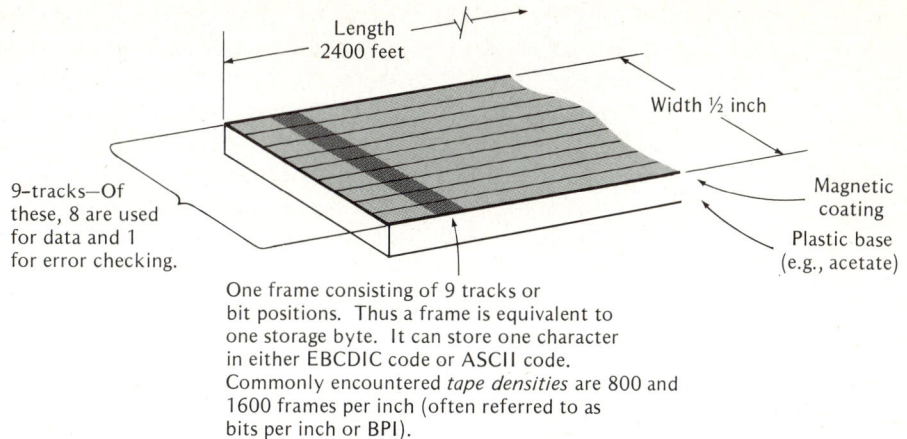

Length — 2400 feet

Width ½ inch

9–tracks—Of these, 8 are used for data and 1 for error checking.

Magnetic coating

Plastic base (e.g., acetate)

One frame consisting of 9 tracks or bit positions. Thus a frame is equivalent to one storage byte. It can store one character in either EBCDIC code or ASCII code. Commonly encountered *tape densities* are 800 and 1600 frames per inch (often referred to as bits per inch or BPI).

Figure 2-12 Section of magnetic tape.

2-12. Whereas data is stored and addressed in internal storage by the individual byte, data on tape is stored by the record (or block of records). Thus to work on an individual field the entire record containing that field must be read into internal storage as a unit. Records on tape are separated by gaps that provide space for the tape drive to start and stop the tape between records. (These are commonly called *interblock gaps* and will use up a great deal of the tape capacity if the records are small.) The rate at which data can be read from or written to tape depends on the tape speed (75 inches per second is common) and the density. Data transfer rates commonly range from about 100,000 to 300,000 bytes per second. This is rather impressive when we consider that, at 100,000 characters per second, this entire book could be read by a tape drive in about 5 seconds.

TAPE PROCESSING Probably one of the most commonly encountered systems in data processing is the company payroll system. This is a typical operation in which transactions (hours worked and other data) are accumulated over a period of time and then processed in a single *batch*. (This type of processing is commonly referred to as *batch processing*.) In its basic form a payroll system involves the processing of two files: the employee master file, which includes each employee's pay rate and other fixed information, and a detail or transaction file, which includes information such as hours worked for each employee. Because of the sequential nature of magnetic tape, data in both files must be organized and processed sequentially. For example, both the master file and the detail file might be arranged in ascending sequence on the basis of employee number. Then corresponding records from each file would be read and processed to produce the paychecks and the updated master file.

A serious disadvantage of magnetic-tape processing relates to the fact that the entire master file must be processed and written to a new tape, regardless of whether or not transaction records exist for each master. If, during each transaction period, virtually every master record has corresponding transaction records, this is no problem. However, if there have been transactions for a very small percentage of the master records, the entire master file must still be read and written on the new master tape. For a large file this can be a relatively inefficient operation and is a drawback of sequential processing as required with magnetic-tape files.

In each processing cycle (for example, each pay period) the batch processing sequence is repeated, as shown in Figure 2-13, in which two processing cycles are illustrated. The output of each cycle serves as the input for the next cycle. In this illustration we see the most recently updated master file and the two outdated master files from previous runs.

USING TAPE FOR DATA BACKUP   Considering the broad extent to which computers are used in business, most companies would be in very serious difficulty if all of their computerized data files were lost. As a result virtually all computer installations have *backup* procedures, which involve preparing duplicate copies of important files on magnetic tape. Very often these backup copies are stored at a different physical location from the computer center itself. (Backup copies would be of little value if they were stored with the originals, and the building burned to the ground.)

Figure 2-13 Updating a tape file.

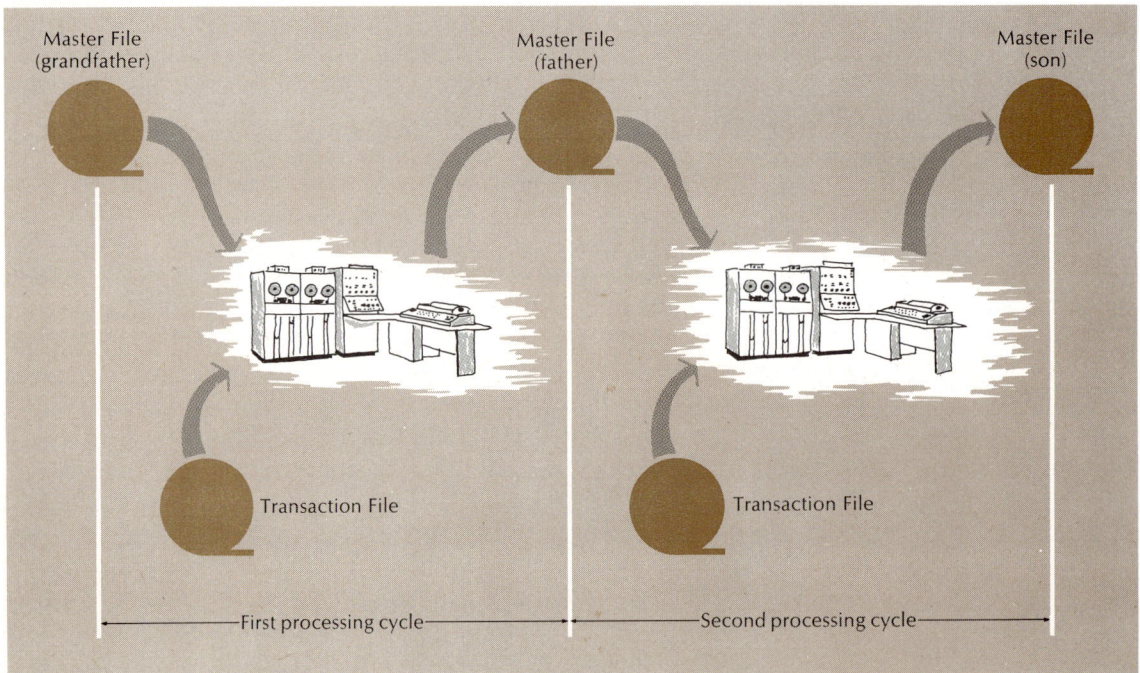

EXERCISES

2.5   What is meant by the statement: "Magnetic-tape files require sequential processing"?

2.6   How does the storage and accessing of data on magnetic tape differ from that within internal storage?

Magnetic-Disk Storage

THE NEED FOR DIRECT ACCESS   As we have learned, the utility of the digital computer is greatly enhanced through magnetic tape. With a tape system vast quantities of data can be handled easily and with great speed. However, tape is seriously limited for many applications in that it is a nonaddressable medium. For this reason all data must be stored sequentially, and processing must be done in that sequence. In many applications it simply is not possible to accumulate a batch and process sequentially at predefined intervals. For example, in an airline reservation system a request for a seat on a particular flight must be handled at once; the customer can hardly be expected to wait until the next batch is processed. In this type of processing the transaction is handled immediately and the seat "inventory" information is updated on the spot. (The automated supermarket example of Section 1 is identical in this respect.) Processing of this type is commonly referred to as *online processing.* Basically it involves *random access,* whereby the computer system is capable of accessing any given record just as quickly as any other.

THE MAGNETIC-DISK CONCEPT   Magnetic-disk storage, like tape, involves two basic components: the disk storage medium and the drive unit. As with magnetic tape, *disk packs* may be removed from the drive and the data stored offline. Disk drive units and their corresponding disk packs are shown in Figure 2-14. The most notable characteristic of a disk drive is its storage capacity, that is, the number of bytes of information that can be stored on a single pack. This is obviously important since it determines the amount of information that an installation can have online at any given time. The capacities of the units shown in Figure 2-14 are 2.5 and 80 megabytes. [By way of comparison, a 2400-foot reel of tape will store approximately 40 megabytes at 1600 bpi (bits per inch).]

The disk pack itself (upon which the data is stored) may consist of a single metal platter about 14 inches in diameter (single platter units are called *cartridges*), or it may consist of a stack of platters (see Figure 2-15). In both cases the surface is coated with the same type of magnetic material as used with magnetic tape. Although each disk surface is a continuous sheet of magnetic material, the design of the drive is such that the surface is divided into circles called *tracks,* as shown in Figure 2-16. This illustration depicts a disk consisting of 400 tracks, which is typical of units in use today. As we might expect, the greater the number of tracks and the more tightly the

(a) Disk cartridge *(courtesy of Dysan Corporation)* and NCR 8250 disk drive *(courtesy of NCR Corporation).*

(b) Disk pack *(courtesy of Dysan Corporation)* and DEC RM03 DEC 80 megabyte disk drive and pack *(courtesy of Digital Equipment Corporation).*

**Figure 2-14
Magnetic disk units.**

information is packed on a track (the *density*), the greater the capacity *and* price of the unit.

By use of special access arms information may be written to or read from any track on any surface. Thus, in contrast with tape, records are addressable and can be accessed in whatever sequence is desired. Typical times to

**Figure 2-15
Cutaway of disk unit.
(*Courtesy of Dysan
Corporation.*)**

locate and access a record from disk storage might range from 20 to 50 milliseconds (thousandths of a second).

These characteristics make it possible to update information in-place. That is, a disk record can be read, processing performed, and the result written back to the original record. Sequential processing via magnetic tape and random processing via magnetic disk are illustrated in Figure 2-17.

**Figure 2-16
Track layout on a
disk surface.**

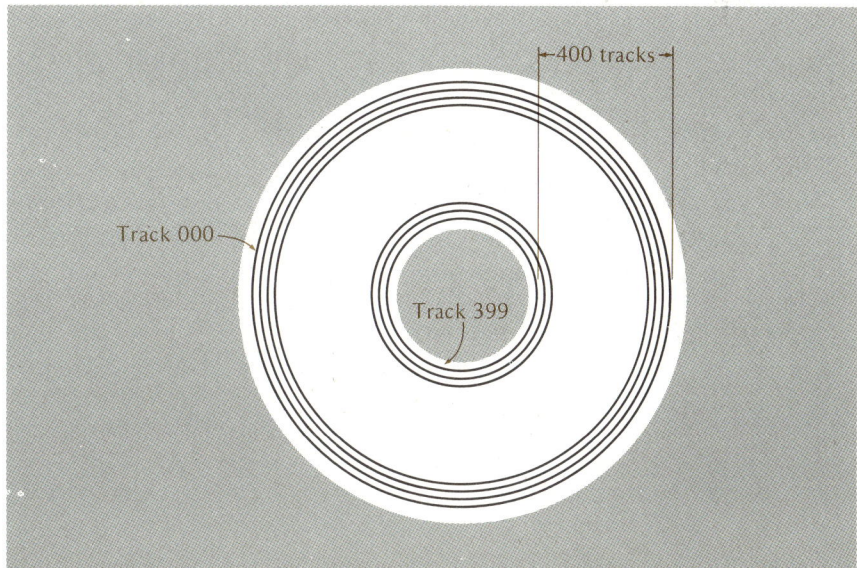

Figure 2-17 (a) Sequential processing via a tape system.
(b) Random processing with an online disk system.

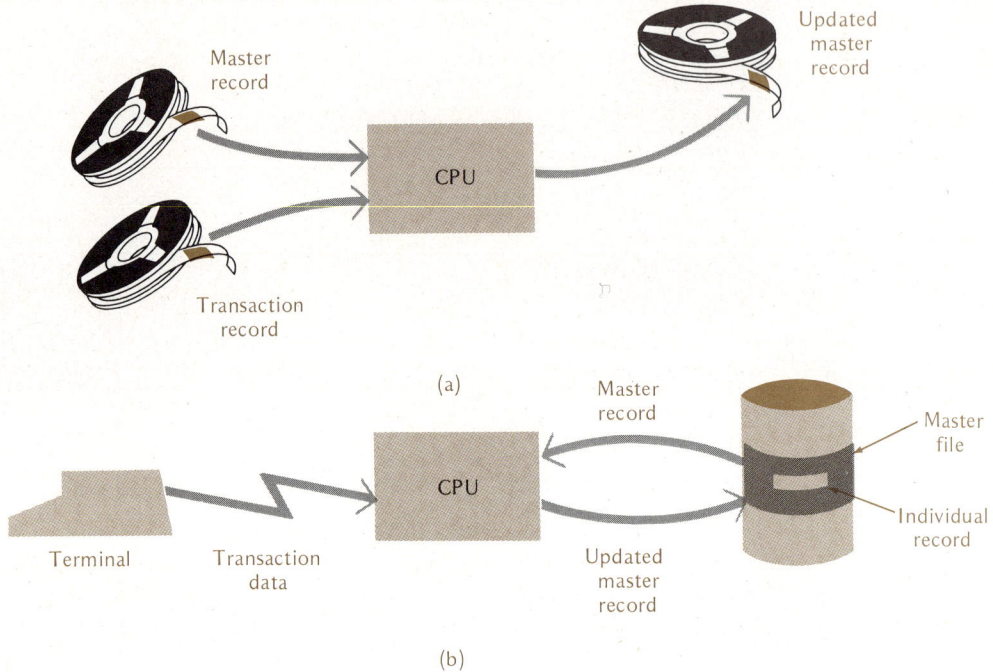

(a)

(b)

EXERCISES

2.7   Distinguish between batch processing and online processing.

2.8   What is meant by *direct access storage device?*

Basic Data Entry Concepts

OFFLINE AND ONLINE DATA ENTRY In general we can consider data collection devices and methods in two broad categories: *offline* and *online*. Briefly, online data collection involves devices such as the UPC reading device in the supermarket that are connected directly to the computer. Offline data collection involves devices such as the card punch through which data is recorded on some medium (such as punched cards) and then entered into the computer later.

For many years almost all data collection was done in the offline mode, generally using the punched card as the basic input medium. With such a system periodic runs are made in which all accumulated data cards are read and processed by the computer. This concept is illustrated in Figure 2-18. As shown, a sales order processing system might involve punching sales information from each sales order into cards. During the night shift the cards for all orders received and punched that day would be collected and processed by the computer to provide appropriate documents for filling the order. This is a typical batch processing type of operation as described earlier in this section. Although batch processing is still well suited to many applications, online data entry and processing have become commonplace.

With an *online* system data is entered directly into the computer via an input device such as a simple terminal. (Terminals, which serve for both input and output, are described in a later portion of this section.) Once in the

**Figure 2-18
Offline data entry.**

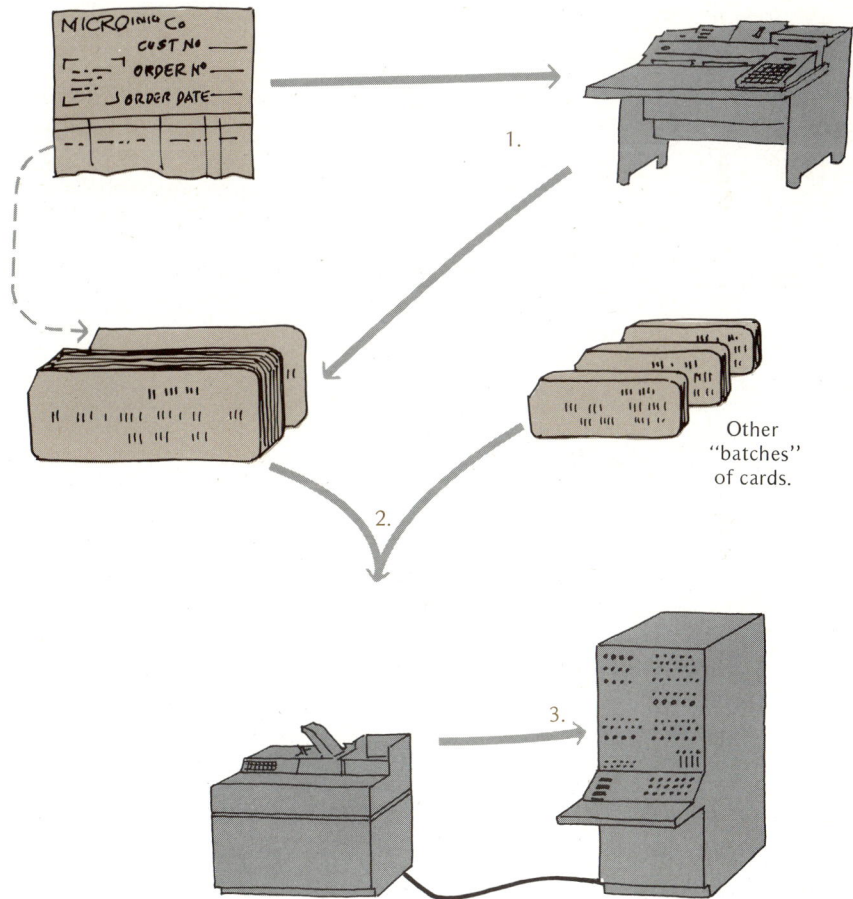

Other "batches" of cards.

1. Input data is punched into cards. Data which is recorded may also be verified at this time in order to ensure accuracy.
2. At periodic intervals, the data stored in the cards is loaded together with other accumulated "batches" into a card reader.
3. Upon reading cards, the data is transmitted to the computer for processing.

computer the information may be stored for later batch processing, or it may be processed immediately. The latter is often referred to as *transactional processing,* and has come into wide use in recent years. The concept is illustrated in Figure 2-19. This section describes a wide variety of input concepts, both batch and transactional oriented. Let us begin with the punched card.

THE PUNCHED CARD For many years prior to the introduction of the computer, the punched card, or IBM card as it is commonly called, formed the basis for automated data processing (see Figure 2-18). The card consists of 80 columns and so is capable of storing a record of 80 characters. The coding method used is

**Figure 2-19
Online data entry.**

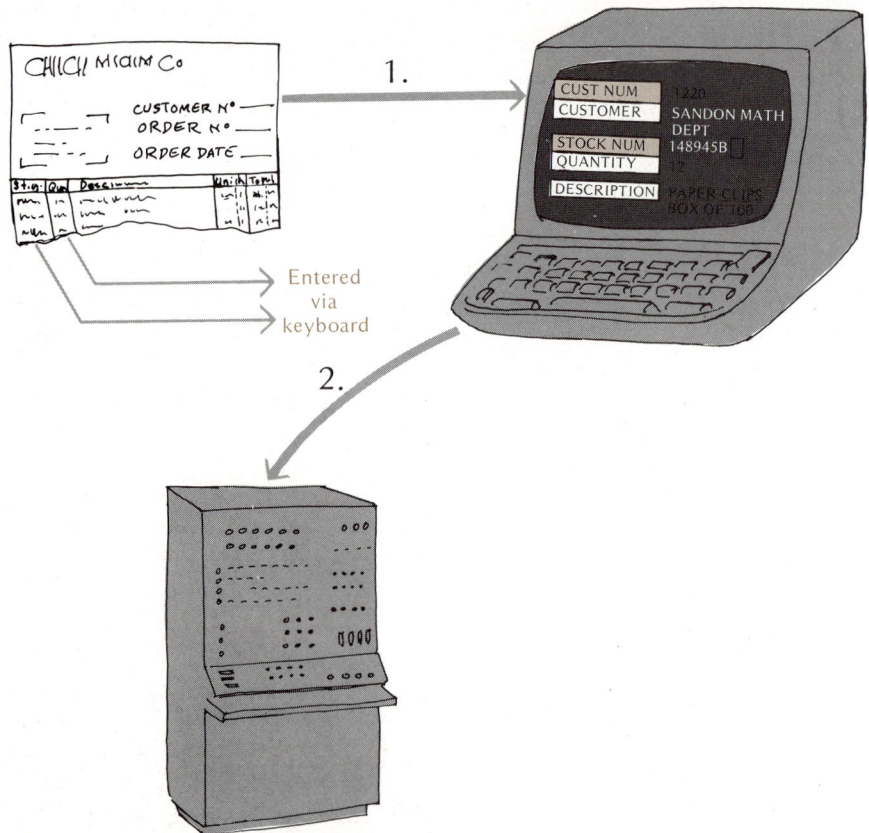

1. Input data is entered via a terminal. Data can be checked and corrected as needed on the spot. Description and pricing information need not be keyed in since such information is already stored in the computer's inventory file.

2. Once verified, the data is stored in the computer for immediate (transactional) processing or for later (batch) processing.

called the *Hollerith code,* named for the early inventor Dr. Herman Hollerith. The card and the associated Hollerith code are illustrated in Figure 2-20.

The card is commonly referred to as the *unit record* because it is normally used to contain data for one complete unit of information. For instance, let us consider the sales order to PQR Wholesale Grocery from Armour Grocery (Fig. 2-21). Note that each entry on the order (each transaction) is recorded on a single card. Thus the three items shown on the form are punched into three separate cards. By inspection we see that some of the information will be common to all of these cards (for example, the customer number, which is 1143), and some will be different for each card (for example, the stock number, which is 135572 for the first record and 228811 for the last). As orders are processed, transaction records are accumulated and processed periodically as part of a batch processing cycle. This is the concept illustrated in Figure 2-18.

The operation of punching cards is performed on a card punch machine, which has a keyboard similar to that of a typewriter. Once punched this information is read into the computer through a *card reader* (refer to Figure 2-18). Card readers are available that read at the rate of up to 2000 cards per minute.

As computer applications became more complex, the disadvantages of the punch card (limited record size, slow rate of input to computer, and cost of

Figure 2-20 Hollerith coding.

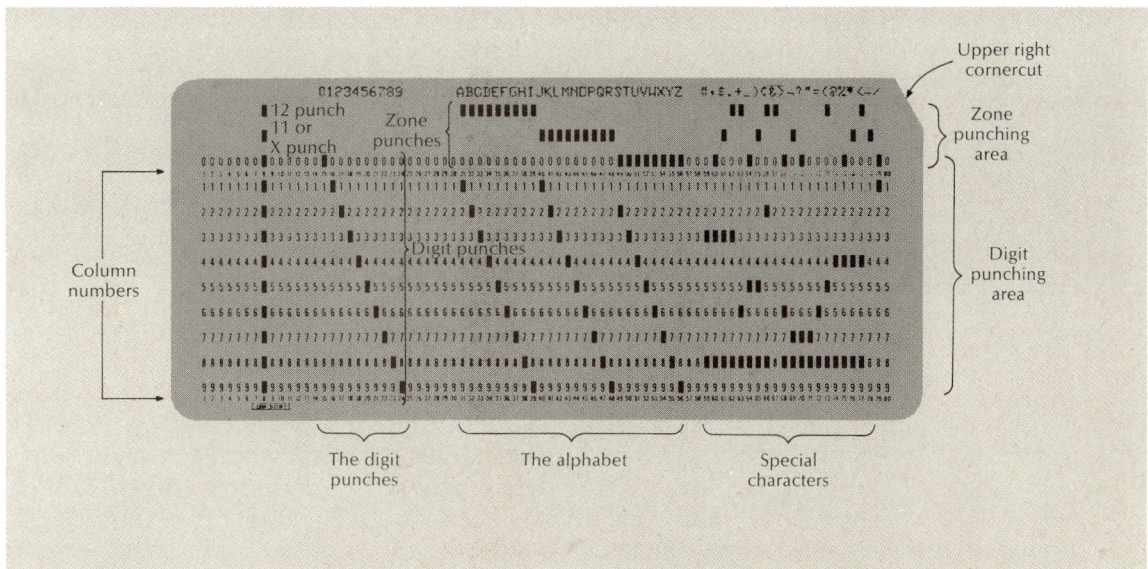

As illustrated, the card consists of two punch areas: zone and digit. The zero row serves both as a zone and a digit. A digit is coded merely by punching that digit position. Letters are coded by a combination of one zone and one digit. Most special characters use three punches in a column.

Figure 2-21 Sales Order Form and the Current Charge card.

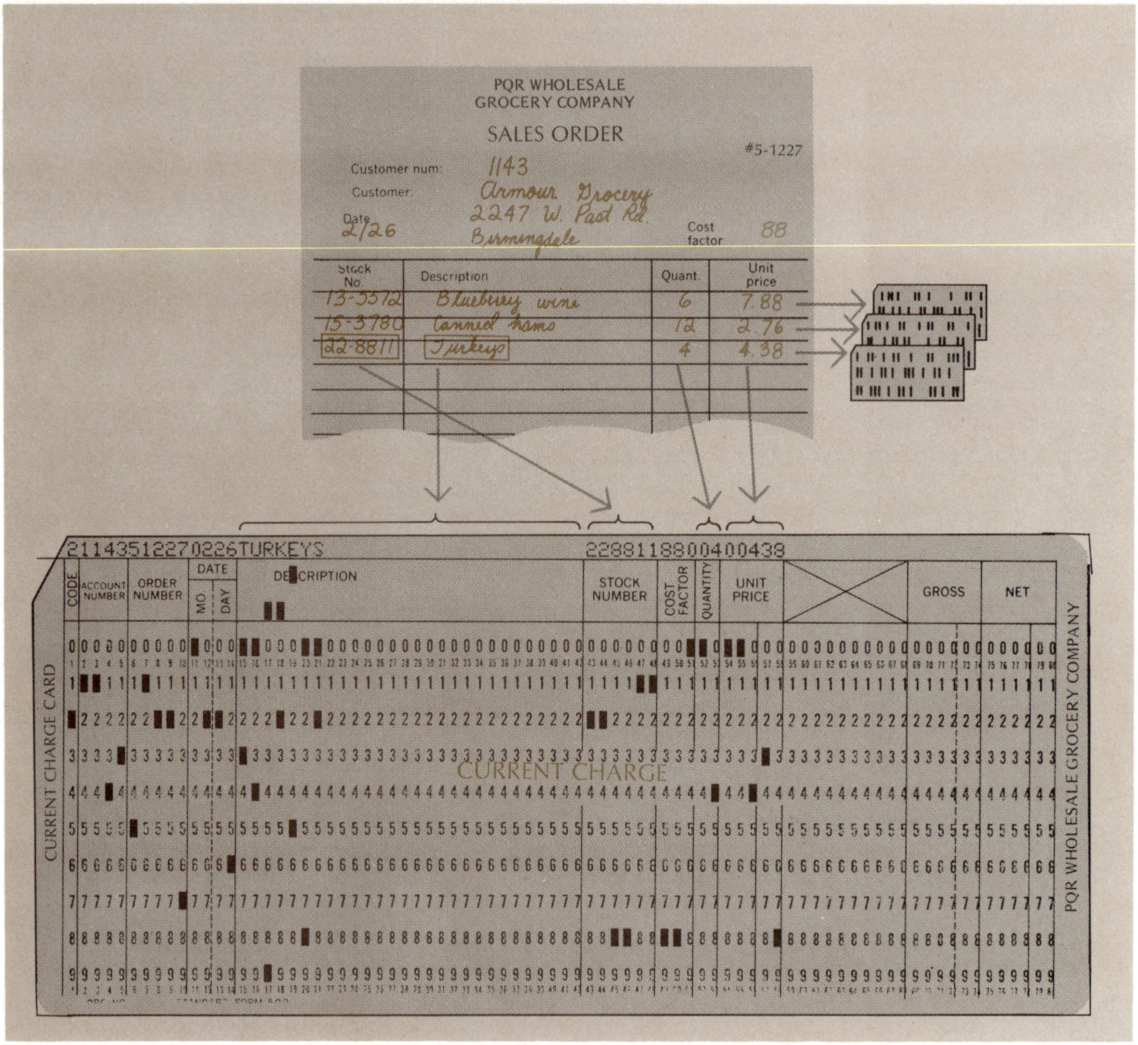

handling) became more significant. With improved technology other methods have become available which, for many applications, are more cost effective in the overall consideration—and in some cases much more so. As a result we see a proliferation of keyboard entry devices that encode information directly onto magnetic disk or tape. The preceding shortcomings of cards are resolved by use of these devices.

With the continually decreasing cost of powerful mini- and microcomputers, it has become possible to incorporate more and more "intelligence" into data entry equipment. The system shown in Figure 2-22 is actually a small special-purpose computer system designed specifically for data entry. As we can see from the schematic representation of Figure 2-22(b), this system includes a number of key stations, all of which enter data to disk storage by way of a special controller.

EXERCISE

2.9   What are some of the advantages of a magnetic medium data entry system over a punched card system?

OTHER INPUT DEVICES   A wide variety of specialized devices is used for entering data into the computer. Bar codes such as the UPC of the grocery industry are employed

Figure 2-22 (a) Key-to-disk data entry system. (*Courtesy of Mohawk Data Sciences Corp.*) (b) Schematic representation of key-to-disk data entry system.

(a)

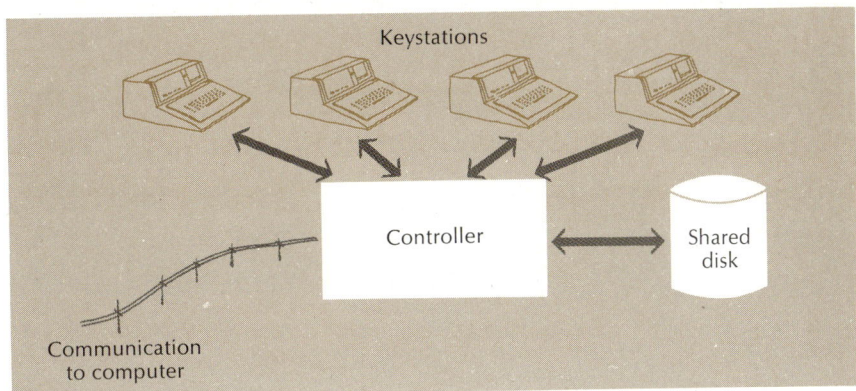

(b)

in many different areas. (Bar codes were first implemented by the railroads in 1967 for automatic car identification.) In some applications the encoded item is moved past a reading element. In others, portable readers coupled to tape cassette recorders are moved across the item. Some libraries utilize automated book lending systems based on bar codes and a centralized computer. In one such system bar-coded labels are affixed to books and other loan material, and also to the library users' identification cards. this concept is illustrated in Figure 2-23.

Magnetic Ink Character Recognition (MICR) has been used by the banking industry since 1959. The technique involves a standardized type font and preprinting of the bank and account numbers across the bottom of the checks. When a check is written and eventually deposited, the transacted amount is also printed. Then all further processing is by special automatic MICR machines.

Figure 2-23   An automated library system. Through use of bar code readers and telephone lines, all lending information can be stored in the computer.

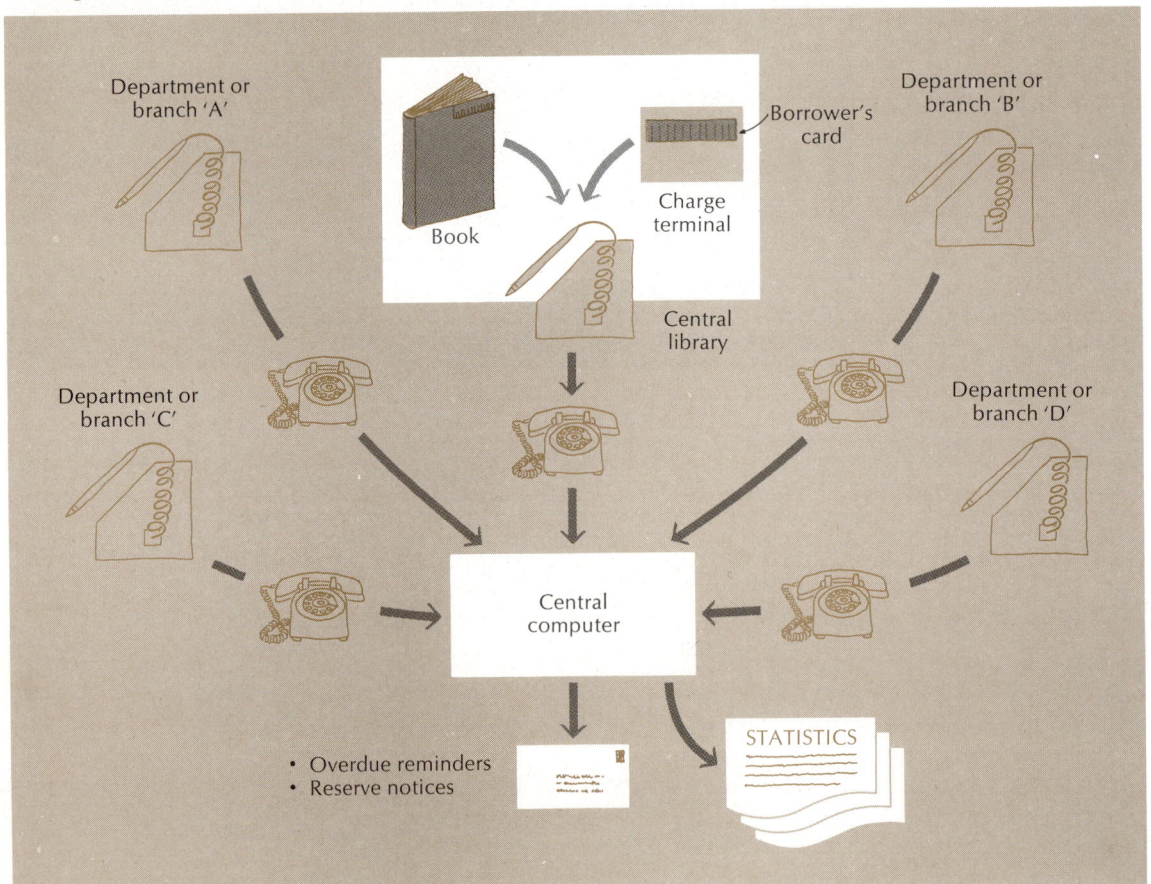

Optical Character Recognition (OCR) is based on machine reading of human-readable information. Optical readers are available that read printed material (printed by other machines), and even hand printing within certain restrictions. The American National Standards Institute (ANSI) has defined the OCR-A font, which is widely used in data processing.

The E-13B font used for MICR and the OCR-A font are shown in Figure 2-24.

Output from the Computer

PRINTED Since the first computers came into use, the standard output medium has
OUTPUT been the printed page. Over the years the average person has learned to

**Figure 2-24
(a) The E-13B type
font. (b) The OCR-A
character font.**

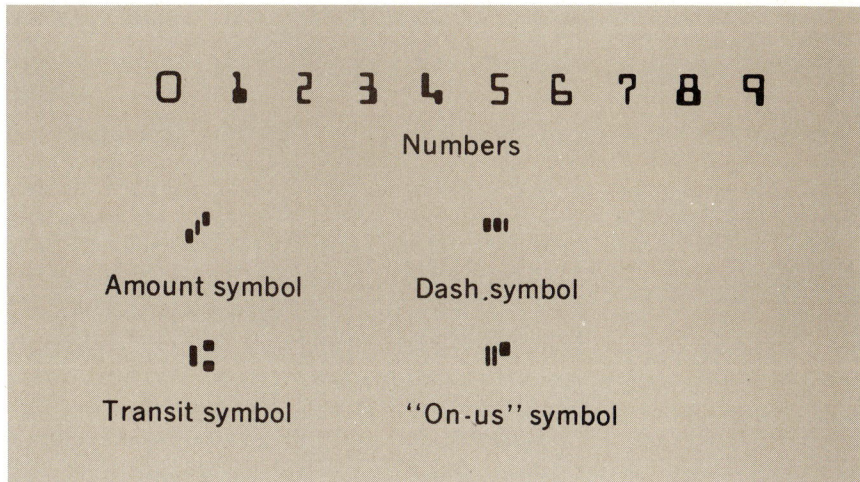

(a)

(b)

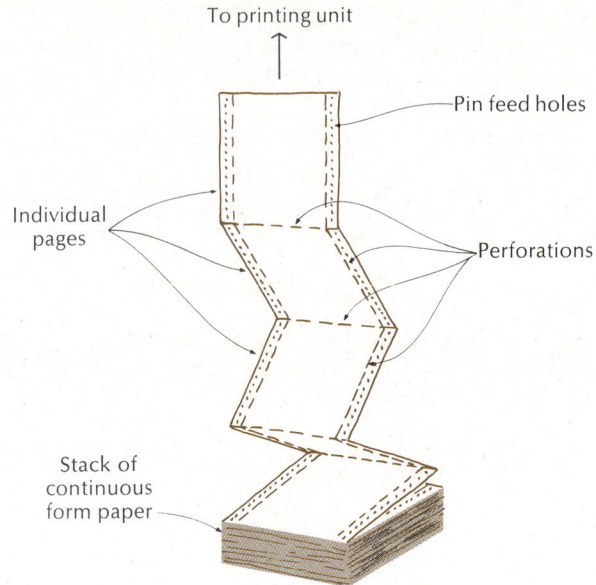

**Figure 2-25
Continuous-feed form
paper.**

recognize computer printout immediately. In general most computer printers are designed to use *continuous-feed forms,* as illustrated in Figure 2-25. This form is actually a single long piece of paper perforated at intervals for easy separation. A special pin feed mechanism is capable of precisely positioning and advancing the paper within the printer. For many applications two or more copies are needed. This need is served by use of multiple-part forms, which are made up of two or more copies separated by carbon paper. With improved technology and continually decreasing costs, we see considerably more versatility in computer-printed output.

There are several ways in which printers can be classified. One classification is *impact,* which prints by means of the impact between a printing element and the paper, and *nonimpact,* in which no physical contact is made with the paper. Many low-cost printers function much like the IBM Selectric typewriter, using a print element embossed with the type characters. For instance, the unit shown in Figure 2-26(a) is called a *daisy-wheel* printer, so-called because the print characters are molded into the ends of radial arms of a print element that has the appearance of a daisy [see Figure 2-26(b)]. Units of this type give high-quality printed output—on a par with that of a good typewriter.

Another technique in wide use is the *dot matrix printing* method. A matrix printer prints a pattern of dots in the shape of the desired character. (This principle is identical to that of many athletic scoreboards.) An illustration of the dot array and some printed characters is shown in Figure 2-27.

Nonimpact printers that use specially treated paper have been used in

Figure 2-26   (a) The Dataproducts D-50 daisy-wheel printer.
(b) Daisy-wheel print element. (*Courtesy of Dataproducts Corporation.*)

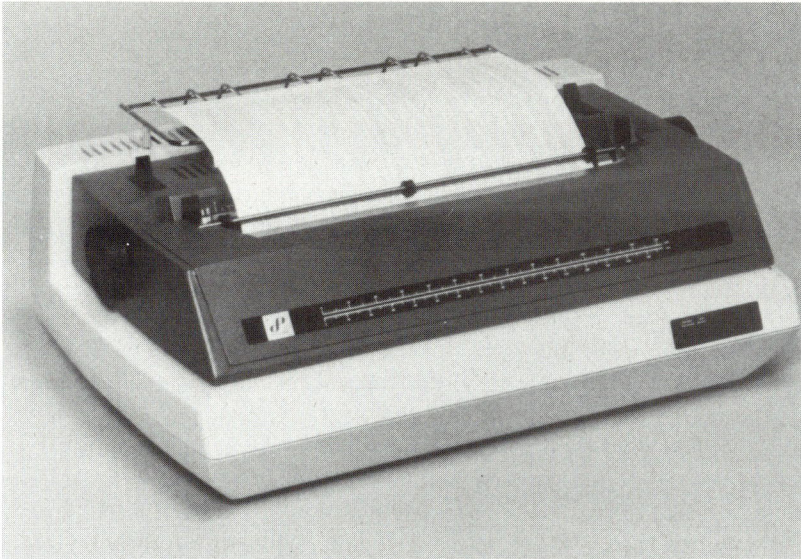

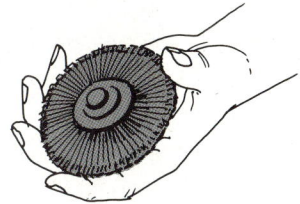
(b)

(a)

the computer field for many years. For example, *thermal* printers use heat-sensitive paper, which is imprinted by contact between selected heated wire ends and the paper. Similarly, *electrostatic* printers print on special electrostatic paper by controlling electric discharges. In general the cost of these units, most of which use the matrix printing principle, is relatively low and so their cost, together with their relative simplicity, is well suited to the low-cost microcomputer market. On the whole the single advantage of impact printers over nonimpact printers is their ability to print multiple copies through the use of carbon paper or pressure-sensitive paper. On the other hand, the mecha-

Figure 2-27
Dot matrix printing.

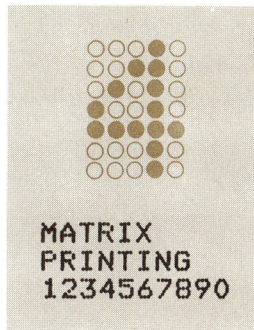

nical printing mechanisms are very intricate, thus resulting in a higher cost and frequency of repair as compared with nonimpact units.

EXERCISE

2.10 What is the difference between an impact printer and a nonimpact printer?

SERIAL, LINE, AND PAGE PRINTERS

Another method by which printers can be classified relates to the amount of information printed during each cycle. That is, some printers print a single character at a time, others a full line, and still others an entire page. As a rule the character printers are the slower ones and page printers the fastest.

Any printer that prints a single character at a time by means of a moving print element is called a *serial* printer. These may be impact or nonimpact; they may also print "solid" letters or use a dot matrix. The daisy-wheel printer illustrated in Figure 2-26 is a serial printer. It prints typewriter-quality output at speeds of up to 50 characters per second via a moving typing element. It is commonly used with computers ranging in size from small micros to full-scale systems. Matrix serial printers are now available that have printing speeds equivalent to more than 200 lines per minute.

For the normal high-volume output associated with the average business data processing center, the high-speed line printer is widely used. As the name implies, each print operation of a line printer involves printing an entire line. This contrasts with serial printers where characters in a line are printed one after the other. Modern line printers will print lines 132 characters wide at speeds in excess of 2000 lines per minute.

One type, the drum printer, uses a rotating cylindrical drum with engraved rows or bands of characters, one band for each printing position. (The drum assembly can be seen in Figure 2-28.) A series of hammers is positioned, one for each band or printing position. As the drum rotates and the paper moves past the printer, hammers are activated in turn, thus causing the printing. The action of the hammer causes the paper to be pressed against the engraved drum, through a ribbon, to effect the printing operation.

For most computer systems the line printer is completely adequate to handle all printed output. However, in some instances huge volumes of printed output are required. To satisfy this need, a number of *page printers* capable of printing an entire page at a time are available. In general, these devices use some type of photographic or electronic technique, and some have speeds in excess of 50,000 lines per minute.

EXERCISE

2.11   Match each type of printer in 1 through 6 with the description, items a–f, that best matches.

1. Matrix	2. Impact	3. Thermal
4. Chain	5. Page	6. Serial

Hammers which impact paper against characters on print drum.

Revolving print drum with inscribed characters.

**Figure 2-28
Hinged drum
assembly of a drum
printer. (*Courtesy of
Dataproducts
Corporation.*)**

a. Requires the use of specially treated paper.
b. The fastest type of printer available
c. Forms characters by an array of dots (much like a football scoreboard).
d. Similar in principle to a typewriter.
e. Includes both serial and line printers; prints by pressing the paper against a print element (or vice versa).
f. Each operation of the printer causes one full line to be printed.

**COMPUTER
OUTPUT
MICROFILM—COM** Overall, our society seems to be characterized by record keeping and pre-serving of printed records. For instance, colleges must store student trans-cript information, businesses must store tax information, and so on. We are becoming engulfed in an ocean of paper. One means for combating this storage and handling problem is the use of *microfilm*. About 30 years ago the DatagraphiX Corporation developed the *Computer Output Microfilm* (COM) process by which computer output could be converted to microfilm. The process, often referred to as *micrographics,* involves writing the output from magnetic tape to photographic film rather than on ordinary paper. It is termed "micro" because the film image is reduced in size to as small as 1/48 of the corresponding printed page size. In general two forms of microfilm are commonly encountered in the data processing field: *roll film* and *microfiche*. Roll film is a continuous length of microfilm on a reel, spool, or cartridge, much like ordinary movie film. With microfiche, or fiche (from the French word meaning "little card"), filmed pages of computer output are mounted in rows and columns on a record card of approximately 4 × 6 inches, as illustrated in Figure 2-29.

**Figure 2-29
Microfiche.**

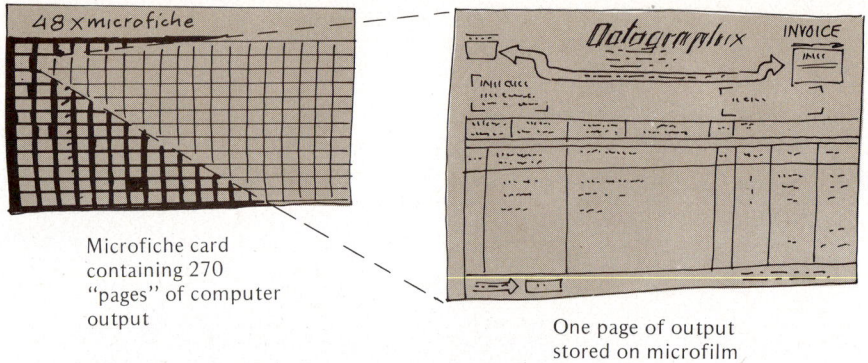

Microfiche card
containing 270
"pages" of computer
output

One page of output
stored on microfilm

Needless to say, if output reports are to be reduced to 1/48 their normal size, humans will require something other than ordinary eyeglasses in order to read them. It is accomplished with relatively low-cost microfiche readers. In effect, such a reader is a projector that allows the selection of a given frame (page of output) to be displayed on the screen.

Like many peripheral operations in data processing, COM has progressed from relatively primitive units to sophisticated systems designed around minicomputers. However, the basic concept still involves the principle of accepting computer output from magnetic tape and converting it to report form on microfilm. This overall notion is illustrated in Figure 2-30. Government agencies with their vast "paperwork" requirements are heavy users, as are banks and many other businesses. The microfiche reader is now encoun-

Figure 2-30 Typical COM system.

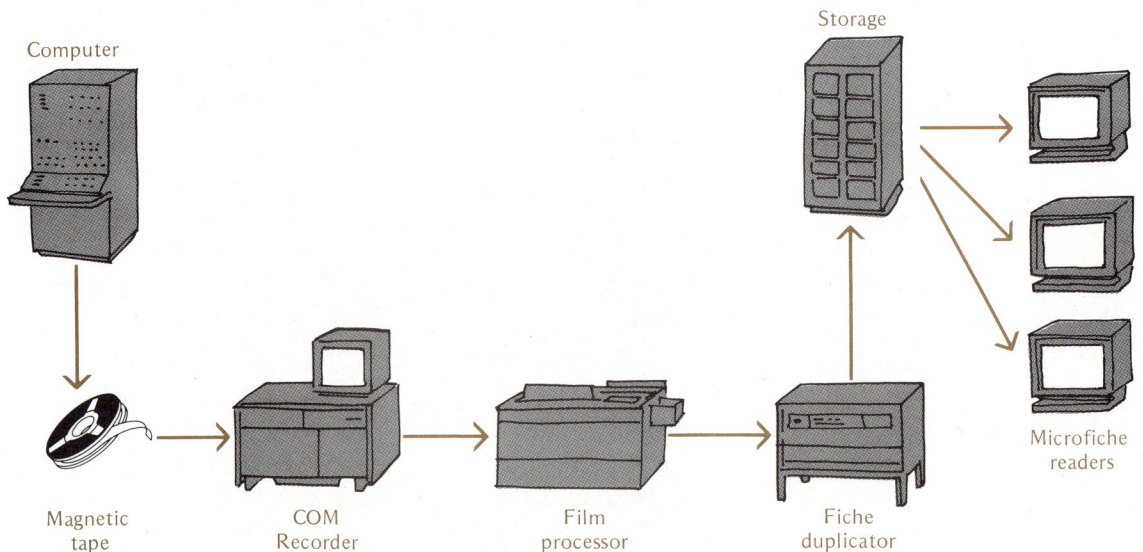

Computer

Storage

Magnetic
tape

COM
Recorder

Film
processor

Fiche
duplicator

Microfiche
readers

tered more and more often by the average person. We see them in such places as libraries, real estate offices and the county assessor's office. In fact, many Federal government reports are available *only* on microfilm. Without the availability of microfilm, the cost of storing and handling the wide variety of reports available would be prohibitive.

It only remains for someone to take pity on the tired newspaper delivery person and use these great advances in technology to lighten his/her Sunday morning load.

EXERCISE

2.12 What are the advantages of microfilm over the printed page for computer output?

Keyboard Terminals

Computer-keyboard-type terminals can be grouped in two broad categories: *hard copy,* which prints output directly to paper; and *soft copy,* which displays results on a television-type screen. Both types find wide use in the computer field. The Decwriter II shown in Figure 2-31 is a widely used dot matrix hard-copy terminal.

The device with which most of us are familiar is the *CRT* (meaning *cathode-ray tube*) terminal. This terminal obtains its name from the television-

**Figure 2-31
The Digital Equipment
Corporation Decwriter
II. A highly reliable
and widely used
terminal, this unit
features a relatively
trouble-free matrix
printing unit which
has a printing speed
of 30 characters per
second. (*Courtesy of
Digital Equipment
Corporation.*)**

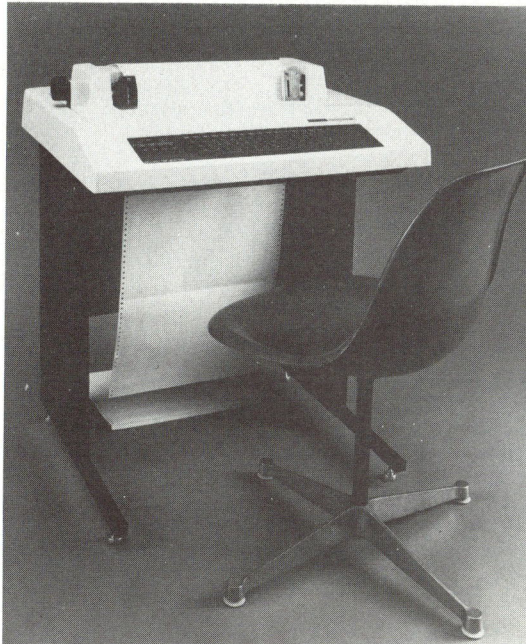

like screen upon which data is displayed. The most commonly encountered CRTs will display 24 80-character lines on the screen (screen size is commonly referred to as 24 by 80). Whereas the input to the computer by way of the keyboard depends upon the operator speed, output to the screen can range up to about 2000 characters per second. At this rate one full screen of 24 lines can be displayed in less than one second. Once the screen is full each new line is inserted at the bottom of the screen. This causes the entire text to be moved up one line, with the top line being lost. With most terminal–computer arrangements this *scrolling* operation can be controlled through appropriate keys on the keyboard. CRT terminals are commonly referred to as *soft-copy* devices because they produce no printed record.

The terminal of Figure 2-32 is called a *graphics* terminal since it is capable not only of ordinary English output but can also display pictorial representations. In addition, it can accept input from the light pen as well as from the keyboard.

Early CRTs were basically typewriter terminal equivalents; that is, they could be used to perform the basic functions of typewriter-like terminals. In a sense they were "dumb"; all "thinking" was performed by the host computer.

**Figure 2-32
Graphics terminal
with light pen. Input
can be either through
the keyboard or via a
light pen. Here the
light pen moves an
object continuously
across the screen.
(*Courtesy of Imlac
Corporation.*)**

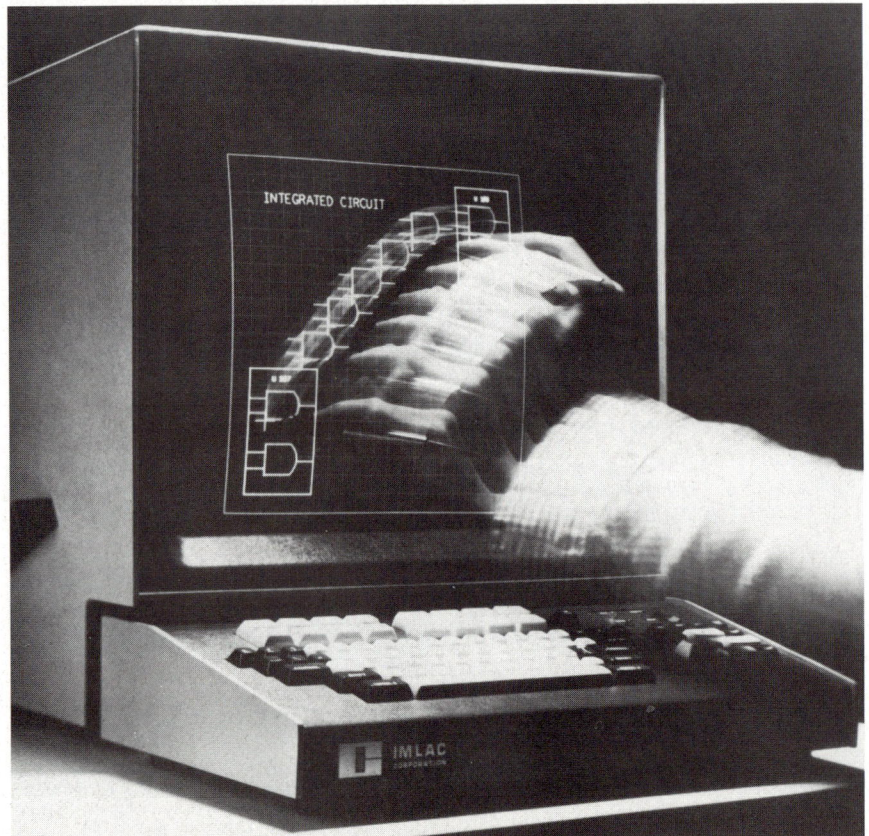

With the advent of microprocessors, the "smart" or *intelligent terminal* made its appearance. In brief, an intelligent terminal is essentially a microcomputer capable of limited data storage and program handling capabilities.

EXERCISE

2.13 What is meant by hard-copy and soft-copy output?

Computer Systems

COMPUTERS CLASSIFIED BY SIZE A fairly common practice today is to classify computers by their cost and size. Although there are no hard and fast rules, the following classifications are typical:

Typical Computer Prices

Type	Purchase Price	Monthly Lease
Large	$3,000,000	$60,000
Medium	1,000,000	20,000
Small	200,000	4,000
Mini	50,000	
Micro	3,000	

In designing a computer system the manufacturer must make many engineering and marketing decisions in order best to meet the needs of the computer users as well as the goals of the manufacturer. For instance, a company purchasing a computer for today will, in all probability, be requiring a larger data processing capability three to six years downstream. Consequently, the manufacturer will design and market a *family* of computers with *upward* compatibility. That is, all programs that can be run on a given computer of the family can be run on any larger computer in the family with little or no modification to the program. In some cases a common family of computers will straddle the range from small to large computer systems. This concept formed the basis for IBM's marketing of the System/360 line introduced in 1964.

Applications for *large-scale* computer systems run the complete spectrum from scientific to business data processing. Similarly, the modes of processing vary widely. For instance, some large systems are dedicated solely to large-scale batch operations. At the other end of the spectrum, others may serve hundreds of online users. The airline reservation system is a perfect example of this type of environment. With the high speeds and enormous processing capabilities of these machines, high-speed magnetic tape is commonly used for input and output. As a general rule the auxiliary storage capabilities of large-scale computers are huge, with capacities commonly measured in the *billions* of characters.

At the high end of the spectrum of large-scale computers we find the extremely large systems sometimes referred to as *supercomputers;* see Figure 2-33. As might be expected, they are larger, faster, and more expensive ($10 million and higher) than large-scale machines. Concurrent with a large installation is normally the need for a substantial, highly trained staff.

Most of the characteristics of the large systems are also true of *medium-scale* computer systems on a scaled-down basis. In general these systems exhibit large storage capacities, both internal and auxiliary, and support a wide range of peripheral devices. They are to be found at all levels of business, industry, and the scientific community. Like large systems, the medium-sized computer installations are usually characterized by a staff that includes personnel for management, systems analysis, programming, and operations.

During the mid-1960s a *small computer* was easily distinguishable from a medium-sized system, not only by price, but also by its relative lack of versatility. However, during the rapid evolution of the computers of the 1970s this changed, and now most small computers have the same capabilities, although on a somewhat reduced scale, as their medium and larger counterparts. And because of their relatively low price (as a rule, less than $200,000) they are used in a wide variety of environments.

EXERCISE

2.14 What is meant by a "family" of computers that are "upward compatible"?

THE MINICOMPUTER Although the first so-called minicomputer was introduced by Digital Equipment Corporation in 1964, their wide use and broad acceptance did not come about until the 1970s. If we asked the question, "what is a mini?," we would

**Figure 2-33
The Cray-1 computer
system.**

Up to four large-scale computer systems serve to feed jobs into this computer or to otherwise concentrate data from multiple terminals. May include internal storage capacity of up to an equivalent of 32 megabytes and up to 48 600-megabyte disk drives. Can perform multiplications at a rate in excess of 10 million per second.

probably come up with a rather nebulus answer. As with the computer field in general, minis reflect the rapid technological evolution that has occurred. Many minicomputer systems currently available have the power and versatility of the large-scale systems of the early 1960s, and of even some low-end medium-scale systems currently available.

The term *minicomputer* is placed in its proper perspective by the following excerpt from a magazine article on the subject.

WHERE HAVE ALL THE MINIS GONE

by Myles E. Walsh

The term "minicomputer" is rapidly becoming an anachronism.* It is not that there are no longer going to be any minis, but rather, there never were any. . . .

MINIS CATCH ON

It has been said, "a minicomputer is a marketing phenomenon." When minis first became available, the trend in computers was for bigger and faster machines. Faced with an attitude like this, the makers of computers that were smaller and slower had to come up with something that would attract attention to their technological "giant-step backward." The term "minicomputer" did just that.

Once the attention of the potential user had been diverted from the bigger and the faster, the manufacturers of the smaller and slower pieces of equipment were able to show the user that in some areas of his business, smaller and slower were better suited and more economical than bigger and faster. And so, minis began to catch on. Yet, minis were nothing more than relatively smaller and slower computers compared to those which dominated the minds of users and the marketplace at the time. As time passed, however, minis got bigger and faster and non-minis got smaller and, in some ways, slower.

From *Infosystems,* July 1978. Reprinted with permission of Hitchcock Publishing Company

*The word *anachronism* refers to anything which has lost its significance with the passage of time.

The minicomputer shown in Figure 2-34 is a powerful business system equipped with a broad range of software. Indeed, to quote the author of the article from *Infosystems,* "The distinction between mini and non-mini, which was never too clear, is now non-existent."

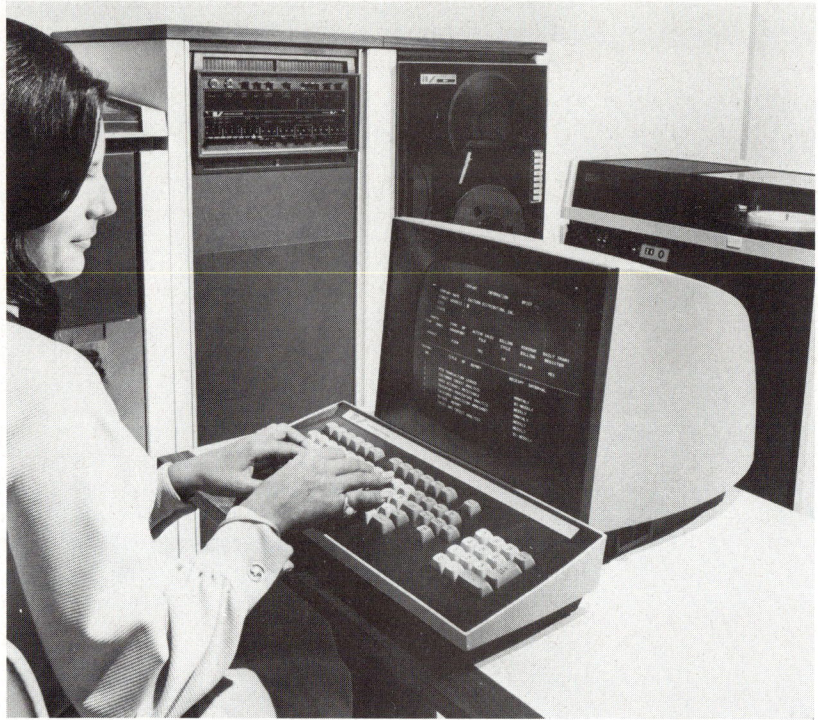

**Figure 2-34
A modern
minicomputer.
(Courtesy of Four
Phase Systems, Inc.)**

EXERCISE

2.15　What is a minicomputer?

**THE
MICROCOMPUTER**
With the coining of the term *minicomputer,* can the microcomputer be far behind? (And what comes after the micro?) Whereas the mini has been with us in concept (if not in name) since 1964, the *microcomputer* or *microprocessor* is a result of recent advances in large-scale integrated circuits (LSI). Introduced by Intel Corporation in 1971, microprocessors have had a huge impact not only on the computer industry, but on many other industries as well. Basically a microprocessor is the control unit and arithmetic logic unit of a computer, all on a single chip less than one quarter of an inch square. It is difficult to conceive that the several thousand electronic components that require a cabinet the size of an ordinary desk can be etched onto such a chip. The low cost (as little as $10) and small size of microprocessors has made it possible to put a "brain" in all sorts of machines. We can even buy a sewing machine controlled by a microprocessor, or an automobile with a microprocessor to optimize the control of the engine and provide better pollution control. There appears to be no end to the possibilities for this amazing device.

When instruction and data memory chips are added, along with input/

output circuitry, the microprocessor becomes a microcomputer (see Figure 2-35). Combine this with a keyboard, a television-like display, and a small disk storage unit (auxiliary storage) and you have a desk-top microcomputer system selling for approximately $2000. In just a very few years both the hardware and software capabilities of the micro have increased at a phenomenal rate. It is truly mind-boggling that these small desk-top units have capabilities exceeding those of large computer systems that cost as much as $1 million just 20 to 25 years ago.

The microcomputer (or personal computer, as it is sometimes called) finds use in a wide variety of applications. It is used by individuals as well as by businesses ranging from small one-person operations to large corporations. Some commonly encountered individual applications include the following:

- Games and entertainment
- Personal budgeting and cash management
- Income tax preparation
- Programmed learning
- Word processing
- Recipe storage and menu planning

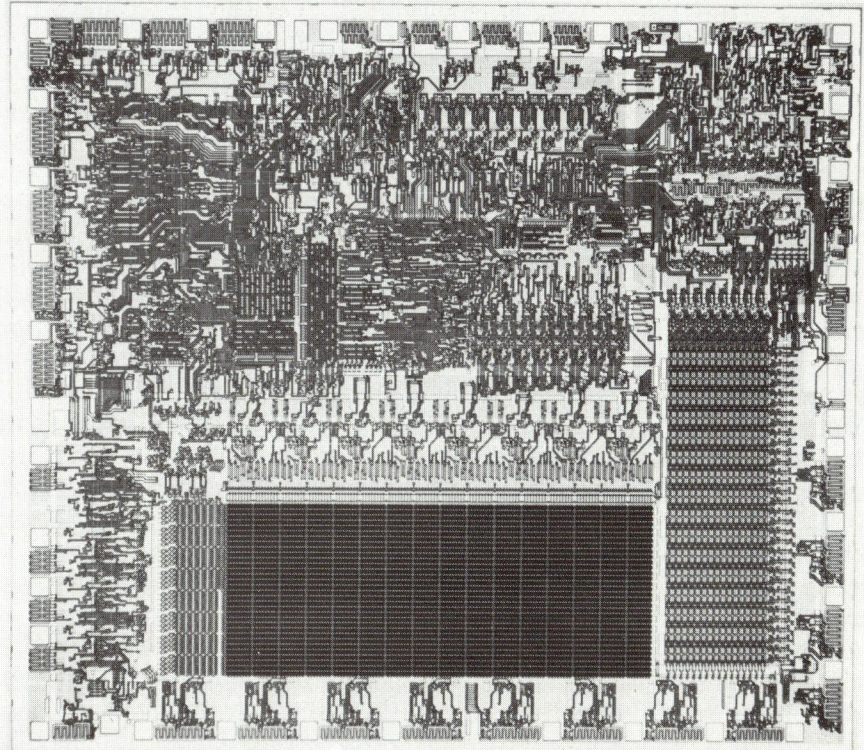

Figure 2-35 (a)Intel 8748 Single-chip micro-computer—includes approximately 20,000 transistors, approximate size is ¼ inch square; for perspective, refer to Figure 2-34. (*Courtesy Intel Corporation*.)

Figure 2-36 The Radio Shack TRS80 microcomputer. (*Courtesy Radio Shack Division of Tandy Corporation*.)

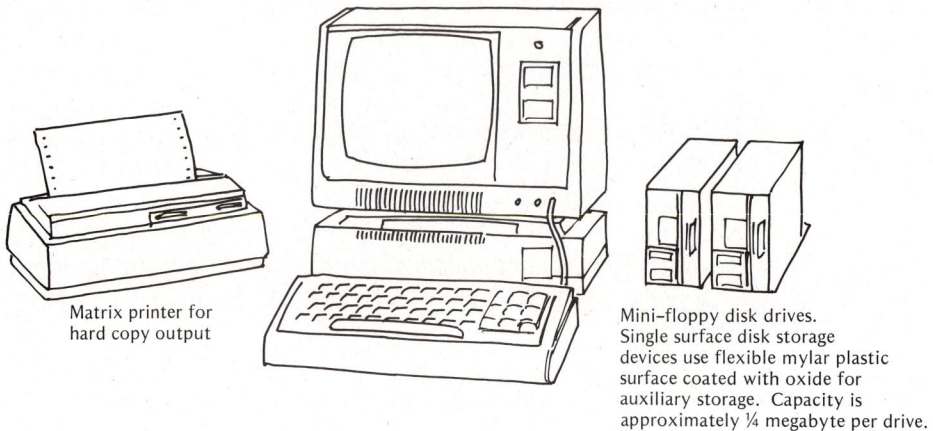

Matrix printer for
hard copy output

Mini–floppy disk drives.
Single surface disk storage
devices use flexible mylar plastic
surface coated with oxide for
auxiliary storage. Capacity is
approximately ¼ megabyte per drive.

Many small businesses and nonprofit organizations use microcomputers to relieve much of the routine record keeping. Some typical applications include the following:

- Payroll
- Accounts receivable and payable maintenance
- General ledger accounting
- Balance sheet and income statement preparation
- Maintenance of customer files
- Word processing

The large number of microcomputers in use and the relatively low cost of micro equipment has caused a virtual explosion in two broad areas. First, a wide variety of hardware items have become available which plug into existing computers. These have increased the versatility of the modern microcomputer severalfold. For instance, one such device allows input into the computer through what is effectively the surface of a special drawing board. Another allows the computer to send computer output to an audio loudspeaker for electronically generated voice output. Second, a huge software industry has sprung up. (Software, the programs which make the computer work, is described in the next section.) These include a wide range of preprogrammed systems that allow the computer to be used for complex applications with little or no knowledge of how the computer works. Many of these software packages, costing thousands of dollars on a large computer, may be purchased for $100 to $200. The reason for the low price is simply the huge size of the market. This software is truly revolutionizing the way in which small businesses handle their office needs.

The present-day "explosion" of the microcomputer is indeed an astonishing happening.

THE SMALL BUSINESS COMPUTER In addition to the preceding classifications of computers, the computer industry has elected to create the *small business computer* category. In general this refers to a complete computer system, usually with applications software (the topic of the next section), which is oriented to business data processing activities. The computer itself may fall in the micro, the mini, or the small computer category. Auxiliary storage devices, usually disk, are standard, together with special software for file processing and common business data processing functions. As a rule they are found in businesses which, only 10 to 15 years ago, would have performed all of their record keeping either manually or with a card processing system. Because of the high cost of programming, many small business systems are sold on a *turnkey* basis. That is, a single vendor supplies not only the machine itself, but also all of the needed software, such as that to handle general ledger, accounts payable and receivable, payroll, inventory, and so on. (As an example, refer to the system of Figure 2-37.) The computer in general, and the small business computer in particular, are revolutionizing the business office. Without a doubt the data processing outlook is bright for the small business.

In Retrospect

The first 15 years of the computer industry saw three distinct "generations" of computers evolve from vacuum tubes to large-scale integrated circuits.

Figure 2-37 Small business microcomputer system. (*Courtesy Radio Shack Division of Tandy Corporation.*)

During the past 15 years computer advances have been at an ever-accelerating pace.

The basic logical components of the modern digital computer are (1) input/output, (2) arithmetic/logic unit, (3) control unit, (4) storage, and (5) auxiliary storage.

Getting information into and out of the computer has always been a bottleneck. As a result many different types of devices are used, ranging from card readers and punches to typewriter-like terminals.

When information is brought into the computer, it must be stored. Numerous devices are used for this; they range from the older magnetic core to the now widely used semiconductor memory. In addition, large amounts of archival-type information can be stored on magnetic tape and disk. Processing of the data, including arithmetic operations and decision making, is carried out by the arithmetic/logic unit.

The overall operation of the computer is directed by the control unit, which can be considered as analogous to a combined switchboard operator and police officer directing traffic. The collection of the control unit, arithmetic/logic unit, and internal storage is usually referred to as the central processing unit, or simply CPU.

Large-scale computers with broad capabilities lease for up to as much as $100,000 per month. At the other end of the spectrum small business computers that have the processing capabilities of large machines of 25 years ago may be purchased for as little as $10,000 to $15,000 *complete.*

The so-called minicomputer came into being in 1964 with the introduction of the Digital Equipment Corporation PDP 8. Some of the mini systems marketed today actually have the capabilities and versatility of many medium-sized computers.

Another of many "computer revolutions" occurred in 1971 with the introduction of the microprocessor—almost a computer on a chip. Microcomputers available today for $2000 to $3000 provide the processing power of large machines of the first generation.

ANSWERS TO PRECEDING EXERCISES

2.1   A logical operation is any operation performed by the arithmetic/logic unit that involves comparing two quantities.

2.2   A bit is a single binary digit (0 or 1); in fact the word bit is a contraction of binary digit. A byte is a unit of storage within the computer that consists of 8 bits.

2.3   Binary information (0 and 1) is stored within the computer by electronic or magnetic components that can be set in either of two states. For instance, 0 might be represented by a capacitor that is uncharged and 1 by a capacitor that is charged.

2.4   Semiconductor memory is faster than bubble memory; however, bubble memory has the advantage of greater capacity for a given size and cost.

2.5   Processing magnetic tape involves reading from one end of the tape to the other; it is impossible to read a record from the center of a tape without reading and checking all records preceding it. Thus the only practical means of processing data on tape is to store it in some type of sequence, then process it from the first record through the last (sequentially).

2.6   Information in internal storage is stored and accessed by the individual character but that on tape by the record. Furthermore, internal storage can be randomly accessed; tape cannot be.

2.7   In batch processing transactions are accumulated over a period of time and then processed periodically. With online processing each transaction is entered directly into the computer as it is received and it is processed immediately.

2.8   Direct access storage usually relates to auxiliary storage devices. It is storage in which a record may be accessed directly without regard to its physical location on the storage medium.

2.9   The advantages of a magnetic medium data entry system over cards are numerous:

1. Record length is not limited to 80 positions.
2. Medium costs are reduced.
3. Data entry is faster.
4. There is less noise, and so operator fatigue is decreased.
5. Editing and accumulating can be performed by the computerized controller.
6. The data is entered directly to high-speed computer input media.

2.10 An impact printer prints by means of impacting between the paper and a print element (the typewriter is the simplest example). A nonimpact printer does not use impact contact between a printing element and the paper. The thermal printer (prints by heated elements) and the electrostatic printer (prints by electric discharge) require specially treated paper. The ink jet printer sprays a fine jet of ink to form printed characters.

2.11 1, c; 2, e; 3, a; 4, f; 5, b; 6, d.

2.12 For large volumes of output microfilm is less expensive in media cost (compared with paper), and it is more convenient and inexpensive to store, handle, and retrieve.

2.13 Hard-copy output is output from the computer that is printed on paper. Soft copy is output that is displayed on a CRT screen.

2.14 A family of computers is a series of computer models, each with a greater capacity than the preceding. Upward compatability means that all software written for a given model will run on any of the larger models. This design philosophy is intended to allow for the user with a growing data processing need who will be upgrading to larger systems as time progresses.

2.15 There is really no good definition that distinguishes between a machine that should be called a minicomputer and one that should be called a small- or medium-scale computer. Refer to the article quoted from the computer magazine *Infosystems*.

ADDITIONAL EXERCISES

2.16 What is the difference between RAM and ROM?

2.17 Operation of computers and computer components is commonly measured in terms of milliseconds (0.001 second) and microseconds (0.000001 second), and now even in terms of nanoseconds (0.000000001 second). If electricity travels at the rate of 186,000 miles per second, how far will it travel in 1 nanosecond? Conjecture about the implications of such short times for the electronic design of computer components.

2.18 Why is the concept of an "upward compatibility" of a computer series important to the computer user? Why is it important to the computer manufacturer?

2.19 **Matching**   Match each item in items a through f with the most appropriate description in 1 through 6.

a. Arithmetic unit
b. ROM
c. Random access memory
d. Control unit
e. Magnetic disk
f. Central processing unit

1. Oversees all operations within the computer.
2. That portion of the computer in which logic and arithmetic operations are performed.
3. Consists of the control unit, storage, and arithmetic unit of the computer.
4. A commonly used auxiliary storage device.
5. A computer storage device from which stored information can be read but not written over.
6. Pertaining to a storage device in which the time required to obtain data is independent of where the data is stored.

2.20 **True–False**   Determine whether each of the following is true or false.

1. Some commonly used computer input devices are the card reader, paper-tape reader, optical character reader, and magnetic core.
2. The speeds of modern card readers and printers have increased to the point where the input and output devices are far faster than the computer itself.
3. The task of directing operations within the computer is the function of the control unit.
4. The control unit, storage, and auxiliary storage make up what is commonly referred to as the central processing unit (CPU) of the computer.
5. Magnetic tape and magnetic disk are commonly used auxiliary storage devices.
6. Internal storage types include core, semiconductor, and bubble.
7. One disadvantage of the magnetic core for internal storage is that it loses its magnetism when the electric current in the wire passing through it is turned off.
8. Auxiliary storage is commonly used to greatly increase the storage capacity of a computer at a moderate cost.
9. An advantage of magnetic tape over disk is that tape records can be processed either sequentially or randomly but disk records can be processed only randomly.

10. The term *software* refers to programs used with computers.
11. One means of categorizing computer systems as large, medium, or small is by their cost.
12. Many medium-scale computer systems have most of the same capabilities that large-scale systems do, except on a scaled-down basis.
13. The most distinguishing characteristic of minicomputers relates to the limited software available with them.
14. The introduction of the powerful microprocessor together with the micro-computer has rendered the minicomputer obsolete.

3

```
021     DATA DIVISION.
022     FILE SECTION.
023     FD  IN-FILE                        LABEL RECORDS OMITTED.
024     01  PAY-RATE-RECORD.
025         05  J-CODE                     PIC 9(3).
026         05  P-RATE                     PIC 99V99.
027         05  FILLER                     PIC X(73).
028     01  PAYROLL-RECORD.
029         05  EMPLOYEE-JOB-CODE          PIC 9(3).
030         05  HOURS-WORKED               PIC 99V9.
031         05  FILLER                     PIC X(74).
032
033     WORKING-STORAGE SECTION.
034     77  EOF                            PIC X(3)      VALUE 'NO'.
035     77  TABLE-LOADED                   PIC X(3)      VALUE 'NO'.
036     77  SEARCH-STATUS                  PIC X.
037     77  X                              PIC X.
038     77  OVERFLOW-MESSAGE               PIC X(41)     VALUE
039             'TABLE SIZE EXCEEDED.  PROGRAM TERMINATED.'.
040
041     01  TABLE-ACCESS-ITEMS             USAGE COMP.
042         05  SUBSCRIPT                  PIC 99        VALUE ZERO.
043         05  TABLE-SIZE                 PIC 99        VALUE 25.
044
045     01  PAY-RATE-TABLE.
046         05  PAY-RATE-TABLE-ENTRY   OCCURS 25 TIMES.
047             10  JOB-CODE               PIC 9(3).
048             10  PAY-RATE               PIC 99V99.
049
050     01  GROSS-PAY-ITEMS.
051         05  GROSS-PAY                  PIC 9(3)V99.
052         05  EMPLOYEE-PAY-RATE          PIC 99V99.
053                                                 (a)
054     PROCEDURE DIVISION.
055     001-MAIN-PROGRAM.
056         PERFORM A100-INITIALIZATION.
057         PERFORM A200-PROCESS UNTIL EOF
058         PERFORM A300-TERMINATION.
059         STOP RUN.   PERFORM H-BONUS.
060
061     A100-INITIALIZATION.
062                                      (b)
063
064
```

Is Seniority ≥ 10 ?

No   Classification = S   Yes

Form   Form

Action to be taken if Seniority is equal or greater than 10.

Resulting action if SENIORITY ≥ 10 will be this or this.

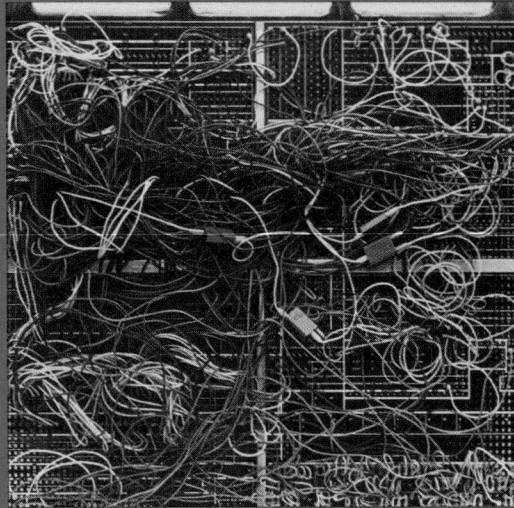

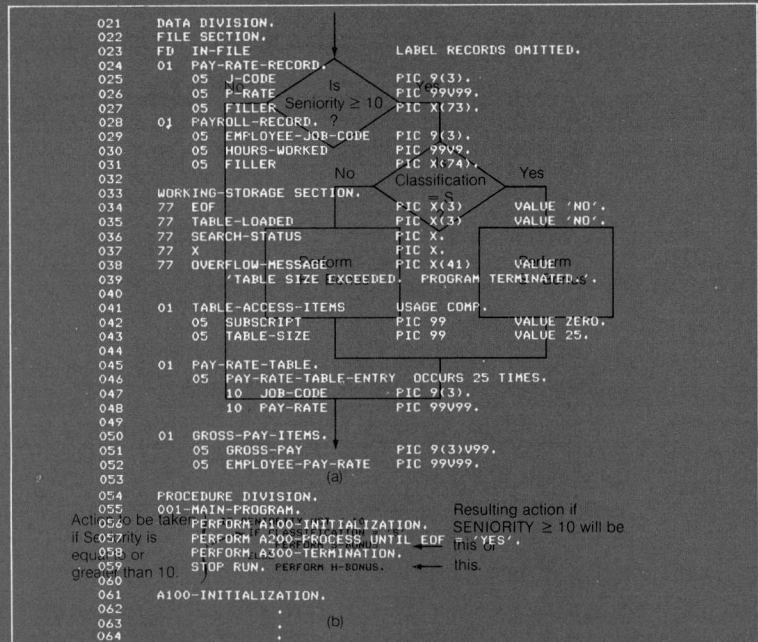

Computer Software and Programming

OBJECTIVES

High computing speed, large storage capacities, and sophisticated input/output capabilities are three of the many hardware features of present-day computers. However, to most users programming systems or *software* are just as important. This section deals with computer software, including user-oriented languages with which we can use the computer to solve problems. Emphasis is also placed on the problem-solving techniques that are used with the computer. From this section you will gain an insight into the following important concepts.

- The principles and features of an operating system and how it improves computer efficiency.
- The nature of computer languages and their classification into three broad categories:

  machine language, which is the form required by the computer
  assembly language, which avoids much detail of the machine language yet gives complete access to the machine features
  high-level language, which is designed for "people use"

- The basic principles of language translation (compiling) in which a program written in a user-oriented language is converted to machine language
- The six basic steps of designing a computer application: *problem definition* (what is to be done), *analysis* (how it is to be done), *programming* (doing it), *testing* (making sure it is correct), *documenting* (describing it), and *production* (using it)
- The principles of top-down design, which involve breaking a large problem into related components and handling these components independently of each other.
- Structured programming methods, which involve orderly techniques for programming
- The use of flowcharts (diagrams) in representing computer program logic
- The nature of pseudocode and its use in preparing a program

Key terminology important to this section includes:

assembler	language processor	pseudocode
assembly language	loop structure	selection structure
Cobol	machine language	source program
compiler	object program	structured programming
flowchart	operating system	supervisor program
Fortran	process structure	top-down design
high-level language		

The Concept of Software

CLASSIFICATION OF SOFTWARE The introduction of the third generation of computers in 1964 (see Figure 2-1) saw not only huge strides in hardware, but also a heavy emphasis on software. Section 2 describes various aspects of hardware. This section is devoted to *software,* the computer programs designed to make the computer work. In many cases a decision is made to purchase one computer rather than another on the basis of quality software available. The best system is not necessarily the one with the best hardware. In a broad sense software can be classified in four general categories.

1. Operating and control programs, which make the computer work. For general applications use, present-day computers are virtually useless without these. They are usually furnished by the computer manufacturer.
2. Applications programs, which are designed and written to handle particular applications. For instance, the inventory control system described in Section 1 might consist of a series of programs written by a software company and purchased by PQR.
3. Programming languages, which are designed by the end user for solving problems and writing applications programs. These are described in greater detail later in this section.
4. Language translators, which convert programs from the programmer-oriented language form to the binary form required by the computer. Language translation is described later in this section.

BASIC CONCEPTS OF AN OPERATING SYSTEM The *operating* system of a computer is a set of programs designed to manage the hardware resources of the computer. Basically the computer hardware is capable of performing relatively simple arithmetic types of operations and rudimentary input output functions. Some of the operations performed by various programs of the operating system are

- Support programming languages, which relieve the programmer of detail.
- Maintain files of data and user programs that are stored on disk in the system *library*.
- Provide for automatic transition from job to job.
- Control the efficient operation of input and output devices.
- In some computers, control the environment such that two or more jobs or users can be running concurrently.

SUPERVISOR PROGRAM The key to an operating system is the *supervisor* program (sometimes called the *monitor* or the *executive* program). In a conventional data processing environment the supervisor is loaded into storage (from a library) at the beginning of the day. It then remains in storage as long as the computer is in use (see Figure 3-1) and either directly or indirectly maintains control of the computer system. Although functions performed by a supervisor vary from system to system, the basic principles of an operating system in general, and of a supervisor in particular, are illustrated by the schematic representation of Figure 3-2. From this characterization we can see that the term *supervisor* appears to be very appropriate.

EXERCISE

3.1   What is an operating system?

Programming Languages

MACHINE-LEVEL LANGUAGES   A wide variety of programming languages (some very specialized) are currently available to ease the programming burden. The choice of a particular language usually depends on the nature of the job being performed and the language capabilities of the computer being used. This will become more meaningful as we study the characteristics of commonly used languages.

In the beginning we had to learn the machine's language and prepare instructions to the machine in exactly that language. Over the next 20 years, through the use of what has become known as *programming systems,* the situation has become reversed to the point where the machine, in a sense, understands the human languages of English and mathematics. The development of these high-level languages has been a major factor in the advance of computer technology.

Regardless of which programming language we use in solving a problem, the program ultimately must be converted to its machine language equivalent for execution by the computer. When programming with a user-oriented language such as Fortran, we may use a form that looks much like an algebraic equation in directing the computer to perform computations. However, in machine language each operation, such as addition and subtraction, must be defined explicitly. Furthermore, programs written for one machine will not work on another machine because of design differences. For

**Figure 3-1
The supervisor in
storage.**

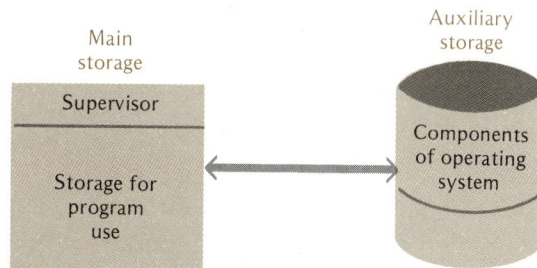

Figure 3-2   Animated representation of an operating system. (*From J. K. Rice and J. R. Rice, Introduction to Computer Science; copyright 1969 by Holt, Rinehart and Winston. Used by permission.*)

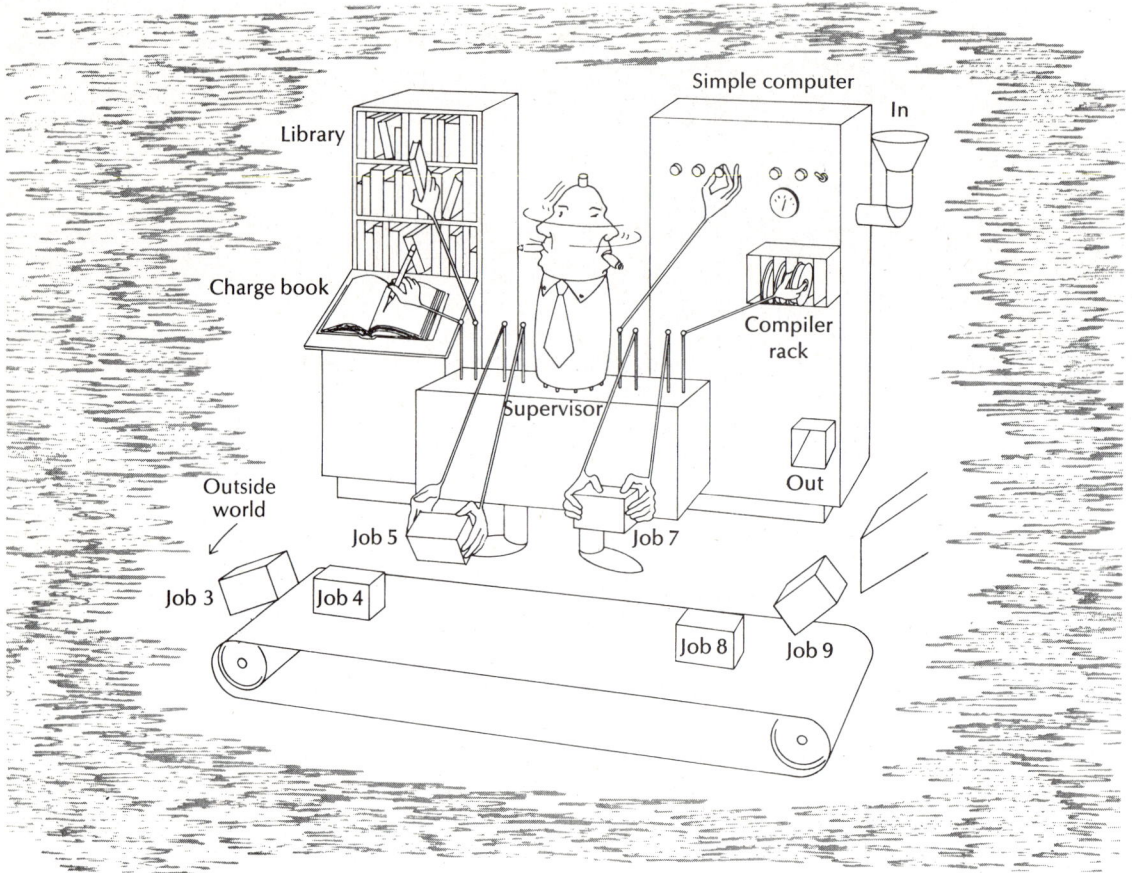

example, the following are typical examples of machine language instructions for adding two numbers:

124130144300	Burroughs B 200
A4733BC	IBM 1401
210538618772	IBM 1620
1010100000000111	Varian 620 minicomputer
010110101010000011000000000111000	IBM 360/370

These forms are indeed clumsy. Because of the immense amount of detail required, few programs are ever written in machine language. More often special *symbolic assembly languages* are used that free the programmer from most of the exacting detail. For instance, the programmer can use symbolic abbreviations to represent storage areas assigned to data rather than binary addresses.

To illustrate the concept of an assembly language, let us consider the following relatively simple task.

> **Example 3-1**   Each record of a data file contains two input fields (call them *a* and *b*). Read each record, compute the sum of *a* and *b*, and print the result.
>
> The detailed sequence of operations required in a computer program would be as follows:
>
> 1. Get the next data record, call the first field *a* and the second field *b*.
> 2. Add *a* to *b* and call the result *sum*.
> 3. Print the values for *a*, *b*, and *sum*.
> 4. Return to step 1.

As we can see from this sequence of steps, this is a relatively simple set of operations (*program*). These exact principles are carried over to the IBM 360/370 assembly language program* shown in Figure 3-3. Although this does not represent a complete program, it is sufficient to illustrate principles. We can see that each instruction consists of three general components:

- *Label.*   Equivalent to the steps numbered above, it provides the means for referring to an instruction or a data quantity.
- *Operation.*   This defines the operation to be performed; for example, read a record, add, and so on.
- *Operands.*   This defines the fields that are to be involved in the operation.

Together with the descriptive comments, this program is fairly self-explanatory.

EXERCISE

3.2   What are the three basic components of an assembly language instruction?

HIGH-LEVEL LANGUAGES   A *compiler* is a much more powerful programming tool than an assembler. With an assembler one symbolic instruction must be written for each machine language instruction assembled, but with a compiler one statement will

---

*The operations RN and WN (for Read Numbers and Write Numbers) are so-called macro instructions. They are not supplied by IBM and would have to be predefined by the programmer.

Figure 3-3   IBM 360/370 assembly language program.

Instr. {	LOOP	RN	A,B	READ NUMBERS FROM INPUT DATA INTO A AND B
		L	7,A	LOAD VALUE IN A INTO REGISTER 7
		A	7,B	ADD VALUE IN B TO VALUE IN REGISTER 7
		ST	7,SUM	STORE REGISTER 7 CONTENTS (A + B) IN SUM
		WN	A,B,SUM	WRITE NUMBERS FROM A,B, AND SUM
		B	LOOP	REPEAT THE PROCESS
Data fields {	A	DS	F	DEFINE THE STORAGE AREA A
	B	DS	F	DEFINE THE STORAGE AREA B
	SUM	DS	F	DEFINE THE STORAGE AREA SUM

produce a multitude of machine language instructions. Another difference between an assembler and a compiler is that the assembler language is so closely tied to the computer's machine language that it is impossible to use the assembler language of one computer on any other computer. This is not the case with compiler languages, which are generally considered *procedure oriented* or *problem oriented* rather than machine oriented.

FORTRAN   In 1954 the concept of the FORmula TRANslating language was proposed. The system was to be designed around statements that were as near to algebraic terminology as was possible. This started a major trend in manufacturer-independent languages, leading to a widespread use of Fortran by virtually all computer makers. However, one problem that quickly became apparent was the tendency of each computer maker to extend its version of the language to make it better than that of the competition. Since most manufacturers have different ideas about the "best way" to do something, the idea of transportability between different machines was jeopardized. The problem was remedied by a standards organization that is now known as the American National Standards Institute (ANSI). Through large working committees composed of representatives of computer users as well as manufacturers, ANSI has been successful in defining a "standard" Fortran to which manufacturers have adhered reasonably well. The most widely used version of the language is Fortran IV, which was standardized in 1966. The most recent standard (ANSI X3.9–1978) was published in 1978 but is commonly referred to as 77 Fortran (since it was originally scheduled for 1977 publication).

To prepare programs in Fortran requires no knowledge of the computer, its machine language, or how it works. The user need know only the rules of the Fortran language itself. In fact, the assembly language program to read two quantities and add them together appears as follows when written in Fortran:

```
100   READ (5,400) A,B
      SUM = A + B
      WRITE (6,500) A,B,SUM
      GO TO 100
```

As we can see, it hardly takes a trained programmer to recognize what this program is intended to do. With the possible exception of the digits 5 and 6 within the parentheses and addition of a few more statements, this program could be run on any computer that is equipped with standard Fortran.

COBOL In May 1959 the U.S. Department of Defense called together representatives from government agencies and computer manufacturers to discuss the possibility of adopting a common language for business data processing. The result was a set of specifications known as Cobol 60. In 1968 ANSI published the 1968 Cobol standard. The currently used version is the 1974 standard.

Fortran is a relatively easy language to learn and use by the nonprogrammer, whereas Cobol, with its vast structure and capabilities, is more oriented toward the professional programmer. However, its design is such that it is quite readable. For example, the following sequence is a portion of a Cobol program to solve the problem of adding two numbers (Example 3-1):

```
SIMPLE-LOOP
      READ INPUT FILE.
      ADD A TO B GIVING C.
      MOVE C TO OUTPUT-C.
      WRITE OUTPUT-RECORD.
      GO TO SIMPLE-LOOP.
```

As with Fortran, this segment of code will work with any computer that utilizes standard Cobol.

COMPARISON OF LANGUAGES With the greater convenience provided the computer user by compiler languages such as Fortran and Cobol, we might wonder why assembly languages are used at all. From the overall point of view compiler languages are far more commonly used in applications areas than are assembly languages. However, for certain types of applications with specialized needs and for preparing system software, assembly languages are more frequently required. This is largely attributable to the features of these languages that allow programmers to make the most efficient use of the computer with which they are working. The advantages characteristic of compiler and assembly languages are summarized in Figure 3-4.

As computers become larger and faster and compilers more efficient,

Figure 3-4   Advantages of compiler and assembly languages.

Language	Item of Consideration	Explanation
Compiler	Program preparation cost	Generally, the cost of all phases of program preparation (coding, correcting and documenting) is lower with a compiler language than with an assembly language.
	Machine knowledge required	Actually, most compiler languages such as Fortran and Cobol can be used without a knowledge of the given computer on which the program will be run. Thus the programmer need not know the machine instructions, the data format, and so on. However, such a knowledge is desirable since it allows the programmer to utilize the system more efficiently.
	Generality of language	Languages such as Cobol and Fortran are industry-wide standards and are not machine oriented. Knowledge gained in a compiler language on one machine is almost 100 percent transferable to the same compiler language used on another machine.
Assembly	Versatility	An assembly language provides programmers access to all the special features of the machine they are using. Certain types of operations which are impractical to attempt using a compiler language are easily programmed using the machine's assembly language.
	Program efficiency	Generally a program prepared by a good assembly language programmer will require less storage and less running time than one prepared by a good compiler language programmer.

the notion of program efficiency becomes less of a factor. Although a clever programmer can indeed produce a better specific program than is obtained through a general-purpose language, the additional programming time and cost are usually unjustified. Overall, the needs and requirements of a given task usually dictate whether a compiler language or an assembly language is more appropriate.

EXERCISES

3.3   What is the advantage of using a symbolic language instead of a machine language?

3.4   List and compare the features of assembly languages and compiler languages.

Language Translation

A SIMPLE ANALOGY   Although assembly and compiler languages differ in many respects, both yield programs that must first be converted to the machine language of the computer to be used before they can be run. This program translation phase is done on the computer by special *language processor* programs that normally are furnished by the computer manufacturer. For compiler languages these translators are called *compilers* and the translating operation is termed *compiling;* for assembly language the corresponding terminology is *assembler* and *assembling.* Throughout the following discussion the all-inclusive term *processor* will usually be employed. To gain an insight into the language processing function, we consider a simple analogy.

Let us assume that we have a large garden that we wish to have cared for by a professional gardener. Furthermore, our neighbor (a close friend) knows an excellent Japanese gardener. Since the gardener speaks no English, our friend, being proficient in both Japanese and English, volunteers to act as a translator. Thus we establish the following procedure:

1. We write the daily instructions in English.
2. The friend translates them from English, the language convenient for us to use, into Japanese, the only language that the gardener understands.
3. Assuming that everything has been translated properly, the gardener carries out the required functions.

The function of the translator is to convert the descriptions and accounts written in English into like descriptions and accounts in Japanese and record them for the gardener. Whether or not our friend has an extensive background in gardening would be unimportant. The primary requirement would be that he have the capability to translate from English to Japanese. Note that the functions of our friend do not contribute directly to garden care. His only purpose is to perform the translation, *not* to carry out the enumerated tasks. These notions can be represented by diagrams as shown in Figure 3-5.

The importance of the idea of changing from a language that is easy for the writer to one that is easy for the user by use of a translator cannot be overemphasized. This is precisely the notion of converting from an assembly or compiler language program into a machine language program via a processor. In the case of the computer language the translating function is

Figure 3-5 Analogy for language translation.

(a) Daily gardening instructions   (b)   (c)

performed by the computer rather than by a helpful neighbor. However, just as the neighbor must have learned the art of translating, so must the computer "learn" how to assemble or compile. This consists of loading the special language processor program into the computer. Then, under the control of the processor, the computer will translate the entire program into machine language. During the processing phase (as during translation in the analogy) none of the instructions are being carried out; they are merely being translated. In essence the language processor program is treating the assembler or compiler program, usually referred to as the *source program,* as data and is producing as output a machine language program, usually referred to as the *object program.* This is presented by diagrams as shown in Figure 3-6.

ERRORS One important feature of assembler and compiler language processors is their ability to detect certain types of errors. Unfortunately these errors fall only in the "use of language" area and do not provide a thinking capability for the programmer.

The gardener analogy can be expanded to illustrate error detection capabilities of the language processor. For example, let us assume that we wish to have a particular tree trimmed and we record the instruction, "Trim the tree." Upon encountering this statement the translator would recognize that the required tree is not specified and would so indicate on the instruction before returning it to us for correction. Thus the translator has detected an error and has aided us—of great importance is the type of error. Here, it is simply a statement that is not completely descriptive of the function to be performed. The translator realized that all of these details must be provided

Figure 3-6   Language translation phase.

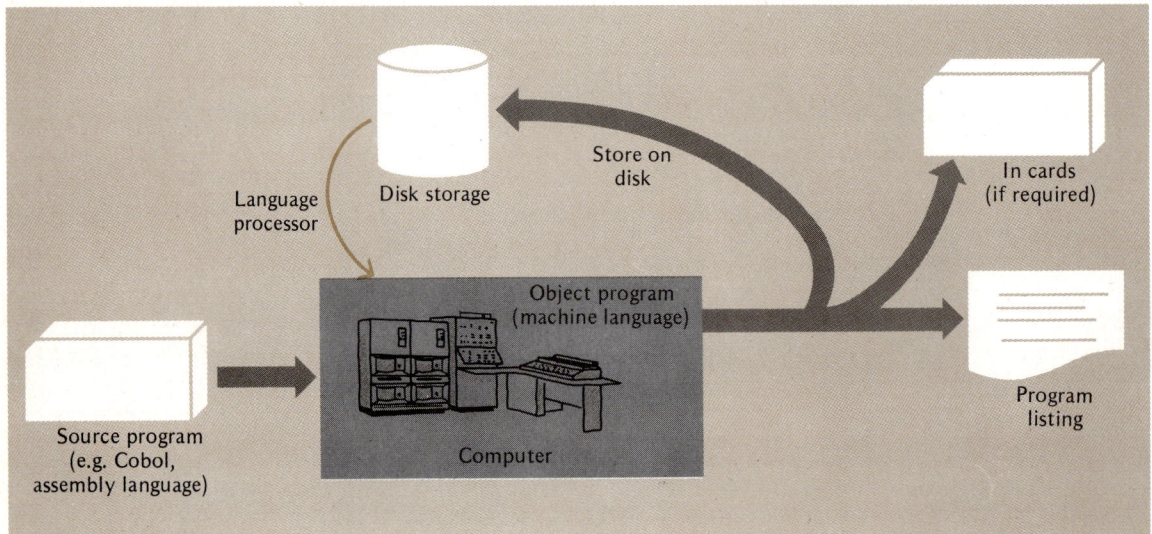

and was capable of detecting such an omission quickly and easily. Now consider two variations of an error of a different type. Assume that we had inadvertently stated "cut down" instead of "trim" and the statement was, "Cut down the third tree from the left." To the translator this is a clearly defined, valid task to be translated into Japanese. Upon encountering this instruction the gardener would perform the task and continue on to the next chore, assuming that we knew what we were doing. On the other hand, if it were illegal to cut these trees without a special permit from the city, the gardener, upon encountering this instruction, would indicate that an error had been made and would not carry the instruction out. These are two distinct types of errors, both of which have their important corollaries in programming.

EXERCISES

3.5   What is the purpose of the language processor (the assembler or compiler)?
3.6   What is the difference between a source program and an object program?
3.7   In preparing a program, the programmer erroneously instructed the computer to calculate the perimeter of a rectangle by adding the width and twice the length (that is, $p = w + 2l$). Would you expect the language processor to detect this error? Explain.

On Solving Problems

BASIC STEPS   With the widespread use of computers in virtually all disciplines, the average person, when faced with a burdensome computational or data processing problem, will frequently respond with, "Let the computer do it." Such a comment usually reflects a basic misunderstanding on two points: (1) The computer is not capable of "thinking" in the usual sense; it can operate only when given a set of detailed instructions written by a programmer. Thus, the computer user must possess a complete understanding of the problem and of how to solve it. (2) Not all problems lend themselves to practical solution on a computer. As we shall see, there are criteria for judging whether or not a given application is, in fact, a realistic "computer application."

The reader should recognize that programmers themselves must "solve" the problem and that the computer is capable of only the most basic arithmetic and logic operations. The creative portion of the overall process remains the task of people; the machine simply follows basic instructions. The coding of instruction sequences for the computer, however, is only one phase of the overall task of problem solution. The general steps can be loosely categorized as:

1.   Defining the problem
2.   Planning and analyzing the solution of the problem
3.   Programming or coding the problem in a computer-intelligible language

4. Testing the program
5. Documenting the problem solution and the program
6. Running the program for production purposes

Figure 3-7 shows a simplification of these steps on a time sequencing scale. In reality the relationship of these individual phases is usually much more complex than illustrated.

PROBLEM DEFINITION The average student of programming seldom recognizes the significance of the problem definition phase since, in a conventional programming course, problems are carefully defined by the instructor. This is hardly the case in an actual business environment. The programming department is commonly faced with such needs from other departments as, "We require a system to report and perform statistical analyses on student entrance examinations." Upon questioning it becomes apparent that persons making requests are (1) not really aware of what they want, (2) uncertain of how their needs can be fulfilled, (3) not very convincing in their need for the results, and/or (4) totally unaware of whether or not the job is economically justifiable. It is the job of the *systems analyst* to resolve these unknowns.

First of all, a careful evaluation must be made of whether or not the problem is actually worth solving. This might sound strange, but in any data processing installation a significant number of job requests are received that are totally impractical. This can occur for a number of reasons, such as:

- The desired output simply cannot be clearly defined, nor can the exact use to which the results are to be put be pinpointed.
- No realistic method of solution is available for the problem. It is important to recognize that the computer itself usually adds little or nothing to conceiving a method of solution. Whereas most problems *can* be solved, the point here is whether or not a *realistic* solution is available.
- It is economically impractical to use a computer. For instance, the value of the results simply might not warrant the cost of preparing and running the program. Sometimes the management of a company, in anxiously computerizing operations, will fail to recognize that some tasks are more efficiently performed manually.

Figure 3-7
Steps of a computer solution.

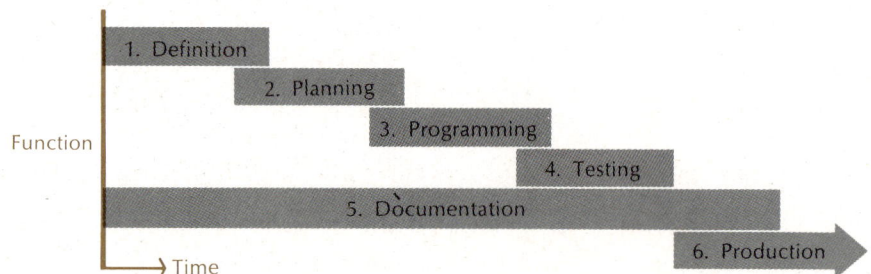

1. Definition
2. Planning
3. Programming
4. Testing
5. Documentation
6. Production

Function

Time

Program planning usually begins during the later steps of the problem definition phase.

PROGRAM PLANNING Once the general method of problem solution has been determined, the actual process of laying out the sequence of events can begin. At this stage details of the input data and output reports are carefully spelled out and documented (another phase of the overall operation that is taking place concurrently). Here the fine points of the solution method are analyzed. Occasionally results of this work will require that ground rules conceived during the definition phase be modified. It is usually during this phase that the choice of a programming language is made.

PROGRAMMING Once the program logic is clearly defined, it is practical to begin writing the actual computer program to perform the desired operations. In some instances some techniques that appeared practical during the planning phase will be obviously impractical when the coding is attempted, thus requiring modifications to the program logic. If the program planning phase has been carefully completed, the coding phase is considerably simplified. In many cases the program planning phase is performed by a systems analyst and the actual programming by a *coder* or *programmer,* a person with less training and experience.

TESTING Once the beginner finally "persuades" the computer to accept a program, process the data, and print results, s/he commonly breathes a sigh of relief and concludes, "On to the next problem!" However, we must never trust the output of a computer simply because it comes from a computer. This is not to imply that the computer is a clumsy, error-prone oaf. On the contrary, modern computers are so designed that very few machine errors go undetected by the computer itself. The problem lies with the programmer in preparing the set of instructions. For example, suppose that a program is being written to update customer charge accounts, and the following directions are to be given to the computer:

```
NEW BALANCE = OLD BALANCE - PAYMENTS + CHARGES
```

Now if the programmer inadvertently coded this as

```
NEW BALANCE = OLD BALANCE + PAYMENTS + CHARGES
```

the computer would not complain, but the customers certainly would. Errors such as these are detected and corrected through preparing and running test data. (More difficult errors may lead to measures as illustrated by the following cartoon.)

DOCUMENTATION Although the preceding phases overlap one another slightly, documentation should be an ongoing process from the beginning. The end result of the documentation should be a carefully written program report. Each computer installation in business or industry has its own rules and format, but most will include such items as the following:

- *Problem definition:* a complete description of the problem for which the program is written
- *Methods:* means and methods used in the program
- *Program usage:* a detailed description of how to use the program, including input format, output format, and special limitations
- *Sample run:* a sample run showing expected output from the sample input

All too frequently, programmers will complete problems and, in their anxiety to proceed to others, will write incomplete reports, if any at all. In documenting work that has been completed, programmers should continually consider these reports from the point of view of a person who needs to use the program but knows nothing about it.

PRODUCTION Programmers will often be ecstatic over the shrewd coding techniques they have used, but everyone else is normally preoccupied with but one thing, the end results. Once a program is completely tested it can be made available as a production program to perform the job for which it was designed. Although we might expect all the preceding phases to end at this point, this does not necessarily follow. Programs are commonly in an almost constant state of expansion and improvement, sometimes even requiring a redefining of the basic problem.

The overall process of problem definition through production is illustrated in Figure 3-8.

Figure 3-8 Solving a problem.

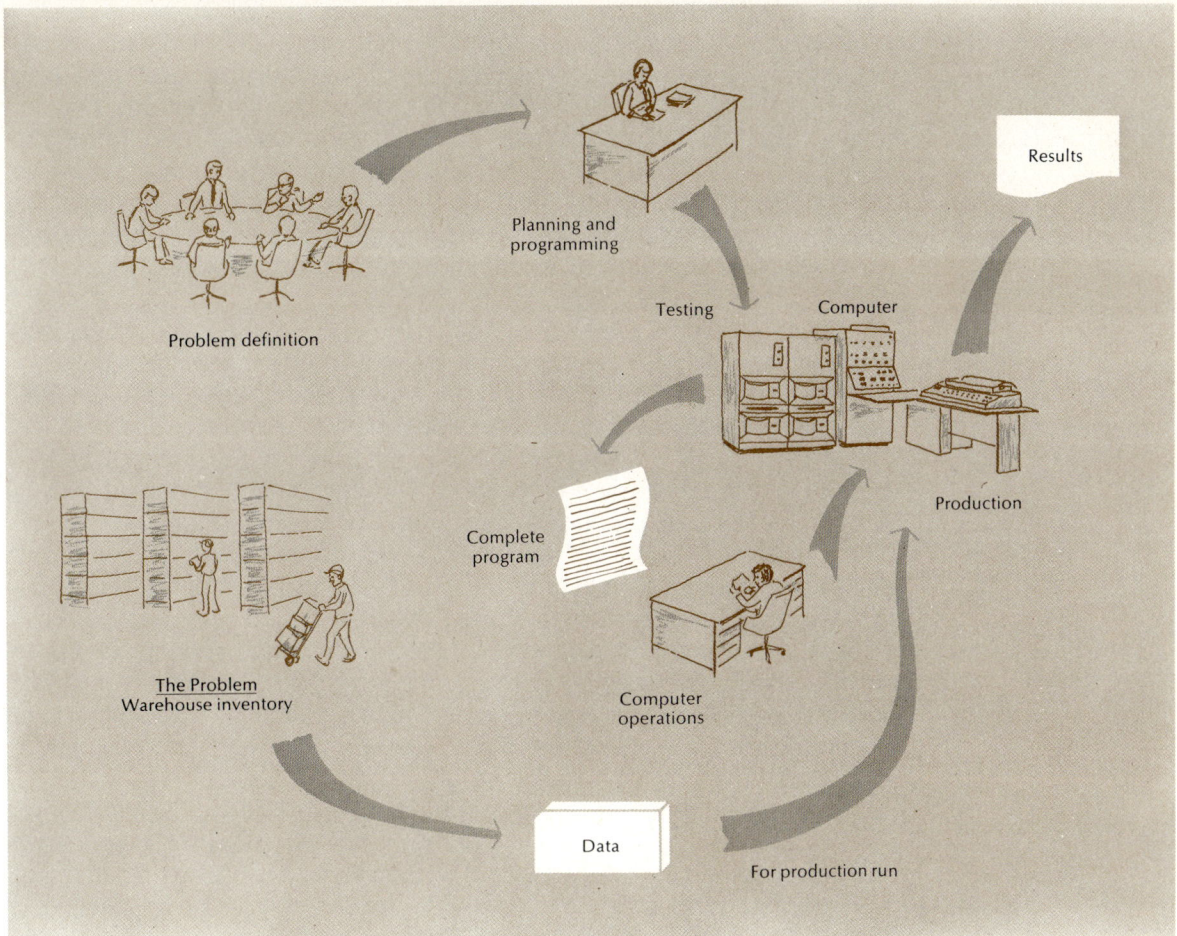

Problem definition

Planning and programming

Testing

Computer

Results

Production

Complete program

Computer operations

The Problem
Warehouse inventory

Data

For production run

EXERCISE

3.8 Describe the six phases in preparing a program.

Problem Definition and Analysis

The purpose of this text is to provide a basic insight into many facets of computer data processing. Readers who pursue programming beyond the introductory level will be utilizing one or more textbooks that specialize in the details of using a given language. In most books dealing with programming examples are widely used to illustrate concepts. In virtually all cases the format is, "Here is the example definition, here is an analysis of the problem, and here is the program solution." Furthermore, programming problems for the student are normally stated clearly, without ambiguity.

This is all well and good; after all, the basics of the language must be mastered before it can be applied to actual problems. But it is at this point—the application of the language to actual problems—that the neophyte programmer first encounters serious difficulties. How does one actually develop the solution to a problem? How can the programmer be confident that the solution that is developed actually solves the specified problem? Program testing is a nasty but necessary job; how can a maximum amount of testing be achieved with a minimum amount of effort? And if, as often happens, the specifications of the problem are changed before the program is completed, can the change be fitted into the framework of the program without destroying it?

These problems loom very large in the world of the professional programmer; after all, it is the programmer's responsibility to produce a program that does the required job. Not only are programmers highly paid, but their work often takes weeks, months, or even years to complete, and until it is completed there is no proof that the program does (or does not do) the job. More than one company has found itself in serious straits because some programmer failed to produce a working version of a critical program. Accordingly, experts in the field of computer science have devoted a great deal of attention to improvement in areas such as better program definition, reduction of programming errors, and simplification of program debugging, modification, and maintenance. A number of techniques have been developed to simplify and accelerate the programmer's work. Many of these techniques are intended primarily for large systems, where a number of programmers are working on individual components of the system, all of which must eventually fit together. Two of them, however, are worth looking at here: *top-down program design* and *structured programming.* It will be impossible to treat them exhaustively here, but enough can be said about them to give an idea of how they work and what they do. Most programmers have been trained to see a program as a logical flow of operations, proceeding from beginning to end and dealing with each problem as it arises—and so that is the way they perform their analyses. This may be adequate for relatively small tasks but generally leads to big problems with large jobs. The result is usually a program that not only is inadequate but is difficult to maintain.

Top-Down Program Design

WHAT IS TOP-DOWN DESIGN? The top-down approach permits the programmer to look at the program functionally rather than logically. It is a technique for defining *what* the program is to do without defining (at least initially) *how* the program will do it. This is illustrated in the following example.

> **Example 3-2**   The Eagle Manufacturing Company wishes to computerize its factory payroll operation. Factory employees are paid according to a complex formula that includes such factors as hours worked, job

classification, employee seniority, and the company's profit in the preceding fiscal quarter. The calculations include tax computations, accumulation of year-to-date figures, and provisions for voluntary deductions. All input and output records have already been defined by the systems analyst; all that remains is to write the program.

To apply the top-down design technique to this problem, the first step would be to portray the overall program in terms of its functions, which is done in Figure 3-9(a). Notice that no details are given at this point as to how the program will accomplish its results. The entire program is represented as a single box, and its function is to convert the input data into the desired output.

The next step is to expand the one-box representation. The expansion is shown in Figure 3-9(b). This expansion may seem to belabor the obvious. It may seem trivial and pointless, but it is not. The whole objective of top-down program design is to permit the programmer to specify the contents of the program one step at a time, with each step being a simple expansion of the previous one. Again, there is no concern with the content of the boxes. The question, "What does the term 'initialization routines' include?," not only is not answered, but it is not even asked. At this point in the program development it is sufficient to know that an initialization routine will be required, and to provide a place for it. Note that the lines connect the lower boxes to the upper box to show that they make up the functions performed by that box. Note also that there is no designation of the sequence in which blocks are executed. The purpose of the chart is simply to show what has to be done by each component of the program.

The procedure continues with the expansion of one of the new boxes. The initialization and termination boxes cannot be expanded yet because their functions are dependent on the main part of the program, so the next task is to expand the "Process Each Employee" block. Figure 3-9(c) illustrates the basic expansion. Here again the same principles appear: simple statements, horizontally aligned, of what the box is to accomplish, with no specific details as to how anything is to be done.

At this point the reader may be questioning the significance of all of this. It is simply this: Very few human minds can grasp all of the details and relationships of a complex computer program. The mind can, however, deal very competently with a small portion of the program, or with a large portion of it broken down into a number of small parts or functional blocks. Top-down program design, then, is nothing more than a technique for taking a large problem, dividing it into a few basic elements, subdividing each element into subelements, and so on until the problem has been broken down into pieces of manageable size.

EXERCISE

3.9　What must be done before the "Initialization Routines" and "Termination Routines" boxes in Figure 3-9(b) can be expanded?

**Figure 3-9
Top-down program
design, Example 3-2.**

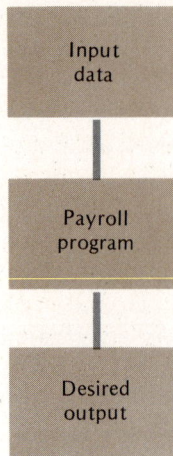

(a)

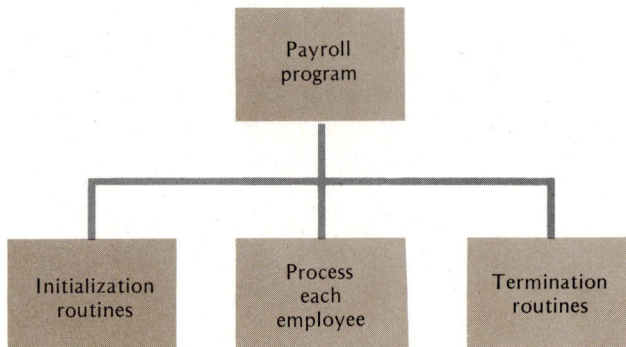

(b)

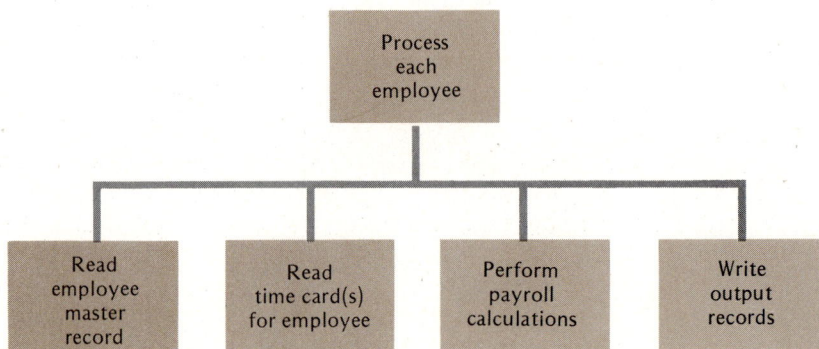

(c)

**FURTHER
EXPANSION OF
THE SOLUTION** Figure 3-10 illustrates the continuation of the process for the "Perform Payroll Calculations" box. While it is not complete, the principle of proceeding level by level is clearly illustrated. The figure also illustrates another important principle of top-down program design—that of dealing with each component on its own level without introducing "sublevel" complexities to confuse the issue. For example, the box that says "Calculate Deductions" does not specify which deductions are to be calculated or how they will be calculated; at that level it is sufficient to know that deductions are to be calculated and that the data will be supplied by a lower level of the program. The same thing is true of the "Calculate Federal Withholding Tax" routine: One of the boxes says "Get Appropriate Tax Rate." There is no concern at that level as to how

Figure 3-10 Continuation of top-down design.

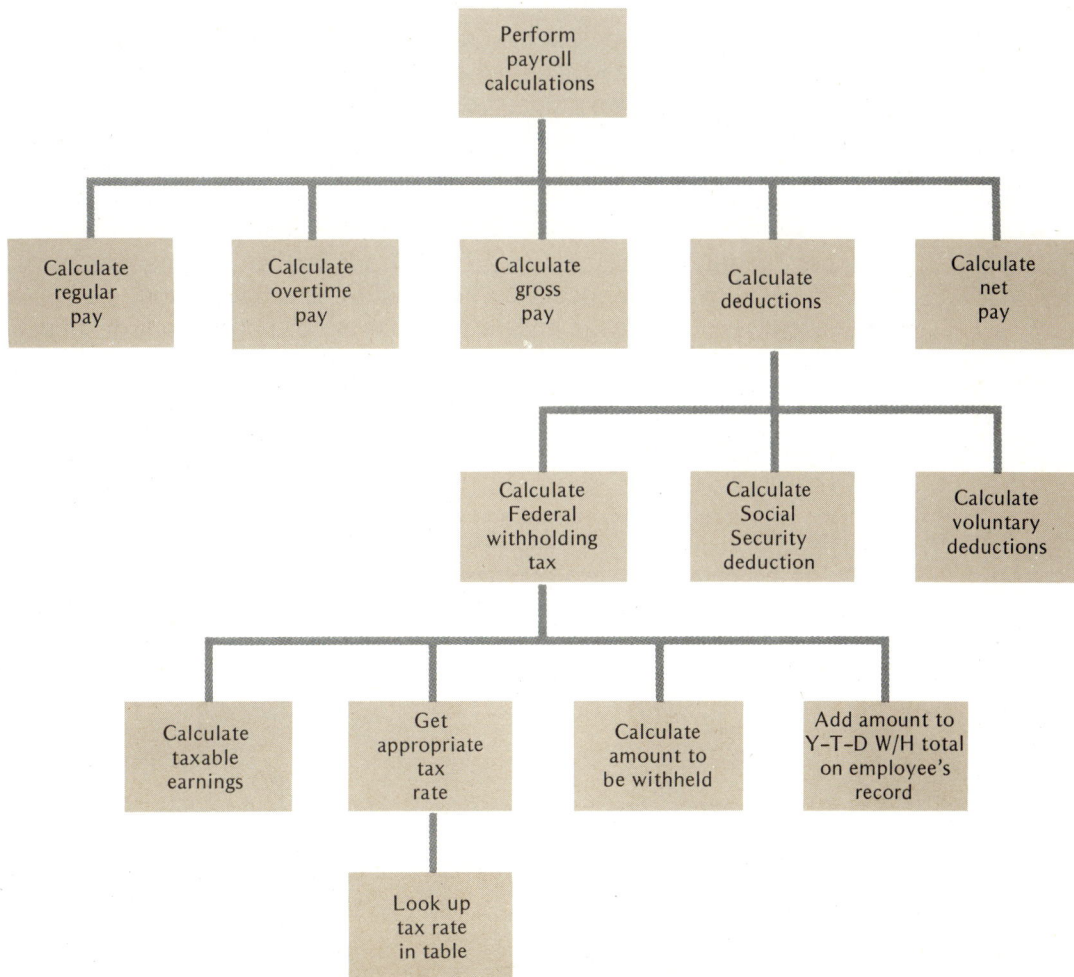

an appropriate rate is determined or obtained; that is the job of the box on the next lower level.

The concept of "separation of levels" is one of the primary strengths of the top-down program design concept. Not only does it permit division of the program into functional blocks without concern for their content, but it also immensely simplifies program maintenance and modification. For instance, assume that the Federal government changes its withholding tax formula. With a well-planned top-down program there is one box whose function is simply to supply the appropriate tax rate. The preceding box is not concerned with how that rate is obtained but only that it is supplied by the box(es) that follow. Thus the only change required to implement the new formula is in a minor and independent part of the program. Similarly, if the city government suddenly imposes a ½ percent withholding tax, the program revision consists simply of adding another box to the row that feeds the "Calculate Deductions" box, as illustrated in Figure 3-11.

With all components of the program neatly compartmentalized, the difficulty of program modification, correction, and testing is significantly reduced. A vital part of top-down program design is the data definition discipline that it imposes. While the programmer may not know at any given level exactly how a block on the next lower level will function, s/he must specify the exact form of the data available to that block and of that expected from it. One very successful tool for this type of data definition is IBM's HIPO (Hierarchy plus Input-Process-Output) technique. HIPO provides the programmer with the means for precisely specifying the input to, and output from, each block. Techniques of this nature ensure that the *what* has been clearly defined; from this, the *how* follows relatively easily and naturally.

EXERCISES

3.10 Explain the necessity for explicitly defining the input to and output from every box in a top-down flowchart.

3.11 The Federal government permits employees to specify an additional amount of money to be withheld for Federal income taxes. What modification is required in Figure 3-10 to provide for additional withholding tax?

**Figure 3-11
Adding a new
component.**

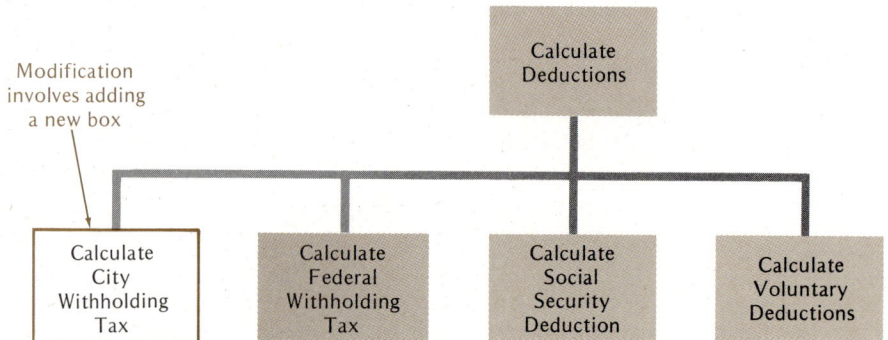

Modification involves adding a new box

Structured Programming

INTRODUCTION   Once a problem has been broken down into basic components, or individual *modules,* then the programming may begin. The first step is to define the *program logic;* that is, now that the *what* has been defined, the *how* must be determined. For instance, referring to the structure chart of Figure 3-10, the Social Security deduction will be discontinued after an employee reaches a certain maximum. Similarly, which voluntary deductions will be calculated for a given employee and what are the methods used in calculation? This brings us to the topic of *program logic.*

Structured programming can be defined as *a set of formalized rules for coding programs.* In general structured techniques are applicable to virtually all languages. However, the most commonly used languages of today (Cobol, Basic, and Fortran) were not designed with structured methods in mind. Although additions have been made to make them more compatible with structured methods, they leave something to be desired from this point of view. On the other hand, the Pascal language was designed specifically as a structured language. Thus, in using structured methods the programmer should be realistic and keep in mind the language that is to be used.

FLOWCHARTING   One of the most common methods of representing program logic is through the use of diagrams called *flowcharts.* With the advent of top-down design and structured techniques, many in programming felt that flowcharts were unnecessary, if not totally useless. However, the key to using any tool, including flowcharts, is careful planning. If flowcharts are used in conjunction with structured techniques, they are very valuable in illustrating program logic.

To illustrate flowcharts let us consider a simplification of the payroll computation of Example 3-2. This example is to read each employee record, calculate gross pay, taxes, and net pay, and then print the results for each employee of the company. The program logic is shown in the flowchart of Figure 3-12. On the left we see all the computations represented by a single *processing* block. The flowchart on the right includes each calculation represented by a single block. We should note that the logic of this flowchart represents an *infinite loop.* That is, it shows no logical end—processing will go on forever. (In reality we know that it would eventually terminate by running out of employee records.) All programs include some means for ending processing since other operations often are necessary. For instance, the company may wish to have the total gross pay printed after the last employee is processed. The means used for terminating the loop depends, to a degree, upon the language being used. Some systems provide ways to detect automatically when the end of the data file occurs. With others, the programmer must write instructions to do the checking.

**Figure 3-12
Simple flowcharts
and flowchart
symbols.**

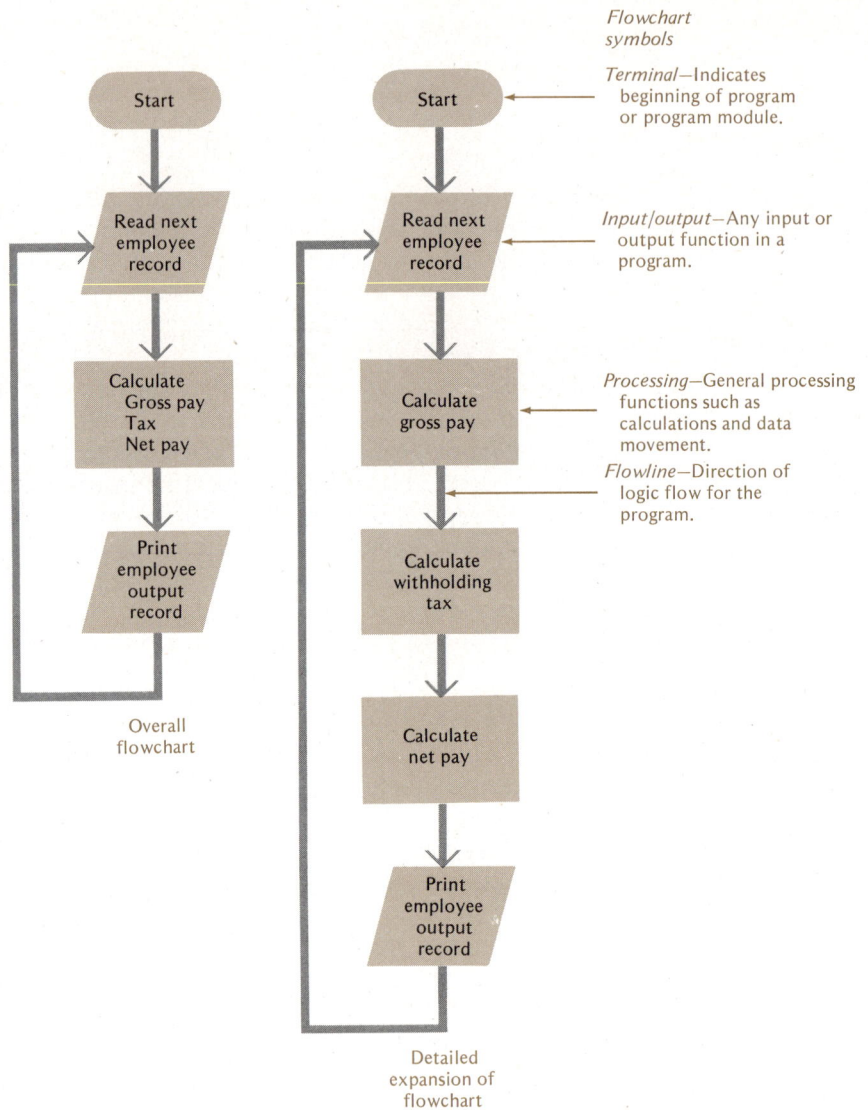

*Flowchart
symbols*

Terminal—Indicates
beginning of program
or program module.

Input/output—Any input or
output function in a
program.

Processing—General processing
functions such as
calculations and data
movement.

Flowline—Direction of
logic flow for the
program.

Overall
flowchart

Detailed
expansion of
flowchart

**STRUCTURED
FLOWCHARTS**   To illustrate the basic principles of structured techniques, let us expand this example as follows: (1) Gross pay and taxes are to be accumulated then printed after processing all employees. (2) If an employee works more than 40 hours in a week, overtime pay must be included. The flowcharts of Figure 3-13 clearly illustrate the logic of this problem. We can see that the solution includes an overall flowchart and a detailed breakdown of the process sequence. The three basic structures of structured programming are also illustrated.

Figure 3-13 Structured flowcharts.

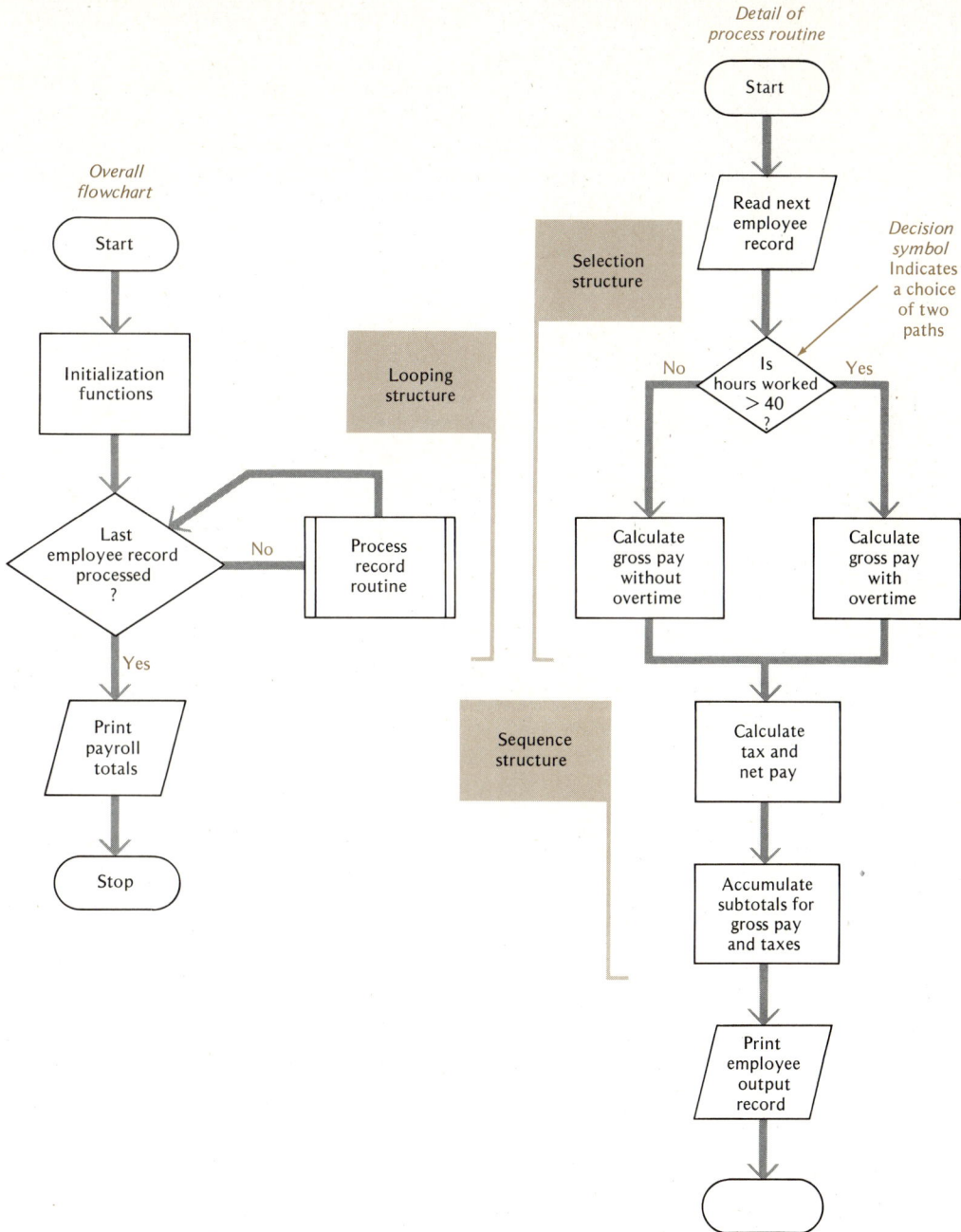

- *Sequence structure*—represents unconditional operations executed one after the other.
- *Selection structure*—selects either of two operations, depending upon a given condition.
- *Looping structure*—specifies that an operation is to be carried out as long as a certain condition exists.

Structured techniques coupled with top-down design represent powerful programming tools and are widely used in business and industry.

Pseudocode

Many users of structured techniques argue that flowcharts simply are not necessary if the problem has been properly analyzed and structured. An alternative to flowcharting is the use of *pseudocode*. Instead of using blocks to represent programming logic steps, pseudocode uses statements that are a cross between actual language statements and ordinary English. Through a stepwise refinement that is virtually identical in nature to that of Figure 3-13, lines of pseudocode can be expanded into the actual program itself. Using the looping DO-WHILE structure, Figure 3-14 represents the first "iteration" of a pseudocode solution. The main processing loop is controlled by the DO-WHILE. This statement directs that all statements down to the END be carried out repeatedly until the specified condition occurs (that is, an end-of-file condition—EOF—is detected). Upon detection of the EOF execution is to break out of the loop, which causes termination of the program. Note that, as with the structured flowcharts of Figure 3-13, no attempt is made to complete *all* of the detail on the first attempt. With the overall structure carefully defined, the next step is to expand further the line of pseudocode: "Process next employee record." This is done in the pseudocode program of Figure 3-15. The final step in the refinement would be to substitute actual programming language statements for each of the English statements.

One important feature of pseudocode as a programming tool is the use of indentation. The same technique is widely used with programming languages themselves. Its sole purpose is to clarify the logical structure of the

**Figure 3-14
Pseudocode example.**

```
                       Perform initialization
              ⎧ DO WHILE not end of data file (EOF)  ⎧ Requires
Processing   ⎨    Process next employee record        ⎨ more
loop         ⎩ END OF DO WHILE                        ⎩ detail
                       Print totals
                       STOP
```

Figure 3-15
Expanded pseudocode
program.

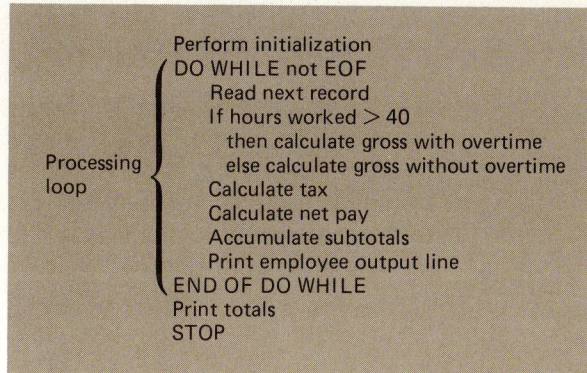

```
                     Perform initialization
                   ( DO WHILE not EOF
                        Read next record
                        If hours worked > 40
                          then calculate gross with overtime
  Processing {             else calculate gross without overtime
  loop                   Calculate tax
                         Calculate net pay
                         Accumulate subtotals
                         Print employee output line
                   ( END OF DO WHILE
                     Print totals
                     STOP
```

program. With this technique we can tell at a glance which statements make up the DO-WHILE loop of Figure 3-15. The differences in clarity would be far greater if this were a longer program covering, for instance, one or more pages.

EXERCISE
3.12 What is the purpose of a flowchart?

In Retrospect

Twenty years ago, when acquiring a computer the primary question asked was related to its hardware capabilities. Now at least as much attention is focused on the software available, with emphasis on the operating system. The operating system with its vast resource management capabilities is the key to the efficient use of the modern digital computer. Through use of a supervisor program, which is always storage resident, automatic control of many functions is achieved.

Programming languages fall into three broad categories: machine, assembly, and high level. Each type of computer has its own machine language. Because of its binary nature and almost infinite detail, practically no programming is done in machine language. Instead, assembly languages and high-level languages are used.

An assembly language allows the programmer to utilize all the machine features through symbolic codes and locations rather than machine codes and binary. However, use of assembly language requires a comprehensive knowledge of the computer.

High-level languages are designed to be machine independent and usable without a knowledge of how the computer works. In general they are much more applications oriented, that is, Cobol is designed for business data processing applications and Fortran is designed more for mathematics-science-engineering types of applications. Before an assembly language or high-level language program can be run on a computer, it must be converted into machine language. This is done by special language translating programs called assemblers and compilers. There is no doubt that the broad use of the computer that we see today is largely due to the simple-to-use high-level languages such as Fortran and Cobol.

The process of putting an application on a computer requires careful planning and study. The six broad steps of such a process are problem definition, analysis, programming, testing, documentation, and production.

Top-down design involves breaking a problem down into functional components. Emphasis is placed on defining *what* the program is to do and breaking this "what" into independent subtasks. During this phase of the analysis little or no emphasis is placed on the *how* of the problem solution; the objective is to break a large problem into small, manageable components.

Structured programming, on the other hand, involves the *how* of problem solution. It is effectively a formal set of rules for writing programs using three basic program structures: process, selection, and looping. Central to structured programming is the single-entry, single-exit concept, that is, each structure or entity of a program must have only one entry point and one exit point.

With good top-down design and structured programming techniques it is often argued that flowcharts are unnecessary. Pseudocode, instead of using flowcharting blocks to represent programming logic steps, uses statements that are a cross between programming language statements and English. Through stepwise refinement the pseudocode is converted to the program itself.

ANSWERS TO PRECEDING EXERCISES

3.1 An operating system is a set of programs, resident in the computer system, designed to maximize the amount of work the computer can do.

3.2 The three basic components of an instruction are label, operation, and operand.

3.3 Simplicity of use. The programmer need not remember various machine codes and determine addresses, since those operations are handled by the assembler program.

3.4 *Compiler languages:*
1. Machine independent
2. Require little or no knowledge of computer
3. Impractical to perform certain functions
4. Programs coded more quickly than in assembly language
5. Normally yield good machine language programs
6. Yield many machine language instructions per statement

Assembly languages:
1. Machine oriented
2. Require thorough understanding of computer
3. Provide access to valuable machine features not available through compiler languages
4. Much time-consuming detail required in preparing programs
5. Can produce better, more efficient programs than compiler languages
6. Produces one machine language instruction per assembly language instruction

3.5 The language processor converts programs from the assembly or compiler language to the machine language.

3.6 The source program is written in an assembly or compiler language (a user-oriented language). The object program is the machine language program resulting from machine translation of the source program.

3.7 The compiler will not detect this as an error since it does not "know" the context of the problem, that is, that the perimeter of a rectangle is determined by adding twice the width to twice the length.

3.8 Problem definition, planning, programming, testing, documenting, and production.

3.9 The "Termination Routines" box could be expanded at almost any time, since the termination routines will deal primarily with output, which will already have been defined. The "Initialization Routines" box, however, cannot be completely expanded until all of the rest of the program has been defined, since not until then will all of the details of all of the initialization requirements be known.

3.10 Each box in a top-down flowchart represents something that is to be accomplished. What that accomplishment is can best be defined in terms of what the box produces (the output), and the data going into the box (the input), which must be sufficient to permit the box to produce the desired output.

3.11 Insert a box between the "Calculation" box and the "Add" box on the fourth horizontal level that says:

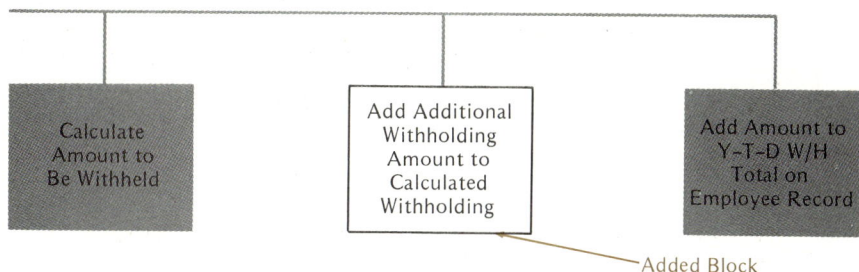

Calculate Amount to Be Withheld

Add Additional Withholding Amount to Calculated Withholding

Add Amount to Y-T-D W/H Total on Employee Record

Added Block

3.12 Flowcharts are used to illustrate the program logic, that is, the sequence and conditions in performing operations.

ADDITIONAL EXERCISES

3.13 Explain the role of the supervisor. How is it "related" to the operating system?

3.14 What is the difference between machine language and assembly language?

3.15 It is said that an assembly language is "one for one" but a high-level language such as Fortran is "many for one." Explain what this means.

3.16 A company, which has all of its extensive applications systems programmed in assembly language, plans to expand its data processing system. Company X is trying to convince the company to obtain a larger, more powerful model of its current X computer. However, Company Y offers a better system for less money. What factors must be considered in making the decision? Explain.

3.17 What is meant by the "ANSI standard" form of a language? Why is it important?

3.18 What occurs when a program is assembled? When a program is compiled?

3.19 What is the basic philosophy of top-down program design?

3.20 Sketch the three basic structures of structured programming and describe them.

3.21 What is pseudocode? Explain how it is used in programming a problem.

3.22 A set of examination papers that have been graded with scores from 0 to 100 is to be searched to find how many of them are above 90. Prepare a flowchart to illustrate this job.

3.23 Each paper in a set of examination papers includes a grade of A, B, C, D, or F. A count is to be made of how many papers have grades of A and how many have grades of F. Prepare a flowchart to perform this function.

3.24 A water company bills certain customers according to the following schedule:

Flat rate	$1.00
Plus	0.20/unit for the first 20 units
Plus	0.225/unit for the next 30 units
Plus	0.30/unit for all in excess of 50 units

Draw a flowchart to illustrate the calculation of the charge on the basis of the number of units used.

3.25 **Matching.** Match each item in a through f with the corresponding description in 1 through 6.

a. Object program   d. Compiler
b. Machine language   e. Macro
c. Assembly language   f. Source program

1. A special program that is needed to convert a high-level language program to machine language.
2. For instance, a program written in Cobol.
3. A capability provided in assembly languages to generate commonly used sequences of code with a single instruction.
4. The end result of compiling or assembling a program.
5. The basic language form from which a computer operates.
6. Closely related to the machine language of the computer.

3.26 **Matching** Match the flowchart symbol in a through f with the corresponding operation in 1 through 10. *Note:* Some symbols may be used for two or more descriptions.

a.

Flowlines

b.

Decision

c.

Terminal

d

Process

e.

Input/Output

f.   Not a flowcharting function

1. Determine if employee is entitled to overtime pay.
2. Halt a program in the event of an error.
3. Obtain gross pay from hours worked and pay rate.
4. Read information from a magnetic tape.
5. Transfer control to another portion of a program.
6. Obtain a magnetic tape from a storage cabinet.
7. Print a report.
8. Count passes through a loop.
9. The portion of the program in which a series of calculations is performed.
10. Check to ensure that a loop is executed exactly 100 times.

3.27 **True–False**   Determine whether each of the following is true or false.

1. The term software refers to programs to be used with the computer.
2. An operating system is a set of programs designed mainly to replace computer operators.
3. A compiler is a prewritten program designed to translate programs written in a machine-independent language into machine language.
4. Cobol is a commonly used machine-independent language used for business data processing applications.

5. One disadvantage of using an assembly language is that programs written for one computer will not run on other types of computers.

6. One advantage of a higher level language over an assembly language is that the program preparation cost for most common jobs is lower.

7. The modern computer can be programmed using compiler languages such as Fortran by a person who has virtually no knowledge of how the computer works.

8. Logic errors, such as subtracting bonus pay from an employee's paycheck rather than adding, generally cannot be detected by the compiler.

9. In using a top-down approach, the programmer first defines *how* the program is to perform the desired tasks.

10. Top-down program design basically involves techniques for breaking a large, complex problem into smaller, more manageable components.

11. The primary problem with top-down design is that a large program is broken down into so many small components that they are difficult to modify at a later date.

12. For all practical purposes structured programming techniques cannot be used with top-down design methods.

13. Cobol and Fortran are well suited to structured programming because of their powerful IF-THEN capabilities.

14. Programming with pseudocode involves "iterative" coding using a combination of actual program statements and ordinary English descriptions.

15. A program flowchart is an illustration of the overall operations to be carried out in a computer program.

16. The recommended procedure in preparing a program is first to code the program in the selected language, and then to prepare the flowchart for documentation purposes.

17. After the overall logic has been flowcharted, details of the program should be defined in the form of more detailed flowcharts.

18. Flowcharting is necessary only for very large and complex problems.

4

Advanced Systems
Software

OBJECTIVES

During the past 20 years the computer has grown from relatively simple uses to highly complex applications. This section presents a brief insight into a variety of advanced topics. Following are some of the important concepts that you will learn.

- The basic theory of multiprogramming, which involves two or more programs in the computer that share it on a priority basis.
- The basic theory of timesharing which also involves two or more programs in the computer but that share it on an "equal time" basis.
- Basic principles of data communication, which involves transmission of computer data over the telephone network.
- The basic concept of sequential and direct access data file organization.
- Principal concepts of database management systems that involve integrating many files into a single organized database.
- The notion of distributing the work load between two or more computers that communicate by the telephone network (distributed data processing).
- The protection of computer stored data from loss or theft.

The following commonly used data processing terminology is found in this chapter.

backup

conversational computing

data communication

database

database management system (DBMS)

distributed data processing

electronic funds transfer (EFT)

indexed file

interactive computing

key field

management information system (MIS)

modem

multiprogramming

remote job entry (RJE)

telecommunication

timesharing

Multiprogramming and Timesharing

IMPROVING SYSTEM EFFICIENCY Programs that make up the operating system described in Section 3 are designed to improve the overall efficiency of the computer. A number of techniques, both hardware and software, are used to get the most out of the computer. One of them involves the concept of *overlapped* operations. For instance, consider the simple programming application illustrated by the flowchart of Figure 3-12. In that example a data record is read, the information processed, and the output record printed. Each of these operations requires a distinct amount of time. Each is performed by a different component of the computer (that is, input device, CPU, output device). If they are performed one after the other, then each of these components will be idle for a period of time awaiting the other to complete its job. Through a combination of hardware and software design these operations take place concurrently. After the card reader finishes reading a card, it "gives" it to the CPU and then immediately begins reading the next card while the CPU is processing the previous one. Thus the printer, for example, might be printing the record for the first employee, the CPU processing for the second, and the card reader reading the third. In this way the overall *throughput* (total amount of useful work) is increased.

MULTI-PROGRAMMING Another means of further increasing the usage of the CPU is through multiprogramming. With the storage-resident supervisor concept we were introduced to the notion of having two programs in storage at the same time: the supervisor for overall system control and the problem program for performing the data processing function. In *multiprogramming* this concept is carried one step further by placing two or more problem programs in storage and executing them concurrently. But although two or more programs may reside in storage simultaneously, the computer is capable of executing only one instruction at a time. Thus, at any given time, only *one* of the programs has control of the computer and is executing instructions. Simultaneous execution of two programs with one CPU is impossible.

The simplest method of multiprogramming is to divide the computer storage into fixed areas or *partitions* and then assign them priority. For instance, a simple system might reserve storage as follows:

- *Supervisor* (first 16K storage).
- *Background* partition (next 56K storage). This partition has low priority. (As such, a program in this partition will be able to run only when higher priority programs are not active.)
- *Foreground* partition (next 56K storage). This partition has high priority.

To gain an insight into the notion of priority and how multiprogramming works, let us consider two jobs to be done in a multiprogramming environment as illustrated in Figure 4-1. Important characteristics of the Report Generation program in Figure 4-1 are its extensive input/output requirements and its minimal CPU needs. Even with the concept of overlapped processing, the CPU will remain idle for significant periods of time. (A program of this type is said to be *I/O-bound.*) With this program the CPU is idle for a great deal of time because it "finishes up" its record and then must wait while the next one is being read. On the other hand, the I/O requirements of the Investment Analysis program are negligible, being almost entirely *processing-bound.* Under control of the supervisor, control of the computer is switched back and forth between the two programs. When the report program is waiting for the next record, control is given to the investment program. When the record is ready, control is returned to the report program. In more sophisticated systems using many partitions ready-to-go jobs are "lined up" in auxiliary storage waiting to be loaded into main storage and executed. (An ordered sequence of objects awaiting service is commonly called a *queue.*) As each is completed, the next program is selected from the queue and placed in storage. By designating a program to be high priority, it can be placed at the front of the queue. If the priority is sufficiently high, some operating systems will even temporarily remove lower priority programs from storage to make room. Upon completion of the high-priority job, the other programs are returned.

Although these functions sound highly efficient, they are not without their problems. Indeed, the process of juggling programs, determining priority, allocating time intervals, and so on can require a significant amount of CPU time, the very quantity the system is attempting to optimize. This "nonproductive time" is commonly referred to as *overhead,* and must be minimized to take full advantage of the operating system.

EXERCISE

4.1   In the multiprogramming example illustrated by Figure 4-1, what would be the consequence of assigning the I/O-bound Report Generator program to the lower priority partition and the Investment Analysis program to the higher priority partition?

**Figure 4-1
Two user programs
in storage.**

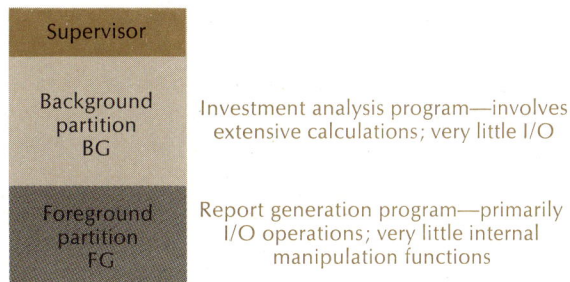

Supervisor

Background partition BG — Investment analysis program—involves extensive calculations; very little I/O

Foreground partition FG — Report generation program—primarily I/O operations; very little internal manipulation functions

ONLINE PROCESSING AND MULTI-PROGRAMMING

In many applications it is important that a number of users be able to communicate directly with the computer and receive rapid response to inquiries. This is made possible by the modern digital computer with large storage capabilities, powerful operating systems, and multiprogramming. For instance, in a banking application tellers require immediate access to customer account information; in an airline reservation system a ticket sales-person requires immediate information regarding space availability; in a college environment a counselor requires entrance examination scores for a student in the office. Through the use of typewriter-like and video display terminals connected to the computer either directly or via telephone lines, such information stored in the system can be instantly available.

A typical multiprogramming system to achieve this is illustrated in Figure 4-2. In this schematic the CPU will normally be processing the lower priority

Figure 4-2
Online processing in a multiprogramming environment.

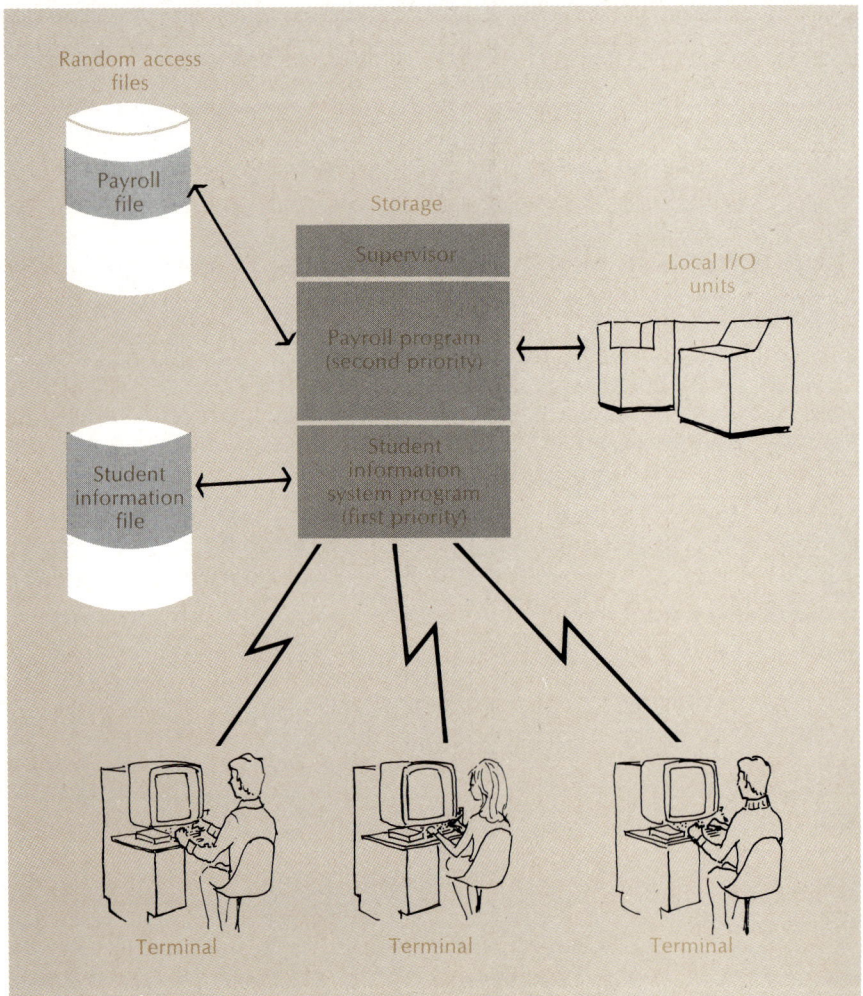

payroll application. However, upon request from a terminal for student information, the Payroll program will be interrupted and control given to the Student Information program. Upon satisfying the inquiry, control will be returned to the Payroll program.

EXERCISE

4.2   What would be the consequence of giving the Student Information program in Figure 4-2 second priority and the Payroll program first priority?

TIMESHARING   *Timesharing,* like much of the jargon in the computer field, has been grossly overused and misunderstood. Rigorously speaking, timesharing refers to the allocation of computer resources *in a time-dependent* fashion to several programs simultaneously in storage. The principal notion of a timesharing system is to provide a large number of users with direct access to the computer for problem solving. The user thus has the ability to "converse" directly with the computer for problem solving (hence the term *conversational* or *interactive* computing). In multiprogramming the principal consideration is to maximize utilization of the computer, but in timesharing it is, in a sense, to maximize efficiency of each computer user and keep him/her busy.

Figure 4-3 is a very simplified representation of a timeshared system. Each user has her/his own communications terminal, portion of storage, and auxiliary storage. In contrast with multiprogramming, where programs are executed on a priority basis, in timesharing the CPU time is divided among the users on a scheduled basis. Each program will be allocated its "slice" of the CPU time (commonly measured in milliseconds) based on some predetermined scheduling basis, beginning with the first program and proceeding through the last. Upon completing the cycle it is begun again so that an individual user scarcely realizes that someone else is also using the computer.

Timesharing is most frequently used for program development and testing. In fact, the Basic language was designed specifically for timesharing systems. Systems that are fully interactive inspect each statement of a new program as it is entered into the computer via a terminal. Errors in usage of the language that are detected are immediately identified to the operator so that the appropriate corrections can be made. The interactive programming and debugging capability of Basic has proved so effective in improving programmer efficiency that interactive versions of the batch-oriented Fortran and Cobol are now available.

EXERCISE

4.3   Multiprogramming and timesharing both involve multiple users in the computer concurrently. What is the basic difference between these two concepts?

**Figure 4-3
Simplification of a
timesharing
environment.**

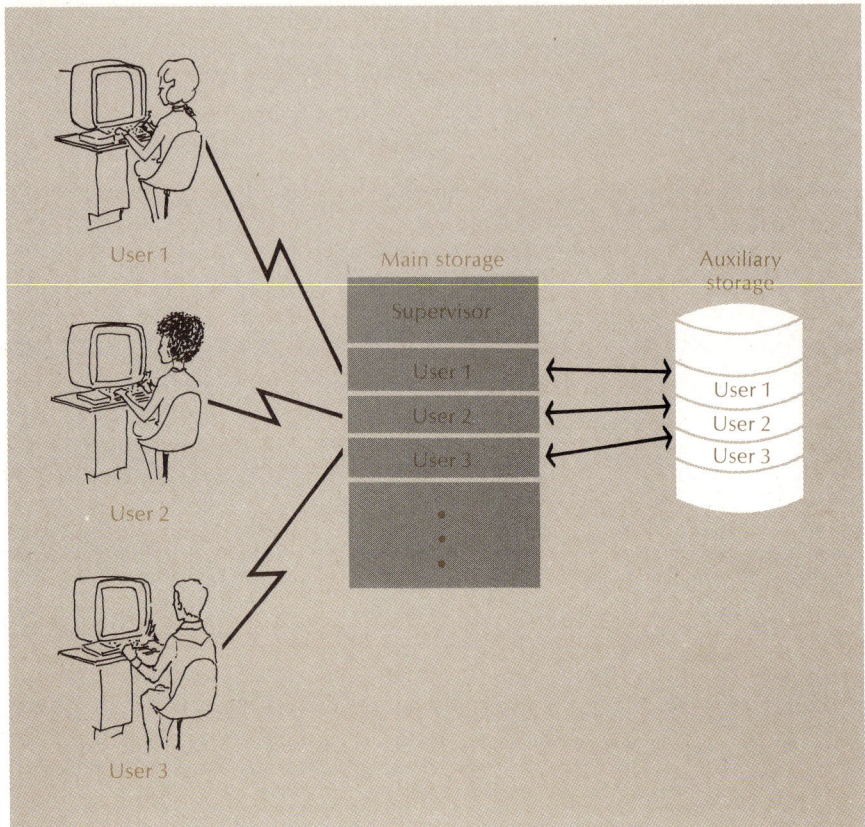

Data Communication

INTRODUCTION   As soon as the first computers became available everyone, from engineers to end users, began dreaming up better ways to utilize them. The development of sophisticated software described in earlier portions of this book is one such example. Another was the notion of using telephone lines to transmit data from a remote location directly to the computer. Thus began the broad field of data communication, the subject of this chapter.

Many of the concepts we have studied in this book rely on data communication—in particular, most of the online capabilities illustrated by numerous examples. However, transmission of data is by no means limited to a terminal communicating with a computer. Indeed, large-scale data transfer between computers is quite common today. Vast computer networks exist that consist of many computers linked by the telecommunications network. The field of data communication has expanded so rapidly that by 1980 expenditures for data communication equipment had exceeded the expenditures for data processing equipment. More and more, the data processing professional is experiencing a need for data communication knowledge.

WHAT IS DATA COMMUNICATION

First of all, let us consider some terminology. *Telecommunication,* as the word implies, is simply the transmission of information over some distance without changing it. (The Greek word *tele* means far, or far off.) The three basic components of a telecommunication system are

1. A *sender (source),* which creates the information to be transmitted.
2. A *medium,* over which the information is transmitted.
3. A *receiver (sink),* which receives the information.

This concept is illustrated in Figure 4-4. For an ordinary telephone conversation the sender and receiver are people and the medium is the telephone circuit. However, in a broader sense the sender and receiver could as easily be machines—in particular, computer devices. Hence we have a "marriage" of *data processing* and *telecommunication,* which we shall refer to as *data communication.* (The term *teleprocessing* is often used in place of data communication; they mean the same—transmission of data without change.) In other words, computer devices "talk to" other computer devices over the communication network. We must recognize that processing is still performed by the computer; the communications network is simply the means for transmitting the data *without* change.

In the business environment, the objectives of most data communication systems are to:

- Reduce the time and effort required to perform tasks.
- Improve the efficiency of entering source data into the system.
- Provide better centralized control over data.
- Reduce the costs of doing business.
- Provide for fast dissemination of information.
- Provide better centralization of some activities while allowing for decentralization of others.
- Support improved management control of the organization.

We have already studied three such systems: the automated supermarket, the centralized library system, and the airline reservation system.

DATA TRANSMISSION

The sender–medium–receiver concept has actually been with us for a very long time, if we wish to be technical about it. Shouting to another person does in fact involve transmission over a distance via the medium "air," which

Figure 4-4
Basic components of a telecommunications system.

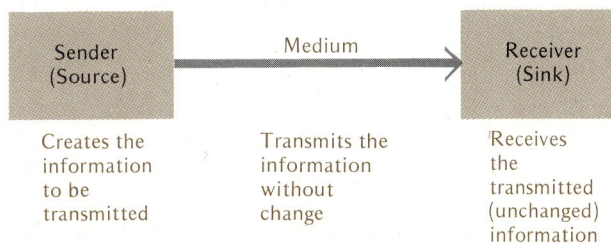

Sender (Source)	Medium	Receiver (Sink)
Creates the information to be transmitted	Transmits the information without change	Receives the transmitted (unchanged) information

carries the sound waves. Needless to say, the use of telephone circuitry considerably enhances the distance possible. However, in order to do this the sound must first be converted into analogous electrical waves before being transmitted. Thus our telecommunication system requires two additional elements, as shown in Figure 4-5. Sound waves are entered into the "converter" and electrical waves that are exactly equivalent are transmitted over the medium. This electric signal is termed *analog* since it is an exact electrical duplication of the sound. (Within recent years digital data transmission has come into use mainly for data transmission.)

The circumstances are very similar when the sender and receiver are computer devices. Now, however, the computer generates *digital* signals, which represent discrete values of either 0 or 1 and are not especially compatible with the continuous analog nature of telephone equipment. Consequently the converting equipment must change the digital signals of the computer devices into the electrical equivalent of voice-like tones, and back again. Electronics people call this *modulation* and *demodulation* of the signal. The units that perform these functions thus are called *modems;* they are illustrated in Figure 4-6, which shows a terminal remotely connected to a computer. The modem at the computer end is usually permanently wired

Figure 4-5 Transmission of digital information through an analog system.

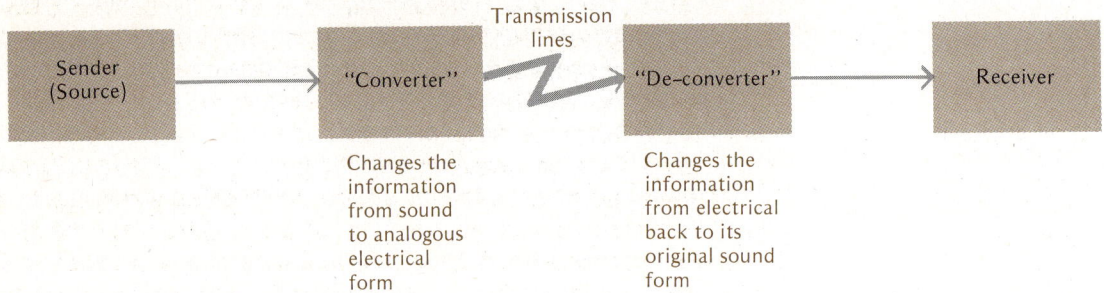

Figure 4-6 Information transmission with conversion-deconversion.

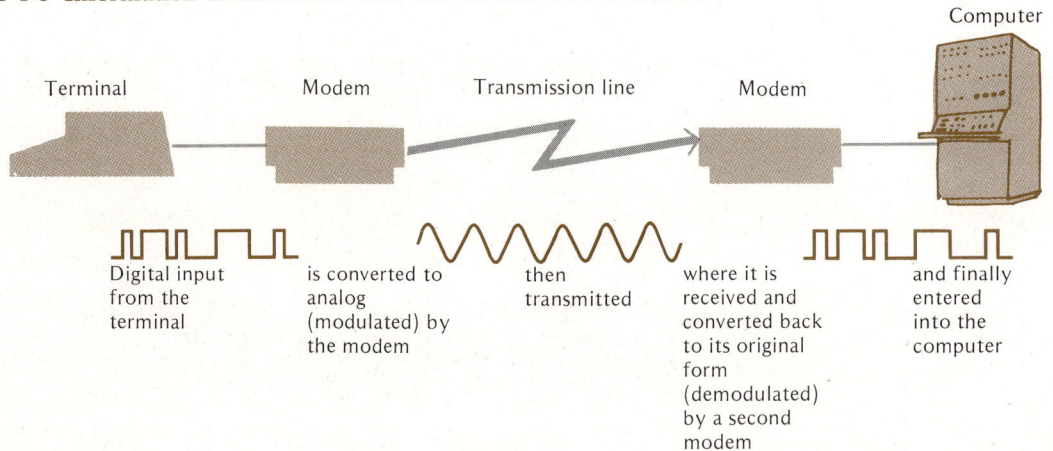

directly into the telephone network on one side and the computer on the other. However, this is not necessarily the case with the terminal. For instance, portable terminals use an *acoustic coupler* in place of a modem, which allows an ordinary telephone handset to be inserted. (A modem and an acoustic coupler are shown in Figure 4-7.)

**Figure 4-7
(a) A modem. (b) An
acoustic coupler.
(*Courtesy of
Anderson-Jacobson
Corporation.*)**

(a)

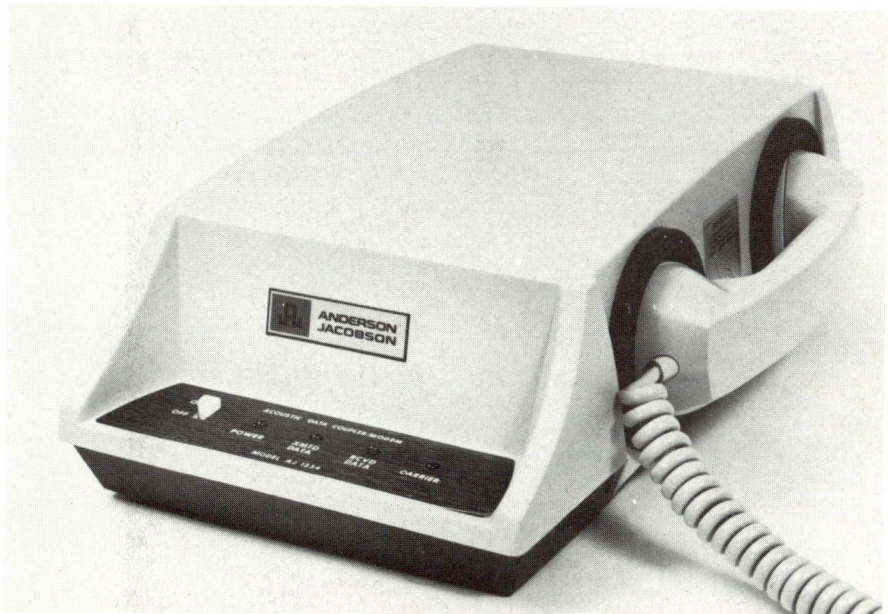

(b)

As we might suspect, the illustrations that we have considered to this point are rather simple. Data communication is an entire field within itself.

EXERCISE

4.4   What is the purpose of the modem?

File Management Principles

THE CONCEPT OF THE KEY FIELD   As we have learned in preceding sections, the processing of data files is a primary aspect of business data processing. Most of this processing involves matching some type of transaction information with corresponding master data. For instance, let us consider a retail store that issues charge accounts to its customers. For convenience, each customer is given a number—the account number. Obviously each charge purchase will involve that account number for the purpose of record keeping. In order to prepare the customer statement (the bill) the Transaction Records (charges) for each customer will have to be associated with the Master Record of the customer. As we can see in Figure 4-8, this is done by using the account number that is recorded in both the Master and Transaction Records. This field, which is common to both, is called a *key field,* and it serves to identify the particular record. As a rule every record in a data processing application will have one or more key fields. This is just as important in modern computer systems as it was with card processing systems of years ago, and with manual systems, which are still in use.

FILE MANAGEMENT SYSTEMS   As we know, a file is a collection of records that are related to each other in some way known to the user of the file. A *file management system* is software that provides the user with the ability to manipulate the file. Whenever a record is required, the user program asks for it and the record is accessed by the file management system. This retrieval might involve simply getting the next sequential record, or it might involve getting a particular record based on a key field identifier. However, it is significant that the file management software

Figure 4-8
Matching transactions records with the corresponding master. Records are matched on the basis of a corresponding key field: a field that is common to both record types.

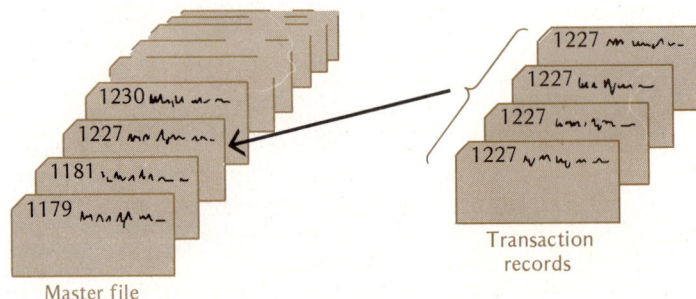

1230
1227
1181
1179

Master file

1227
1227
1227
1227

Transaction records

does *not* know what the record format is. This information is contained in each program and is hardly needed by the file management system, which simply passes records back and forth. Furthermore, file management systems are not designed with the ability to recognize that some data records are logically related to others (for example, Figure 4-8). Again this is controlled by the program. Now we should not take this to imply that file management systems are trivial, do-little programs. On the contrary, many of them are quite sophisticated, and certainly very valuable to the user. However, these points are critical to the distinction between file management and database management, as we shall learn in this section. Let us first consider three methods of file organization that are basic to conventional file management systems: sequential, random, and indexed. To illustrate these methods let us assume that we are working with an employee master file. Each record within the file includes the employee's Social Security number, which is used as the key field.

EXERCISE

4.5   The Department of Motor Vehicles (or some such agency) in every state maintains a record on every registered driver in the state. What probably would be used for a key field in such a system? Why not use the person's name as the key field?

FILE ORGANIZATION AND PROCESSING CONCEPTS

In a broad sense there are two basic ways of accessing data from files. One is *sequential access,* in which the records are processed in the order in which they are stored. Files on magnetic tape are necessarily processed sequentially. For most applications sequential files are sorted on the key field prior to processing. The other accessing method is *random access,* in which the records are processed in whatever order is required. For instance, the supermarket example of Section 1 revolves around processing information for cornflakes (or whatever other product the customer purchases). The record for cornflakes may be located anywhere in the file. It might be the 273rd record, for example, and so the system must be able to access it directly without looking at the preceding 272. Concepts of sequential and random file accessing are illustrated for the employee master file in Figure 4-9.

Figure 4-9(b) illustrates accessing a record by its position in the file. For most applications this is impractical. For instance, the user wants the record for Social Security number 133-44-1121 and has absolutely no interest in the fact that this might be the fourth record in the file. Thus some method is required to relate the key field to the actual location. Two common methods for doing this are hashing and indexing. Using *hashing,* some mathematical method is used to operate on the key field to produce the location of the record in the file. For instance, 133-44-1121 might hash into record location 4. The other method is through *indexing.* We are all familiar with the concept of an index. For instance, if we wished to find the description of UPC in this book,

Figure 4-9 (a) Sequential file.
(b) Accessing records by relative file location.

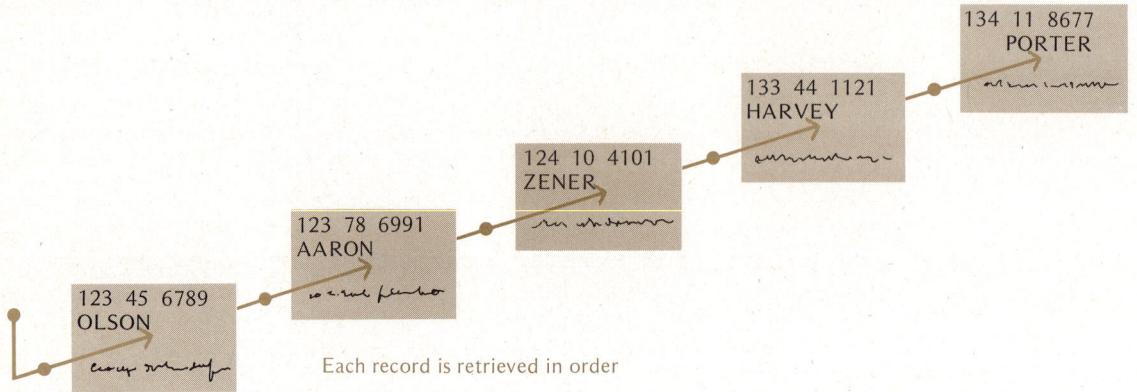

Each record is retrieved in order

Example: Get the next record

(a)

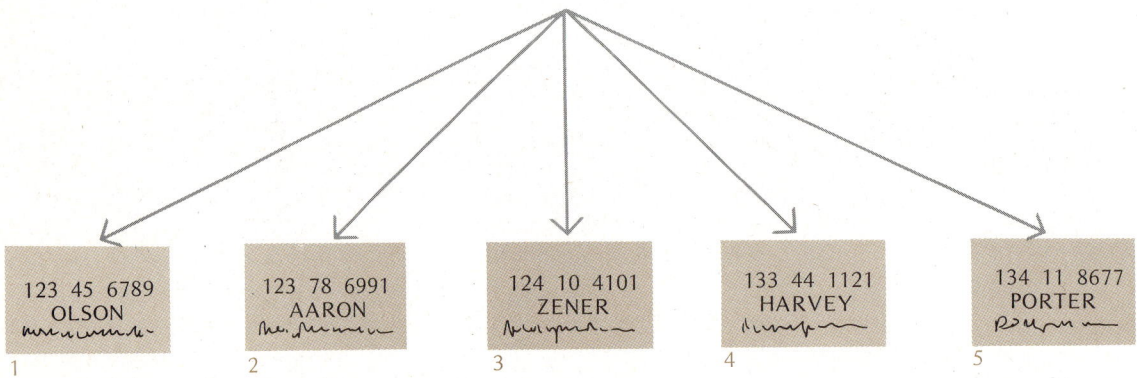

Each record is retrieved by its relative location in the file.

Example: Get the 4th record.

(b)

we would turn to the index, look up UPC, read the page number, then turn directly to that page. Indexed files use exactly the same principles.

The principles of hashing and indexing are illustrated in Figure 4-10.

EXERCISE

4.6   What is meant by random processing?

Figure 4-10 (a) Random accessing using hashing.
(b) Random accessing using an index.

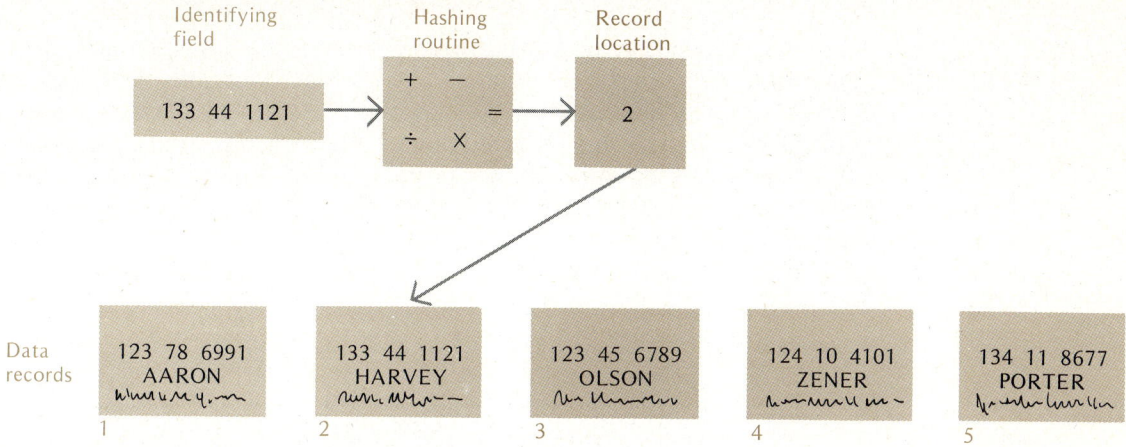

Each record is retrieved by using a hashing algorithm that
computes the record location from the identifying
field (key field).

Example: Get the record whose social security number is 133 44 1121

(a)

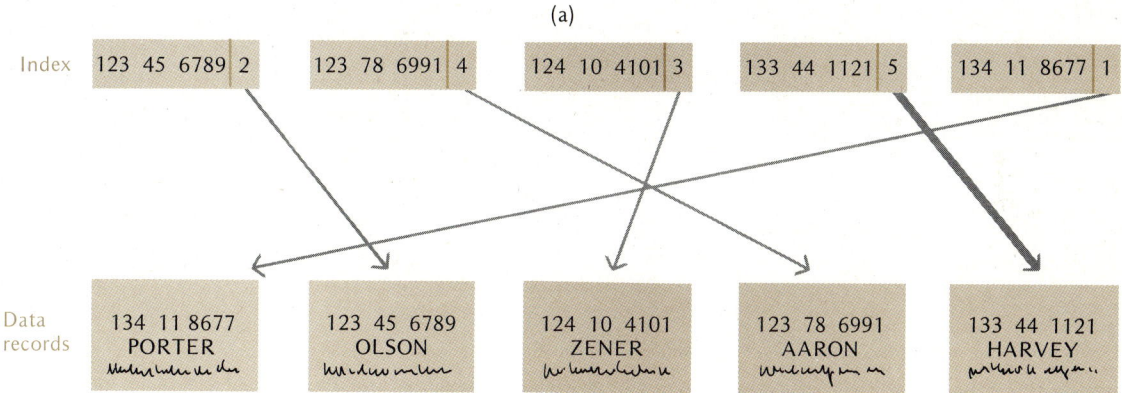

An index (directory) to the file is maintained.
Each record is accessed by finding its
location in the index.

Example: Get the record with a social security number 133 44 1121.

(b)

Database Management Systems

AN EXAMPLE APPLICATION   What is a database? In general we might say that all the files that make up the data processing system of a company form their database. However, the term *database* is now used in a much broader and more comprehensive sense. To appreciate this let us contrast a "conventional" data processing system consisting of one or more separate files for each application with a database system in which a single large collection of data serves all applications.

> **Example 4–1**   Prime Research Corporation carries on a number of research projects at its main office and several branch sites. The data processing department for Prime has developed several systems for performing normal accounting and report generation functions. Among the many files in the system are the following:
>
> 1. Department File—sample record contents
>   a. Department description and function
>   b. Budget information
>   c. Projects in progress
>   d. Names of employees in the department
> 2. Project File—sample record contents
>   a. Project description
>   b. Financial data
>   c. Names of departments participating
>   d. Personnel assigned to the project
> 3. Personnel File—sample record contents
>   a. Personnel and professional data
>   b. Payroll information
>   c. Department to which assigned
>   d. Project(s) to which assigned

Associated with each of these three files is a set of programs for preparing required reports as illustrated in Figure 4-11. Here we see that each file is processed virtually independently of the other files and each will include its own set of processing programs (such as Program C in Figure 4-11) for processing that file.

There are three major problems with systems of this type. The first relates to the fact that data in different files cannot easily be shared. Thus processing that requires data from two or more systems (sets of files) can be clumsy, and in many cases very inefficient. This results in another problem: redundancy of data between files. In order to produce desired reports many fields from a given file are often duplicated in others. For instance, referring to the example definition, both the department and personnel files contain information about

Figure 4-11 Conventional processing.

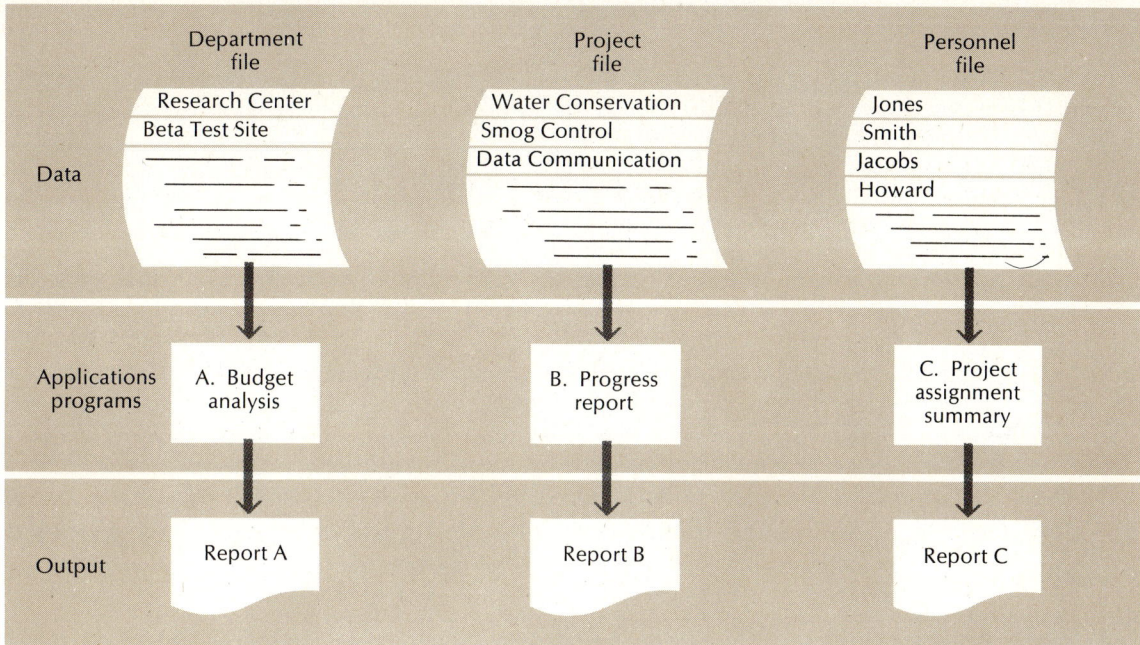

Department file	Project file	Personnel file

Data

Research Center	Water Conservation	Jones
Beta Test Site	Smog Control	Smith
	Data Communication	Jacobs
		Howard

Applications programs

A. Budget analysis

B. Progress report

C. Project assignment summary

Output

Report A

Report B

Report C

projects. Unfortunately, duplication of data across files can lead to inconsistencies. (For instance, a correction might be made to a field in one file but not to the same field in another file.) The third problem associated with conventional file systems is that records in the files do not describe the record format. Each record is merely a string of characters. Thus each program written to process a given file must include the record definition for that file.

THE CONCEPT OF A DATABASE

If we were to survey the software market today, we would find a large number of database systems available. However, some of them would be little more than highly sophisticated indexed file management systems. What then is meant by database system? In a nutshell, a database system has the following characteristics.

- It is a single collection of all data used by a company (for example, a combination of all files used by Prime Research).
- It is organized and structured in other than ordinary multiple file form.
- Its organization permits access to any or all data quantities by all applications with equal ease.
- Organization is such that duplication is minimized, if not eliminated entirely.
- It involves the concept of separating the data definition from the applications programs and including it as part of the database.

• It provides for the definition of logical relationships that exist between various records in the database.

A DATABASE EXAMPLE   To illustrate the elementary notion of how a database works let us consider a grossly simplified version of a database for Prime Research Corporation in which the original three files are collected in a single large online "file" or database (refer to Figure 4-12). Although the original files retain some of their identity they are now interrelated by system pointers, which allow easy processing of data within two or more of the files. Conceptually, the easiest way of achieving these pointers is by record addressing, which is provided to the programmer by random access storage devices. For instance, the Water Conservation record in the Project File includes all of the necessary information on that project. It also includes two address areas: the first contains the disk address of each department record relating to this project, and the second contains the disk record address for each employee working on the project. With this data organization information in the Department or Personnel Files is readily available when processing the Project File. For instance, preparation of a report involving project expenditures and the salaries of assigned employees can easily be prepared.

Management Information Systems

One of the keys to a successful business organization is timely information and the use of that information in decision making. This was a fact of life in

Figure 4-12 Pointers in a database system.

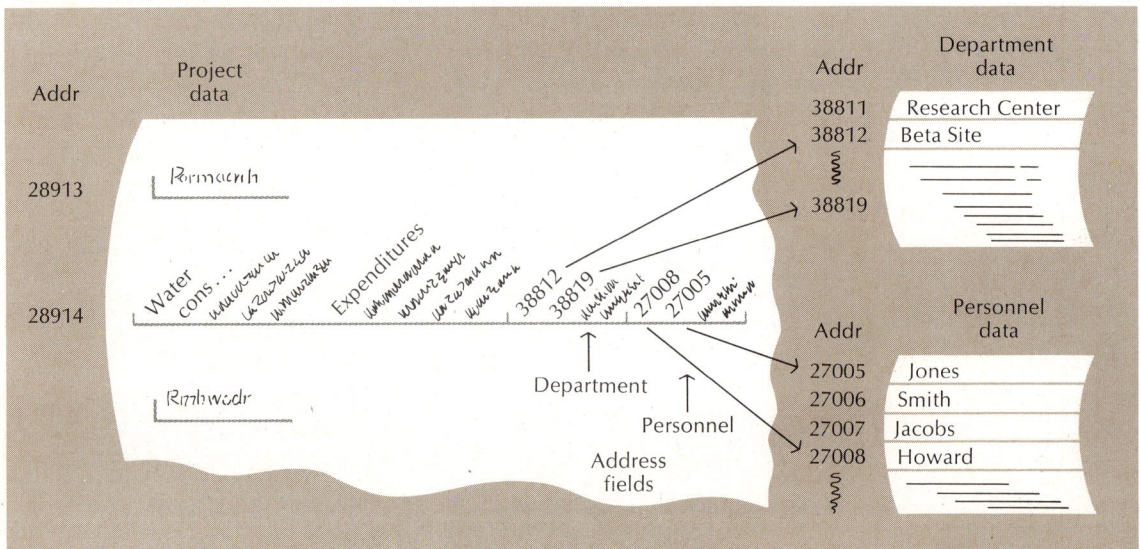

business long before the age of electronics, and is even more pertinent today. Obviously the computer in general, and database management systems in particular, offer a powerful capability for obtaining needed information. The combination of database management, online real-time processing, and telecommunications can be used to provide all levels of company management with powerful tools in managing the company. In this respect we must not limit our thinking to information such as payroll summaries and quarterly profit and loss statements. Indeed, a comprehensive information system must provide the following.

- *Top management* requires information for long-range planning, establishing company goals, and setting policy. For these purposes computer simulations must provide management with information for predicting and planning company activities. This involves not only the financial status of the organization but also its relationship to the general business environment and appropriate economic forecasts. For instance, all of these factors would be of prime importance to top management in deciding whether or not to build a new manufacturing plant.
- *Middle management* requires information for implementation of decisions and plans of top management. This involves allocating resources of the company, delegating authority and responsibility for operations, and exercising overall control of the company. For instance, a middle manager might be required to respond to a bid specification for the manufacture of certain electronic equipment. If the bid is too low, the company loses money; if the bid is too high, the company loses the contract. Accurate, up-to-date material, labor, and production costs are absolutely essential in preparing a competitive proposal.
- *Low management* requires information necessary for the daily operation of the company. Production quotas must be achieved, materials orders placed, personnel must be managed, and so on. If any facet of the operation begins to falter or fall behind schedule, timely information must be available to pinpoint the problem immediately so that corrective action can be taken.

A system of this type is commonly called a *management information system,* or MIS. Conceptually, the objective of an MIS is to provide the means for timely information to be integrated into the functioning of a company for planning, decision-making, and control purposes. In reality total MIS systems as envisioned by many proponents have been slow in materializing. To implement MIS far more is needed than a powerful computer and a solid database management system (DBMS). The concept of integrating an information system into a company must permeate virtually all levels of the company or else the total concept will achieve considerably less than the objectives. Furthermore, in many cases it simply may not be economically feasible, or even practical, to integrate into a single information system.

Distributed Data Processing

DISTRIBUTED ACCESS TO A CENTRAL COMPUTER

By combining the capabilities of multiprogramming and data communications it is possible to serve a large number of users in a variety of ways. For instance, a large computer managing a large database can handle online processing from both local and remotely located terminals. It can concurrently accommodate batch processing from both local and remote card readers and line printers. As an example, a large company might consist of a main facility and two branch facilities. The main facility houses a large computer that does all data processing for the company. However, each branch facility has a card reader and printer for submitting their own jobs to the computer. (This is commonly called *remote job entry,* or simply *RJE.*) This concept is illustrated in Figure 4-13. This is a widely used technique; note that it gives distributed *access* to data but actual processing is centralized. Furthermore, tight central control over the entire system is possible.

EXERCISE

4.7   Remote job entry (RJE) and online remote transaction processing both involve remotely located, online terminals. How do they differ in basic principle?

DISTRIBUTING THE PROCESSING LOAD

Referring again to Figure 4-13, if the remote terminal is "smart"—for instance, a small computer—then some of the processing can be performed at the remote site. Systems of this type have been available for a number of years. This represents a step in the direction of decentralization of processing capability, or *distributed data processing* as it is called. In the early days of computing the trend was for a business to "adjust" the organizational needs (the problem) to fit available computer hardware and software resources (the solutions). Now more and more we are seeing a trend toward truly tailoring the computer resources to solve the problems. Distributed data processing is a significant step in this direction. In any large company that involves two or more different geographic locations many data processing functions are better served through centralization. These might include such operations as handling employee benefits, legal reporting, and vendor contracting. Other functions might be far more efficiently handled at the individual sites through distributed processing capabilities. These could include such operations as order processing, accounts receivable and payable, and payroll. However, it is important to recognize that local processing is not independent of the central system. Needs such as this have given rise to computer networks. Such distributed systems have become increasingly common during recent years, partially because of the following circumstances.

- The cost of computer hardware has decreased dramatically as computing power has *increased.*
- The cost of online storage has decreased and capacities have increased.

Figure 4-13 A simple data processing network.

Local I/O

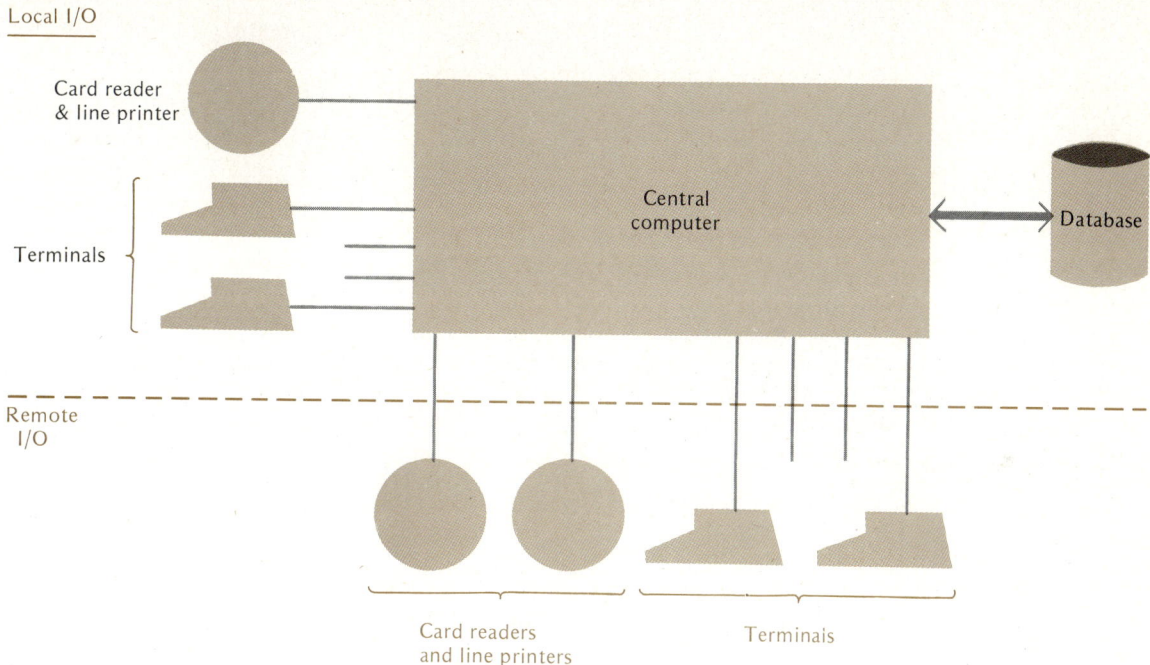

Card reader
& line printer

Terminals

Central
computer

Database

Remote
I/O

Card readers
and line printers

Terminals

- Sophisticated operating systems and database management systems have become available.
- Data communications equipment and techniques have come into wide use.
- End users have become more knowledgeable and sophisticated and demand better capabilities.

To illustrate a truly distributed data processing system let us consider a manufacturing company consisting of the following three geographically separated branches.

- Company central site
- Manufacturing branch
- Sales branch

We will assume that all company files are to be maintained at the central site, that companywide data processing is performed at the central site, and that local processing is performed at the branch sites. The system represented by Figure 4-14 will function in this way. This is a very simplified form of *hierarchical* distributed processing. Local processing, such as inventory control of raw goods (data at the manufacturing site) or sales summaries (data at the sales site), is performed at the respective secondary (local) site. Companywide

Figure 4-14 Example of a simple distributed data processing system.

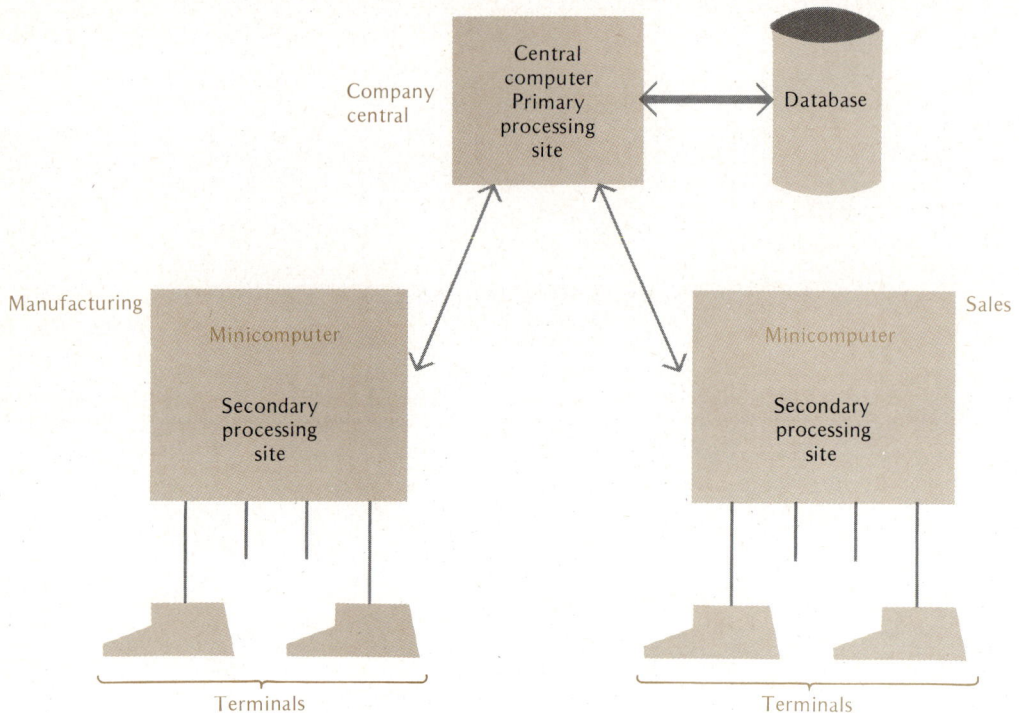

processing functions would be performed at the primary site. For example, the overall company general accounting and employee payroll might be processed centrally. Also, the central system manages the database. Access by the secondary sites to the database is through the central system. There may or may not be a direct communications link between the secondary sites.

EXERCISE

4.8   Would the remote job entry system illustrated in Figure 4-13 be a distributed data processing system? Qualify your answer.

DISTRIBUTING THE DATABASE   Although the system of Figure 4-14 is close to the real thing, such a network without a distributed database is only "partially" distributed. For instance, certain items of the information regarding sales order processing should properly be stored and processed at the sales site where they can best be managed. To illustrate this concept let us assume the following regarding our company.

- Each of the sites has database capabilities.
- Data of interest to us include customer data, order data, and product line data.

- A complete customer database is maintained at the company central site but segments are duplicated at the sales site.
- A complete order information database is maintained at the company central site but segments are duplicated at the sales site and the manufacturing site.
- A complete product line database is maintained at the company central site but segments are duplicated at the sales site and the manufacturing site.
- All sales order and customer information originates at the sales site.

The overall concept of this distributed system is illustrated in Figure 4-15. As we can see, the complete database is stored only at the primary site. For those segments of the main database that are required at the local levels, duplicate copies are maintained at the respective secondary locations. Thus most of the locally required processing can be performed at the local level without access to the central database. Any information that cannot be processed at the secondary level is "moved up" to the central site and

Figure 4-15 Distributed data processing with distributed database.

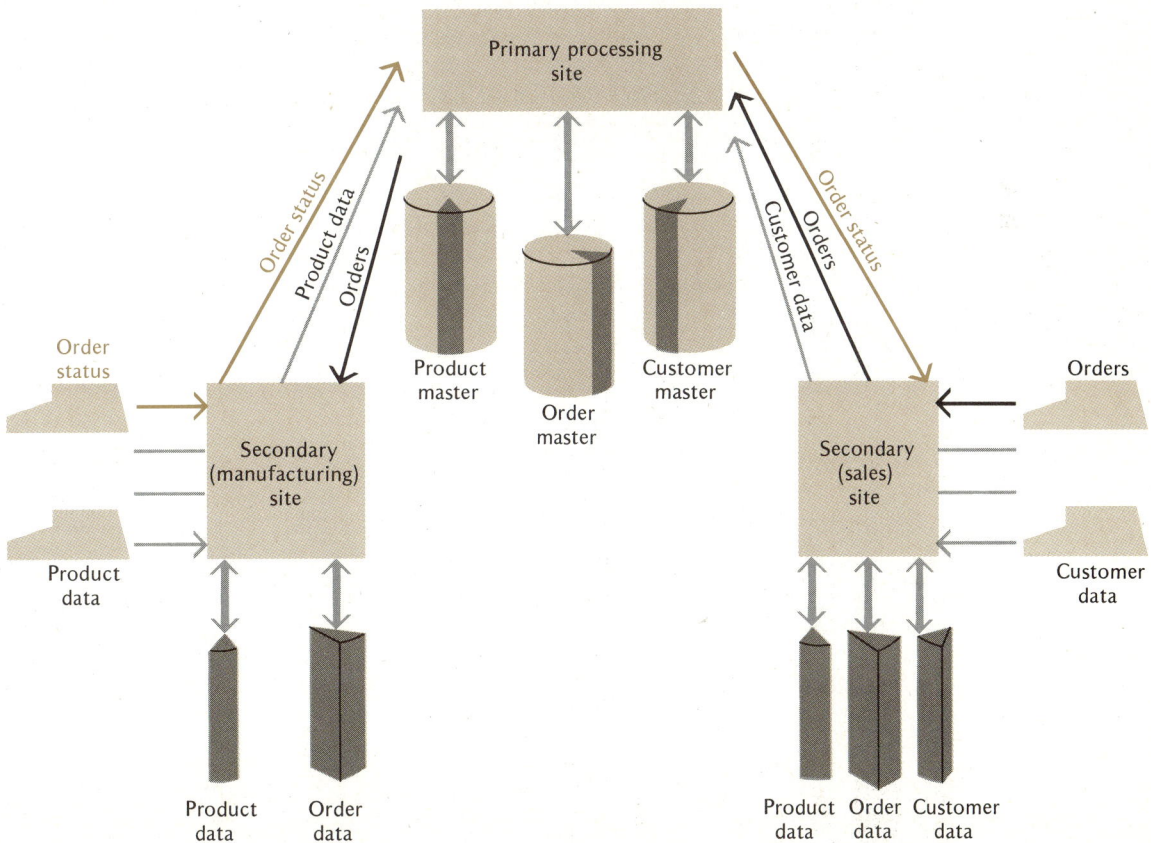

processed at that level. In other words, we have a *hierarchy* of processing levels—and thus the terminology, hierarchical distributed data processing.

At first consideration computer networks and distributed data processing might appear to be appropriate only to very large corporations. The preceding descriptions certainly sound as though they apply to large, sophisticated computer systems. This is hardly the case. With the low-cost, sophisticated minicomputers now available, these techniques appeal to a wide variety of medium-sized businesses.

EXERCISE

4.9   The system of Figure 4-15 involves maintaining duplicate copies of portions of the central database at the secondary sites. It could be argued that this is contrary to the basic philosophy of a database management system. Explain.

Computer Networks in Our Lives

ELECTRONIC FUNDS TRANSFER   Ten to fifteen years ago experts predicted that we would soon become a "checkless" society and that most money transactions would be electronic in nature via vast computer networks. Indeed, with more than 30 *billion* checks being handled daily there has been considerable pressure to devise methods for reducing this paper flow. The notion of transmitting money transactions electronically from the computer of one bank to the computer of another is commonly referred to as *electronic funds transfer,* or *EFT.* By avoiding the handwritten document (the check) this technique has much to offer in the way of reducing paperwork and improving overall efficiency. However, EFT has not become widely used as quickly as many had predicted, for various reasons. One reason relates to cost. Officials of the Chase Manhattan Bank indicate that for most transactions checks continue to be the cheapest payment instrument other than cash. Another reason relates to fear of security problems and loss of control and privacy by consumers.

A CONVENTIONAL CHECKING TRANSACTION   Let us consider what takes place with the writing of a check. We will assume that a customer has made purchases in a store and has written a check for the amount owed. This is a simple procedure—one that we encounter every day. Now, what happens to the check once the customer gives it to the store?

Figure 4-16 is a simplified representation of the route followed by the check. As we can see, the piece of paper does some traveling. At each stop it must be processed and handled. At the banking clearinghouse it must be separated from thousands of other checks and sent on to the proper bank. Although high-speed processing machines are in use to speed these operations, there remains a tremendous amount of paperwork to be handled. The final step in the process is, of course, return of the check together with a statement to the customer.

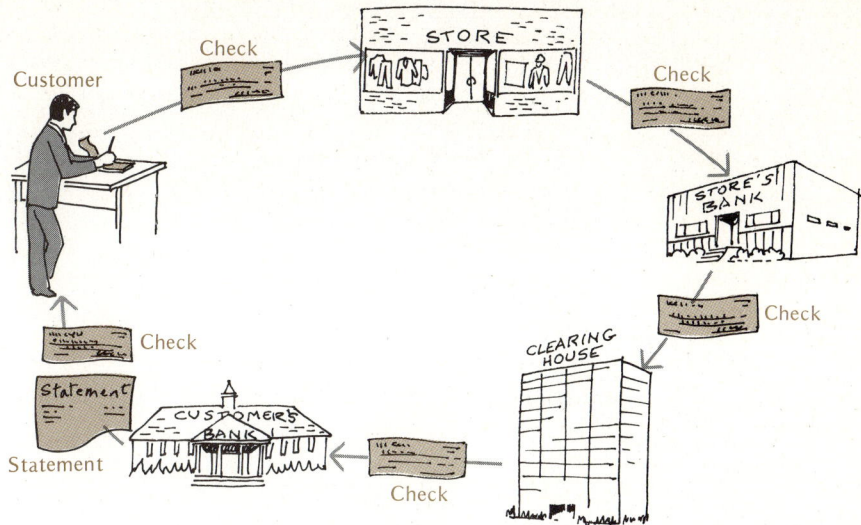

Figure 4-16 The cycle of a check transaction.

AN ELECTRONIC TRANSACTION

Now let us assume that our customer is functioning in an EFT environment. To use this system our customer will have been issued an EFT card similar to the VISA or MasterCards with which we are all familiar. The visit to the store for purchases now appears as illustrated in Figure 4-17. In this case the following occurs.

- The charges together with identifying information from the card are transmitted to an automated clearinghouse location over the communications network.
- The computer at the automated clearinghouse has communication links with all member banks. The customer account is debited by the amount of the transaction and the store account is credited with that amount.
- The customer receives periodic statements of all transactions.

The computer coupled with the communications system is truly coming of age.

EXERCISE

4.10 List some of the factors that might concern you about electronic funds transfer.

Data Security

FILE PROTECTION

Considering the extent to which the computer is used in most businesses, the loss of significant amounts of data could be very serious. In fact, many companies would suffer disastrous consequences, and perhaps even bank-

Figure 4-17   Simplification of a transaction via an EFT system.

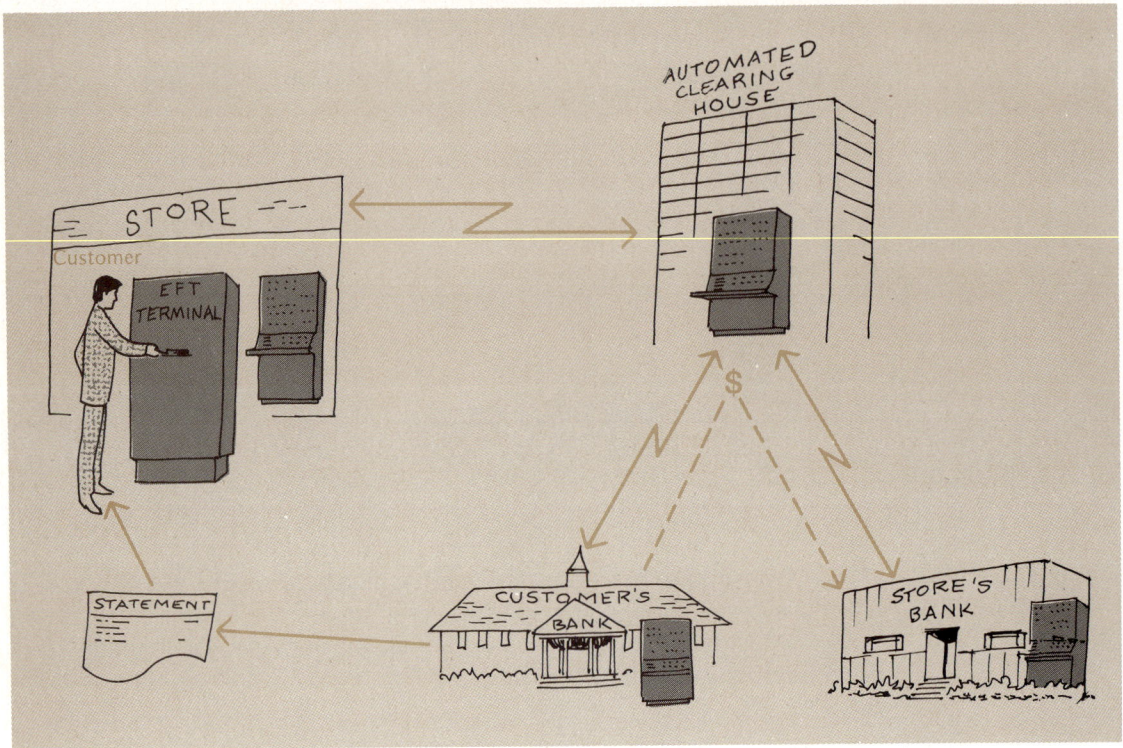

ruptcy, if all of their computerized files were irretrievably lost. In general, data files, whether online or offline, must be protected against loss, which can occur in any of the following ways.

- *Physical loss*   Disk packs or tapes, for instance, can be destroyed by flooding or fire.
- *Equipment failure.*   Occasionally components of the computer will fail, which can result in the loss of data stored on disk or tapes that are being processed.
- *Sabotage or vandalism.*   In the minds of some (such as disgruntled employees or extremist groups) the computer center appears to be the ideal place in which to cause trouble.
- *Software failure.*   Most sophisticated programs have "bugs." Although usually few in number, they sometimes can cause loss of data.

To a large extent data files are protected by *backup* procedures. This involves making duplicates of critical files on a periodic basis (see Figure 4-18). In most modern computer installations backup runs are usually part of the normal operational procedures. In general, backup procedures depend

Figure 4-18
File backup.

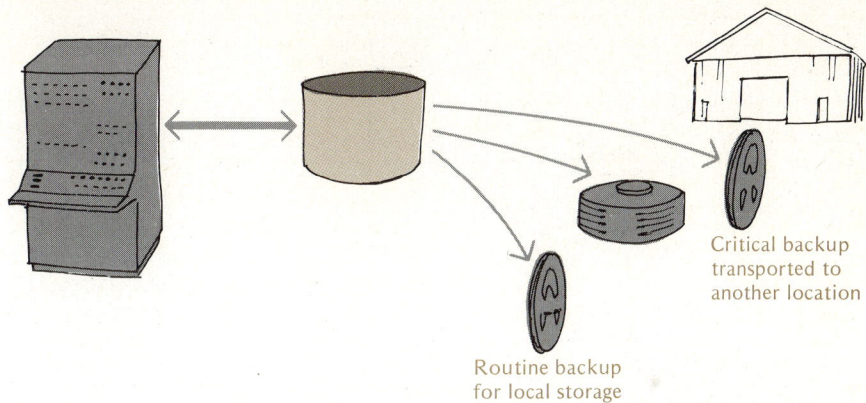

Critical backup
transported to
another location

Routine backup
for local storage

on the importance and activity level of individual files. For instance, online files that are continually being changed will frequently be copied to magnetic tape on a daily basis. On the other hand, files that do not change as rapidly might be backed up on a weekly basis, with the backup procedure being performed on the weekend.

EXERCISE

4.11 One of the disk drives of an online system suffers what appears to be a temporary failure and corrupts the disk pack. Since it is the busiest portion of the day, the operator quickly replaces the corrupted pack with the backup pack and restarts the computer to minimized lost time. Comment.

SECURITY OF INFORMATION FROM MISUSE

Computer networks, distributed data processing, and remote access to computers provide business and government with powerful tools. For example, paperwork can be reduced, services can be improved at lower costs, and criminal information can be made readily available to law enforcement agencies. On a broad basis there exists the potential for a vastly improved use of our overall national resources. The key to all of this is wide access to a very broad base of data. Unfortunately this powerful tool with its potential for so many good uses provides equal opportunity for uses that are bad. EFT systems, for instance, provide the ideal environment for electronic theft of money; and central data banks are an open invitation to invasion of personal privacy (see Figure 4-19).

Newspapers and magazines report all types of computer-related crime. Some may appear to be harmless game playing or just snooping; others are clearly fraudulent. The following are some of the typical problems that have been encountered.

- A student figures out the password or other entry code to a central computer system and uses computer time via a portable terminal. The activities are quite "innocent" and include writing some programs and

**Figure 4-19
Desirable and
undesirable access to
a database.**

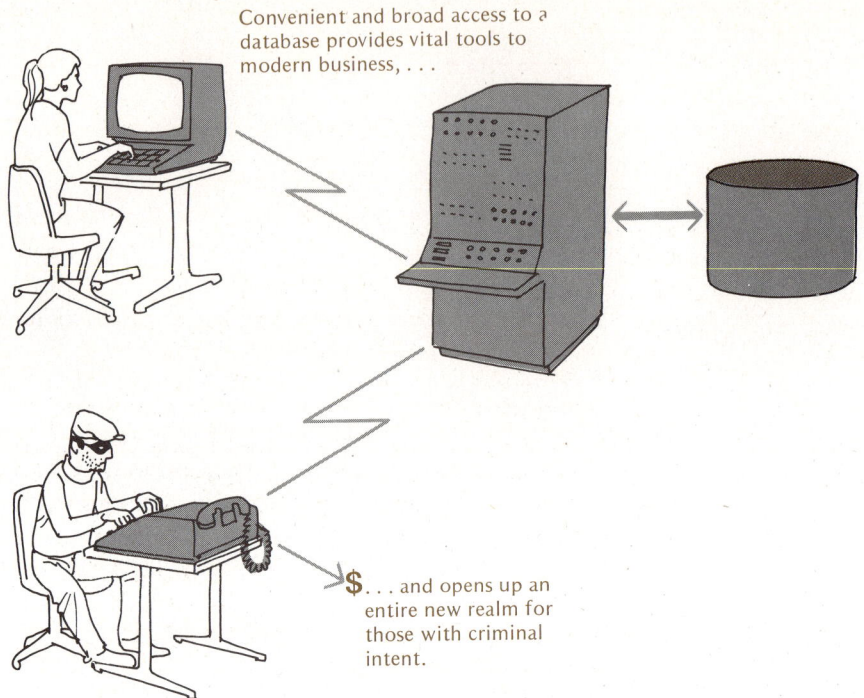

Convenient and broad access to a
database provides vital tools to
modern business, . . .

$ . . . and opens up an
entire new realm for
those with criminal
intent.

playing tic-tac-toe with the computer. No harm is done to either software or hardware.

- A systems analyst feels that he has been dealt with unfairly by the company and desires to "even the score." This is accomplished by making subtle changes to critical processing programs, which, over a period of time, corrupt the database.
- A consultant breaks the entry codes to a system and copies programs costing hundreds of thousands of dollars to write. Copies of the programs are sold to competitors.

As computerized databanks become more and more common and as access via remote terminal becomes more available all types of data misuse are bound to occur. The misuse of computerized data is so foreboding that during the first few months of 1979 more than 100 pieces of legislation relating to data security and privacy were introduced in state legislatures.

EXERCISE

4.12 Of these three examples of "misuse" of the computer or its data which do you feel represent(s) illegal activities that could be prosecuted in a court of law and which are merely in the "unethical" category?

SECURITY MEASURES FOR PROTECTION OF DATA

An article in the November 5, 1979, issue of *Computerworld* began as follows:

> There's good news and bad news when you talk about computer security in the 1980s. The good news: computer security systems will be better than ever. The bad news: computer criminals will also be better than ever.

Most experts readily admit that there is no way to stop the experienced thief from accessing and stealing information from a computer system. However, it is possible to use techniques and systems that will make it difficult to steal. The key element to any good security system is to make it so costly in terms of time and resources to commit the crime that the crime loses its appeal. Furthermore, the crime can further lose appeal if the security system is designed to make apprehension of the thief highly likely.

Most online computer systems with remote terminals rely on *identification codes.* Such a code may be a simple password consisting of several letters that will permit a user to gain access to the computer for writing programs, or it may be much more elaborate. Some systems require a terminal identification code, a user identification number, and special access codes to various files. (Refer to Figure 4-20.) However, the more complex the security and password arrangement, the clumsier the system will be for authorized users. This is obviously contrary to the intent of an online business system.

Auditing techniques to verify business records and prevent theft were used by business long before the electronic computer. To *audit* simply involves confirming the validity and accuracy of transactions in the records of a company. Auditors are especially concerned that each financial transaction can be traced through every step of the system and that some traceable record is kept at each point. This is commonly called an *audit trail.* These

Figure 4-20 Security codes to protect authorized access to data.

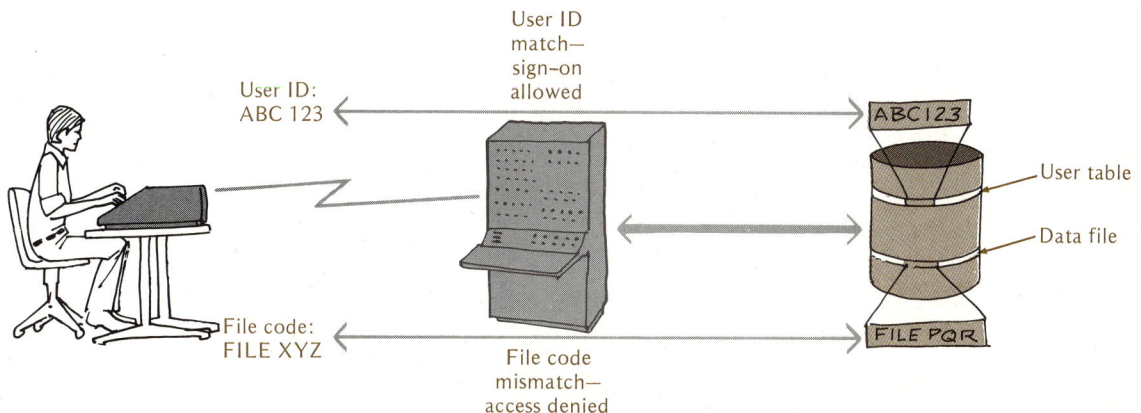

User ID
match—
sign–on
allowed

User ID:
ABC 123

ABC123

User table

Data file

File code:
FILE XYZ

File code
mismatch—
access denied

FILE PQR

principles apply whether the record-keeping system is manual or compute-rized. The primary difference, as a rule, is that computerized systems are capable of handling tremendous volumes of data. Therefore, the auditing system should be integrated into the overall software system. Although ex-perts agree that it is impossible to prevent computerized theft, properly designed auditing systems can almost always make it possible to track down the culprit.

EXERCISE

4.13 A company uses an online system with a large number of remote users. A security expert has installed a very clever sequence of codes and passwords that should be almost impossible to "crack." The company therefore feels that the data is secure. Do you agree? Comment.

Personal Privacy

Without a doubt, personal privacy is the most controversial subject discussed in this book. The capability of the computer and computer networks to compile and process massive databanks promises tremendous potential for both good and bad. Many articles, and even books, are available. The following observation from the *Harvard Law Review* is typical:

> Recent innovations and business methods call attention to the next step which must be taken for the protection of the person, and for securing to the individual what Judge Cooley calls the right "to be let alone."

Sound like a response to the influence of the computer in our society? Not really: that observation appeared in the December 15, *1890,* issue of the *Review.* Now, nearly 100 years later, it is even more appropriate than when it was written. The amount of information on each of us that is stored in modern databanks is staggering. Figure 4-21 illustrates some of the multitude of databanks that contain personal data about us. Is it necessary to have so much information stored? This is a sticky question. Many feel that most agencies request more information than is necessary for the particular need. On the other hand, a lending institution has the right to learn if a person borrowing money is likely to pay it back. The Internal Revenue Service has a right to information to ensure that each taxpayer has paid her/his share of taxes. Hospitals need information in order to treat patients properly. In fact, many of the services that we expect—indeed, we demand—would not be available without large databases. However, high on the list of priorities must be protection of the individual and her/his privacy.

During the early 1970s the concept of a *national databank* was widely discussed. Such a system would involve a massive central system containing

Figure 4-21 Personal data stored in data banks.

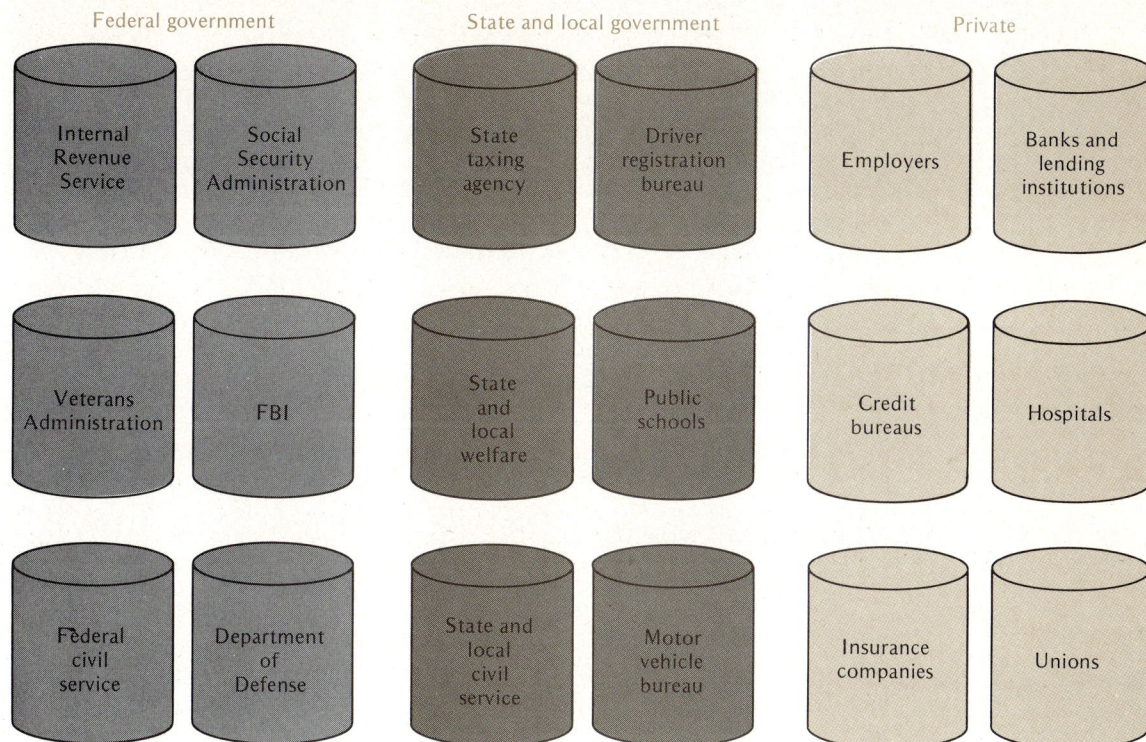

Federal government   State and local government   Private

| Internal Revenue Service | Social Security Administration | State taxing agency | Driver registration bureau | Employers | Banks and lending institutions |

| Veterans Administration | FBI | State and local welfare | Public schools | Credit bureaus | Hospitals |

| Federal civil service | Department of Defense | State and local civil service | Motor vehicle bureau | Insurance companies | Unions |

complete information on every U.S. resident. It was argued that one central system would avoid duplication and allow for better control of confidential information. Proponents loudly argued the many merits of such a system, most of which were quite valid. But the potential for misuse of this centralized information was generally considered far too dangerous to our way of life. Control of information is critical to a totalitarian form of government.

Fortunately the national databank concept appears to have settled into oblivion. In its place we have a myriad of relatively independent data systems. Most of them are necessary to our society. All of them must be controlled against misuse. Information is the key to our highly sophisticated society. Proper control of that information is essential to the continued existence of our way of life.

In Retrospect

Two basic approaches to effective utilization of the computer are multiprogramming and timesharing. Table 4-1 compares the two concepts.

**Table 4-1
Comparison of
Timesharing and
Multiprogramming**

Timesharing	Multiprogramming
Users share CPU time on a scheduled basis	Users share CPU time on a demand basis
Prime objective: keep user busy (maximize response)	Prime objective: keep computer busy (maximize throughput)
Person–machine interaction is emphasized	Minimal person–machine interaction
Rapid response time is of primary importance	Response time is not a consideration (usually slow)
Response generally implies partial completion of computing requirements	Response implies completion of computing requirements

Data communication involves the transmission of data over the telephone network. However, computer devices are binary in nature and the telecommunications network is analog. Thus modems are used to convert the digital signals to analog for transmission and to reconvert at the receiving end for input to the computer.

Conventional file management concepts involve sequential, random, and indexed file organization techniques. A sequential file is usually arranged in order according to some key field. Processing of the file proceeds sequentially from the first record through the last. It is not possible to process the records of a sequential file in a random sequence. In contrast, random file organization methods may use either indexes or hashing algorithms operating on the records' key field to determine the physical location to which each record is assigned.

In more recently developed database systems all of the files of an installation are integrated into a single large system. Included within the database is a complete definition of all data characteristics, thus removing such information from applications programs.

Extensive database management systems form the basis for management information systems, which can provide timely, comprehensive information to all levels of company management.

Distributed data processing involves the decentralization of the data processing operations of an organization. This is achieved through networks of computers that communicate with each other via the telephone system. Data processing functions, including entry, processing, transmission, and storage of data, can be handled locally or centrally, depending upon which is the more efficient.

Timely, readily available information represents the basic lifeblood of virtually every business. Unfortunately the more accessible data is, the greater the security problem. Generally speaking, security of computerized information may be considered in two broad categories: security from loss and security from misuse.

In general the best safeguard against loss of data files is regular backup procedures. Online files that are constantly changing are often backed up daily. More comprehensive backup is commonly performed weekly.

The objective of most security measures is to make computer theft sufficiently difficult to discourage it and, when the theft *is* successful, to provide a high probability of apprehending the thief.

In recent years considerable concern has been expressed over the gathering, storage, and exchange of computerized personal information about each of us. As a result much attention has been given to ensuring against invasion of privacy by computerized systems.

ANSWERS TO PRECEDING EXERCISES

4.1   The Investment Analysis program is CPU-bound since it involves very little I/O and much computation. If it is given first priority very little "CPU idle" time will be available for the Report Generator program. Effectively, the Report Generator program would have to wait until the Analysis program had been completed. Generally speaking, I/O-bound programs are given high priority and CPU-bound programs are given low priority.

4.2   The online component must have top priority or else the response time will be degraded. This is inconsistent with the entire notion of a rapid-response online system. No problem is encountered if the payroll calculation is delayed slightly, but great inconvenience can result if the remote inquiry is not handled immediately.

4.3   In a multiprogramming system users are scheduled on a priority basis; in a timesharing system they are scheduled on a time-scheduled basis.

4.4   A modem converts the computer signal to analog at the transmitting end and from analog to digital at the receiving end.

4.5   The driver license number. People's names are a bad choice as a key field since the data processing agency has no control over the names that are "issued." Consequently there is no way to avoid duplication.

4.6   Random processing is the processing of transactions on demand, as opposed to collecting them in batches and running them periodically.

4.7   Although RJE involves remote entry of jobs, it is handled in a batch processing environment. Online remote transaction processing, on the other hand, involves handling each transaction as it occurs.

4.8   No. Remote job entry is, as the name implies, *job entry*. It allows distributed access to the computer but the processing remains central, not distributed.

4.9   The basic philosophy of a database management system is to minimize duplication of information. In a distributed system such as this one, data is duplicated at the secondary level. It would be of utmost importance to ensure that all copies of duplicated data are the same as the master.

4.10   Items that would concern me would relate to the security of my money (unauthorized transfers out of my account) and further loss of privacy. That is, anyone who could gain entry to the system (legally or illegally) might "snoop to their hearts' content." If I were a bank manager I would be concerned about remote "electronic" theft of bank funds.

4.11   This sounds like poor judgement. If the disk drive has failed once, it might fail again and should not be used until checked by an engineer. If the installation has a second backup copy on tape (which is common), then it would be safe to bring the system up but by using another disk drive. If there is not another copy, one should be made before the backup is placed online.

4.12 All of them could be prosecuted. The "innocent" use of computer time actually represents theft of computer resources that have a monetary value. The others are clearly criminal acts.

4.13 The password system might be very sophisticated but what about the large number of remote users? Each user will require knowledge of the codes and passwords. The more people who know, the more difficult it is to keep the passwords and codes secret. In this respect we might conclude that if one person knows, it is a secret; if two know, it is news.

ADDITIONAL EXERCISES

4.14 What are the main similarity and the main difference between multiprogramming and timesharing?

4.15 A college computer center is set up to use three partitions: P1, P2, and P3. Partition P1 has the highest priority and P3 the lowest. The computer is to be used concurrently for instruction and administration with requirements for the three partitions as follows:

- Administrative processing: roughly an equal balance between processing and I/O.
- Instructional control system: handles all instructional input and output, and job scheduling; primarily I/O.
- Instructional processing: language translation and program execution; primarily internal processing.

Assign these to the respective partitions and justify your answer.

4.16 What are the basic components of a telecommunication system?

4.17 What is the difference between an acoustic coupler and a modem?

4.18 What is a key field?

4.19 How is a record accessed in an indexed file?

4.20 The system of Figure 4-14 is said to be only "partially" distributed. Explain what this means.

4.21 Describe the various ways in which data stored in a disk file can be lost.

4.22 What is a national databank? What are its good and bad points?

4.23 **Matching**   Match each item in a through h with the corresponding description in 1 through 8.

a. Multiprogramming	e. Remote job entry
b. Distributed data processing	f. Management information system
c. Backup	g. Data communication
d. Timesharing	h. Database system

1. Involves users sharing a computer on a time-scheduled basis.
2. Necessary to ensure that files will not be lost.
3. Uses multiple computers to share the work load

4. Involves submission of jobs over telephone lines for batch processing on a central computer.
5. Means sharing a computer on a priority basis.
6. Involves the integration of files into a single comprehensive file system.
7. The transmission of computer information over the telephone network.
8. Requires a comprehensive database management system.

4.24 **True–False**   Determine whether each of the following is true or false.

1. In a multiprogramming environment the program with the heaviest computation load would be assigned to the highest priority partition to ensure that the processing gets done.
2. Multiprogramming involves high-speed processing by a computer of many programs, one after the other.
3. In a timesharing system users can communicate directly with the computer via terminals, but in multiprogramming systems they cannot.
4. Where a programmer would think in terms of a "job" in a multiprogramming environment, s/he would think in terms of a "terminal session" in a timesharing environment.
5. In a timesharing environment only one program can be active at a time.
6. Rapid response time is very important in the design of a multiprogramming system.
7. Data communication involves transmission without change of computer data over a communications system.
8. The primary purpose of modems is to improve the transmission of data over the telephone system.
9. In an indexed file data records may be stored in random order but the index is in sorted sequence.
10. Although it is possible to use two or more indexes for a file, it generally is not very practical.
11. Sequential files are poorly suited to random processing.
12. It would not be practical to use a database system on a magnetic-tape computer system.
13. One drawback of database systems is that data stored in various files is not easily accessed.
14. One important feature of a database management system is that the data characteristics (such as format) are included within the database.
15. A good DBMS could probably be considered an essential cornerstone of a management information system (MIS).
16. It is imperative to back up online systems on a daily basis.
17. Special identification codes are commonly used to prevent unauthorized access to online disk files.
18. As a general rule the wider the access to computerized files, the more difficult it is to protect the files.
19. The powerful capabilities of the computer for checking all transactions of a company has made embezzlement a thing of the past.
20. An online system with remote access can be made completely secure with a good set of identification codes and passwords.
21. It is unlikely that a national databank will ever be set up in the United States because of the personal privacy issue.

5

System Design
and Development

OBJECTIVES

In previous sections we have studied many aspects of data processing including various types of hardware, the concept of system software, programming languages, and computer applications. We will now turn our attention to integrating many of these concepts while gaining an insight into the management and use of a computer system via another case study. The important concepts which you will learn in this chapter include the following.

- The importance to a company of carefully planned system design and development
- The characteristics of a system "life cycle"
- The importance and value of the feasibility study
- The importance and value of the detailed study and analysis
- Preparation of a time schedule for a system installation
- The computer selection procedure including use of a bid specification
- Methods of financing: rental, lease, third-party lease, and purchase
- Typical staffing needs for a data processing department
- Program preparation and testing
- Installation of the computer

Key terminology which is important in this chapter includes the following.

acquisition schedule	detailed study phase
bid specification	development phase
computer financing	feasibility study
lease	installation phase
purchase	system analysis
rental	system life cycle
third-party lease	

The Life Cycle of a System

INTRODUCTION Every business whether engaged in service, sales, manufacturing, or whatever must process data in order to exist. Even a small, informal operation such as a student performing minor repairs to automobiles in order to stay in college involves a certain amount of data to be processed. For instance, the student must maintain a record of hours worked and parts purchased in order to properly charge the owner of a repaired automobile. Obviously, the processing needs of a large repair garage are much greater, involving many of the data processing systems described in earlier chapters. As most businesses grow, their data processing needs grow. For a very small company, manual record-keeping methods are normally quite adequate. However, a larger company will require the use of automated methods. We studied these concepts in the first section describing the evolution of the PQR grocery business.

The process of planned expansion and/or redesign of data processing systems to match the growth of a company is important to the success of the company. Unfortunately, all too often, the company focus is elsewhere. For instance, a manufacturing company directs its attention to the manufacture of its goods; a sales-oriented company directs its primary attention to sales and marketing; and so on. As a result, data processing systems often develop piecemeal and without overall coordination. Most successful companies consider their data processing systems a vital component of the organization and handle them accordingly.

Within the past several years, low-cost computers and applications software have become available. Although these hardware and software components represent a tremendous boon to the small businessperson, they still require considerable system study and planning to be implemented. Stages of the "life cycle" of a system are illustrated in Figure 5-1. Let us consider each of these in more detail.

FEASIBILITY STUDY The feasibility study is intended to define problems, not to determine solutions. The overall data needs of the business must be identified. Then existing systems are examined to determine whether or not they are satsifying these needs in an economical way. If not, preliminary examinations are made to determine how the system should be modified to achieve its goals. The end result of a feasibility study might be any of the following:

Figure 5-1 A simplified life cycle of a data system.

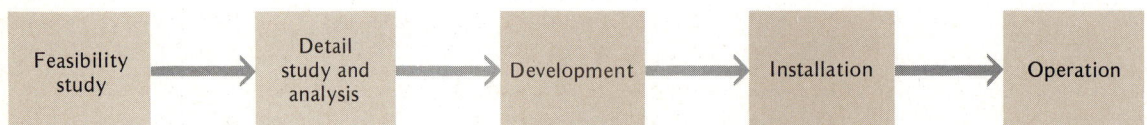

1. The existing system is adequate to meet company needs.
2. The existing system is adequate but needs some minor changes in order to do the job properly.
3. The existing system is adequate but it is not being implemented as it was designed and employees are not attempting to make full use of it.
4. The existing system is inadequate to do the job and requires major restructuring.

The final report of the feasibility study will include recommendations regarding steps to be taken.

DETAILED STUDY AND ANALYSIS During the detailed study stage, each of the problems identified by the feasibility study will be analyzed. Final decisions will be made regarding overall handling of data within the company, computer hardware and software requirements, and personnel needs. Bid specifications for all equipment and software to be obtained from outside vendors will be prepared. During this segment of the system life cycle a detailed timetable will be prepared covering all aspects of the conversion process. Input from all departments of the business will be crucial to a successful detailed study and analysis phase.

DEVELOPMENT Once final decisions are made, the plan must be carried out. Unfortunately for the data processing department, it is usually not possible to suspend all ongoing operations until the new system is completed and operating. Often software is prepared and tested by renting computer time on another computer. In this manner, programming and testing can proceed without seriously impairing the ongoing data processing needs of the company. It is frequently possible to build basic components of the company data base and basic processing programs on a computer belonging to the manufacturer or some other agency.

INSTALLATION At some point the new computer hardware and software must be installed. This is sometimes done by running the old and new computer systems in parallel and gradually shifting applications, one-by-one, from the old to the new system. The installation can be considered complete only when major software systems are operating and the old computer has been removed.

OPERATION Once the system is installed and certified, it becomes operational and thus becomes a working component of the company. This is not to imply that the system is complete, never again requiring modification. We must remember that Figure 5-1 is a *simplified* representation of a system life cycle. Indeed, development and installation are ongoing processes which continue for the remainder of the system's useful life.

All of these concepts regarding a system life cycle usually appear to be somewhat abstract to the beginner. Furthermore, the "textbook" system study and installation rarely occur. To gain a broader understanding of each of these phases and of the problems which commonly occur, let us consider a case study.

Case Study Definition

INTRODUCTION TO THE XYZ CONTRACTING COMPANY Located in a large metropolitan area, the firm of Xiezopolski, Yamagiwa, Zboyovsky, and Associates (commonly termed XYZ for obvious reasons) is a building contracting company capable of contracting for anything ranging from an individual home to condominiums to an office building. The firm employs approximately 250 people in the main office and a branch office. The staff includes a small engineering section, the clerical and accounting department, and a large field section. The company had its founding in 1960 by Mr. Yamagiwa, who began as a small-home remodeling contractor. Although much of the company's phenomenal growth was carefully planned and directed, the computer and data processing needs were somewhat neglected along the way.

By 1977, the following major application areas involved the use of services and computer time from firms specializing in such applications.

1. Payroll
2. Accounts payable
3. Accounts receivable
4. General ledger
5. Project progress analysis
6. Engineering analysis

A number of business factors during the 1970s forced the management of XYZ to reassess their computer needs. A very brief investigation revealed glaring inefficiencies in the existing uncoordinated system.

BUSINESS ACCOUNTING FUNCTIONS During the early years of XYZ, most of the ordinary business bookkeeping operations were performed manually or with the aid of a basic accounting machine. However, by the time the company reached the size of 100 employees, the existing semiautomated payroll system became overburdened. After considerable investigation, the business manager recommended that XYZ contract with Business Accounts Service Bureau to take over accounts payable and accounts receivable as well as payroll. Business Accounts was a local independent company (possessing a medium-size computer) with "a computer and associated services for hire." Although Business Accounts was quite willing to prepare a computerized system tailored specifically to the needs of XYZ, the management of XYZ felt that it would be far more economical to use the standard payroll and accounts payable and receivable services already available. This required some minor modifications to the information network of XYZ so that the raw data to be processed was in a form compatible with the Business Accounts standards. Once the system was implemented, a courier service would deliver a record of the XYZ daily activities to Business Accounts at the end of each day. At prescheduled times throughout the month, appropriate processing runs were made and the results returned to XYZ. For instance, hourly rate construction workers were paid weekly, clerical employees were paid twice per month, and salaried employees were paid once per month. Checks for each category of employee were run by Business Accounts and delivered as scheduled. For an agreed-upon monthly fee, the complete service was provided to XYZ. This solution to these data processing needs was an ideal one for XYZ for a number of reasons, the two foremost being:

1. The volume of processing was too great to be handled by the semiauto-mated methods used previously, but not enough to justify acquisi-tion of a computer.
2. The XYZ management was relatively nonknowledgeable about compu-ters and was fearful of "ending up in the computer business" when their expertise was in the contracting business.

However, XYZ found it necessary to establish a data clerk position to coordin-ate activities between XYZ and Business Accounts. The overall process is illustrated in Figure 5-2. This system served the needs of XYZ adequately and, in fact, management was quite pleased with the simplicity of the operation. On the other hand, the complaint was sometimes voiced that this method of servicing data processing needs forced XYZ to conform to the Business Accounts methods and was not really tailored specifically to the needs of XYZ. After less than two years of operation, XYZ hired an experienced programmer as a general data processing coordinator to serve as an advisor in such areas as system design and activity coordination and to perform a limited amount of programming.

PROJECT PROGRESS ANALYSIS As the construction business became more competitive and building costs spiraled upward, the management of XYZ became increasingly aware of the need for continually monitoring the progress of each project. It finally got to the point where the manually maintained progress charts and reports simply could not supply sufficient and timely reports required by the firm. To satisfy this need, XYZ contracted with a small service bureau which specialized in this particular field. The task of tailoring the available services to the needs of XYZ and coordinating the overall process was assigned to the newly hired data processing coordinator.

ENGINEERING ANALYSIS As the complexity and size of construction jobs performed by XYZ increased, the engineering staff encountered a continually expanding need for comput-ing services. Although most of the extensive engineering work requiring

Figure 5-2   Using a service bureau.

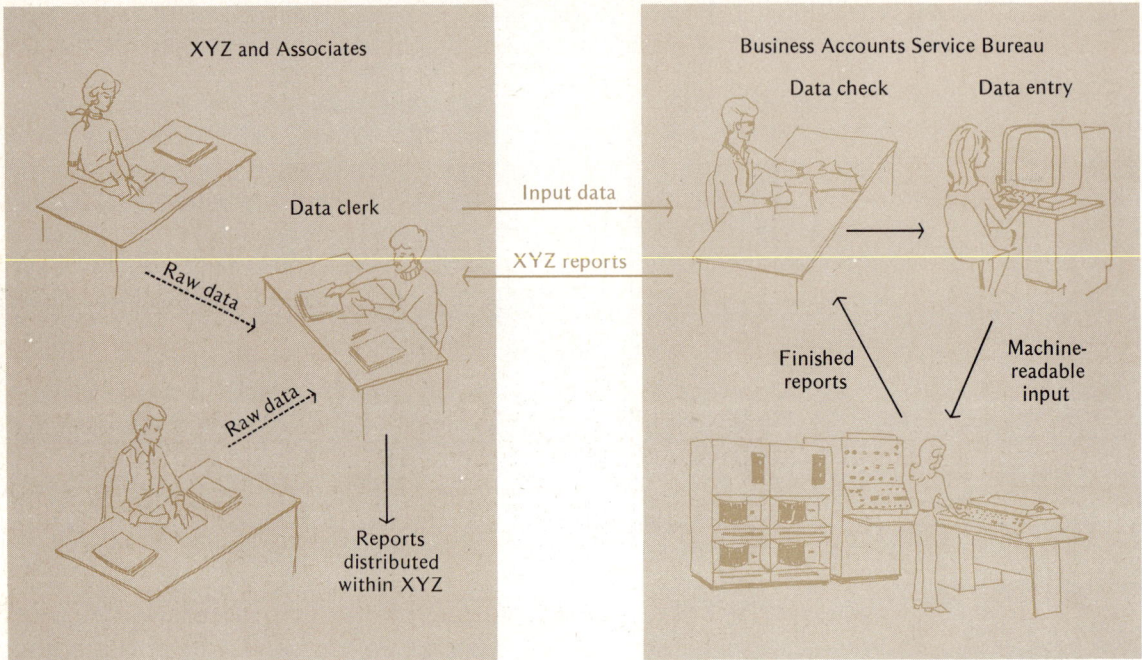

computer analysis was farmed out to another firm, XYZ entered into a contract with a timesharing service via a CRT terminal located in the main office of XYZ.

THE EXISTING SYSTEM By 1975, therefore, the computing and data processing needs of XYZ were handled as follows:

1. Business data processing (payroll, accounts payable, and accounts receivable): performed by Business Accounts Service Bureau.
2. Project progress analysis: performed by a second service bureau.
3. Engineering analysis: the bulk of computer analysis performed by an engineering firm; some analysis performed locally by terminal and computer time purchased from a timesharing service.

Staffing within XYZ to handle these needs consisted of the data processing coordinator and the data clerk. Their places in the firm are illustrated by the organizational chart of Figure 5-3. The manner in which the data processing services evolved (without overall planning) saw the data processing coordinator reporting to the business manager.

As time progressed and the demand for computer services increased, a number of problems became apparent.

- Whenever work loads increased, business data processing needs were given first priority, thus creating friction with other departments.

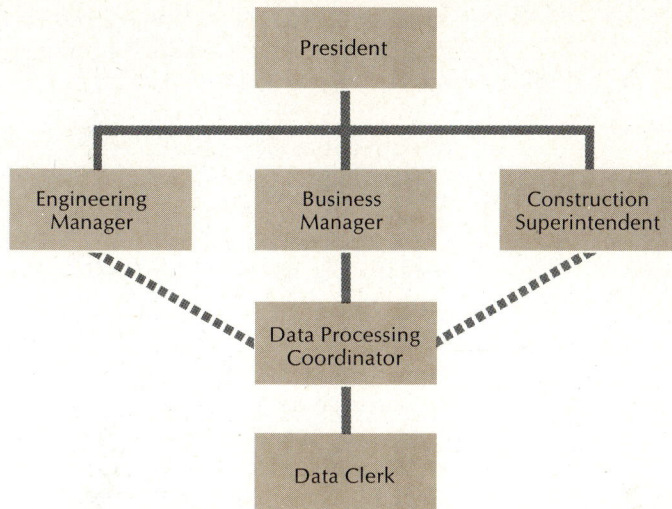

**Figure 5-3
Organizational chart
for XYZ.**

- The activities were fragmented; XYZ was obtaining computer services from four separate companies.
- The timeliness of many reports began to lag.
- Management desired a more extensive and timely project progress analysis.
- The engineering staff felt that more in-house analysis should be done using interactive terminals.
- And so on.

EXERCISE

5-1   In your opinion, what should be the principal factor in deciding whether to use a service bureau or to install a computer to satisfy data processing needs of a company?

A Long-Range Feasibility Study

PRELIMINARY STUDY   Before proceeding further, the president of XYZ decided to hire a data processing consultant to assist in a study and to provide computer expertise which the firm sorely lacked. The first action of the consultant was to recommend that a study team be set up, consisting of the following individuals in addition to himself.

1. Business manager
2. Engineering manager
3. Construction superintendent
4. Data processing coordinator

The consultant emphasized the importance of a preliminary study which was supported at the highest levels of the company. The purpose of this study was severalfold:

1. To summarize all of the current computer-related activities.
2. To determine what data processing improvements are actually needed.
3. To determine if projected improvements appeared to be practical and economically justifiable.
4. To make a preliminary recommendation about further action to be taken.

A 45-day period of time was allocated for each team member to scrutinize his/her area of responsibility and, with the assistance of subordinates, draw up a "wish list" of potential computer applications. These summaries were then brought together and presented at a work session of the study team. Each application was discussed, argued, and subjected to the following questons:

*   Is the information required to generate the desired reports available or could it be made available?
*   Will the output really be used or will it merely receive lip service?
*   Does the desired report or function appear to be economical?
*   Does the desired report or function appear to be practical; will it fit into the system?

The preliminary study findings presented to the president indicated that the computer services currently being provided by service bureaus together with several new applications of primary importance should justify the acquisiton of a computer system. Some of the points the consultant emphasized were:

1. The need for increased data handling capacity and handling speed was imperative.
2. Acquisition of a computer would not reduce computer and data processing costs but would increase them. However, over the long term, the cost increase would be more than offset by increased productivity in a number of areas.
3. A detailed study should be performed to set a realistic time schedule and determine the type of equipment which would best suit the needs of XYZ. The notion of getting "super equipment," merely because everyone else was, must be avoided at all costs.
4. A crash program would lead to nothing but trouble; a carefully planned, realistic schedule must be determined. The overall project, consisting of preliminary planning through final acquisition of the computer and transferring existing applications to that system would require at least 18 months.

EXERCISE

5-2 In your opinion, what are the principal advantages and disadvantages of a committee such as that formed for the data processing study?

DETAILED STUDY AND ANALYSIS

Following approval of the president, the study team was commissioned to perform a more detailed study to include firm recommendations and a time schedule. This detailed study was considered in two phases: phase 1 was a detailed analysis of the information needs of XYZ, and phase 2 was a determination of the hardware, software, and personnel required. The first step of phase 1 involved identifying and documenting the basic objectives of the study. At first consideration, this might appear to be trivial, since the objective is obviously to study the company's computer and data processing needs. However, consider that a detailed study may take anywhere from a few weeks to several months, that it will involve a substantial amount of valuable time of the company's employees, and, finally, that the action taken will significantly affect the company for years to come. Then it becomes imperative that study objectives and a time scale be carefully determined. Basic objectives include items such as the following.

- Document all aspects of each current computer and data processing application.
- Cost analyze the current operation.
- Project computer and data processing needs for the next three to five years.
- Perform cost analysis on future needs.
- Summarize all benefits of a new system. From a dollar-and-cents point of view, some of these will be tangible. For instance, reducing the cost of providing timesharing services to the engineering department can easily be measured. Other benefits, such as improving customer service, may be very intangible.
- Prepare a preliminary specification for acquisition of a computer.
- Analyze personnel and software needs.

In the case of XYZ, three months were scheduled for this phase of the study. In performing it, each department manager delegated to his/her key personnel specific studies to be carried out. Weekly department meetings were scheduled to hash and rehash all phases of the initial findings. (The purchasing agent suggested that special "combat pay" should be provided for these Friday morning sessions.) The president of XYZ had emphasized that no domains should be considered sacred and that everyone should attempt to be completely objective in viewing what would best serve the company.

At the end of the three-month period, phase 1 of the study was completed. These findings strongly suggested the following.

1. That acquisition of a small computer with online capabilities was not only feasible but was economically advisable.

2. That the following business data processing applications be ready when the computer is acquired:
   a. The batch processing payroll system, with only minor modifications to its existing form.
   b. A completely new online general ledger, accounts payable and accounts receivable system.
3. That a comprehensive project scheduling system be prepared for implementation upon computer acquisition. This substantial project was to be a joint operation with three other construction companies.
4. That existing engineering applications be converted for the new computer.
5. That phase 2 of the detailed study and analysis begin immediately, with ultimate acquisiton of the computer scheduled for 18 months.

EXERCISE

5-3   What factors must be considered in determining whether or not a particular application is suitable for computerizing?

Planning for a New Installation

ACQUISITION TIME SCHEDULE   In preparing a time schedule, the consultant had emphasized the importance of allowing sufficient time for each step. He pointed out that the majority of new installations do not meet their timetables because of unrealistic assessments of how long given tasks will take. It is imperative to recognize that day-to-day business activities must continue concurrently with the planning, preparation, and installation of the new system. With this in mind, the study team adopted the acquisition schedule shown in Figure 5-4. Each of the five general activities shown in 5-4 was further broken down into a more detailed schedule. To ensure that the schedule was met and to alert the management to any schedule slippage, monthly progress reports were required by each department manager.

To the neophyte, this schedule might appear to provide more than adequate time. However, the experienced professional in data processing will recognize that, in general, a complete system conversion will normally require from 12 to 30 months, depending upon the size and complexity of the installation.

SELECTION OF A COMPUTER SYSTEM   In general, there are two ways of selecting a computer system. The first is described in the accompanying article from *Small Systems World;* the second is the method used by XYZ which is described in the paragraphs which follow. (This article should not be interpreted to imply that IBM equipment does not match equipment from other manufacturers. The fact is that IBM computers are of the highest quality and are backed by a large corporation—IBM—which has an excellent reputation for reliability and good service.)

Figure 5-4 Overall acquisition time schedule

	Mar	Apr	May	June	July	Aug	Sept	Oct	Nov	Dec	Jan	Feb	Mar	Apr	May	June	July	Aug
Preparations of specifications and selection of a vendor	▓	▓	▓	▓	▓	▓	▓											
Systems definition and analysis						▓	▓	▓	▓	▓	▓	▓	▓	▓				
Personnel training									▓	▓								
Programming and program modification											▓	▓	▓	▓	▓	▓	▓	
Installation and testing																		▓

A Political DP Decision

"By far, the biggest decision factor in the implementation of any data processing system today is political."

I used to think this statement would be very controversial, but it turns out most people agree, once they know the whole story. Very rarely are the technical considerations of a system given much weight in the final decision as to which system to implement. I hear it in almost every class: "A lot of what I am here for is just an exercise. My boss has his mind made up that we're going with vendor X and I just need some backup information to justify the decision."

This is also the environment where many of the decision makers today are accustomed to the very large mainframe presentations and are very much mainframe oriented. So when the system designers come to them with configurations that involve multiple minicomputers, the decision makers, not understanding all of the capabilities of today's minis, are reluctant to go that route and therefore go the sure way of sticking with the big mainframe.

This is especially true of selecting IBM because in almost all environments, "you can't be wrong if you pick IBM." Even though the system may not work as well as you originally thought, or is inefficient, or definitely the most expensive, it is still the feeling in many corporate environments that because it is IBM it is okay.

That is not to say that going with IBM is wrong. For many users it is the best and only choice. Those are the users who are not in a position to develop their own software or to support an operational system once implemented.

One only has to look at the help-wanted ads in any of the newspapers or industry tabloids to see the same areas of expertise requested by everybody—namely, communications programmers, data base programmers and network analysts. Since IBM has provided for accommodating most of these potential problems already, the extra costs and, in many cases, the inefficiency of their software is still a bargain because the resources may not be available to the user to do it otherwise.

Next month we'll put some of these comments into a wider perspective and give them some more practical consideration.   **—Ken Sherman**

Copyright by *Small Systems World*, Chicago, Ill.

The first step in selecting a computer was to prepare a *bid specification* for prospective vendors. The bid spec included both broad and detailed data processing needs, such as the following.

Hardware

- The CPU shall include 6 timesharing terminal ports with capability for expansion to 16.
- Removable disk storage capability with an online capacity of at least 100 million 8-bit bytes.
- One-line printer with the following minimum capabilities:

  1. 600 lines/minutes alphanumeric printing speed.
  2. 132-print-position line.
  3. 64-character printing unit.

Software

- Programming languages: The vendor may make recommendations regarding programming languages. However, minimum requirements are:

  1. For business data processing: Cobol or RPG II.
  2. For online programming: Basic, or interactive Fortran.

- Languages must conform to ANSI standards or, where appropriate, to detailed definitions in Section VI of this specification.
- The operating system shall have the capability for simultaneously serving as:

1. A timesharing system supporting interactive computing from terminals.
2. A Batch processing system accepting programs from any input device for a queued batch processing operation.

- The disk storage file structure shall be standardized so that files created through one language can be processed by programs in any of the other languages without format conversion.

Other Requirements

- The vendor must provide six person-weeks of education and training on the proposed system for XYZ employees.
- The vendor must make available to XYZ test time on a computer similar to the one proposed. This is to allow for program preparation and testing prior to delivery of the computer.

Also included as part of the bid specification was the schedule shown in Figure 5-5.

Upon completion of the specification, it was made available to computer manufacturers on June 1, 1981. During the two months which followed, conferences were arranged with various vendors to clarify points of the specification and to provide insight into the needs of XYZ and Associates. Upon receipt of all proposals, the XYZ management evaluated them in light of

Figure 5-5
Computer acquisition schedule

Activity	Start	Finish	XYZ	Vendor
			Action by	
Issue bid specification to vendors	6/01/81		x	
Vendor confers with XYZ officials as required	6/15/81	8/01/81	x	x
Proposals due from vendors	8/01/81			x
Evaluation of proposals	8/01/81	9/01/81	x	
Announce top three bidders	9/01/81		x	
Run benchmark tests	9/01/81	9/15/81	x	x
Final evaluation	9/15/81	10/01/81	x	
Award contract	10/01/81		x	
Personnel training	11/01/81	2/01/82	x	x
Prepare and test software on vendor's computer	1/01/82	8/15/82	x	x
Installation and testing	7/26/82	9/01/82	x	x
Acceptance of equipment	9/01/82		x	

Figure 5-6   Steps in the selection of a system.

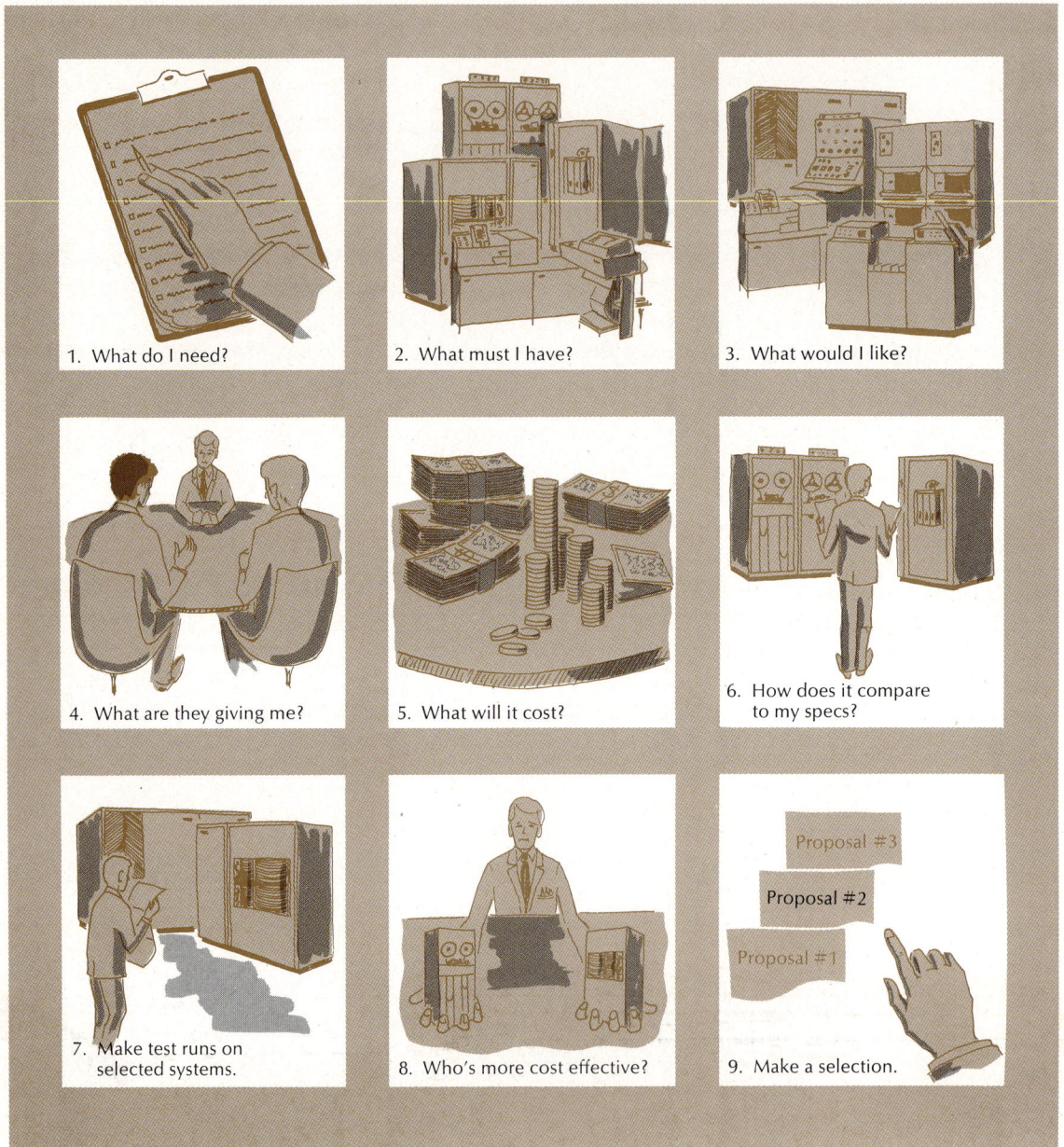

1. What do I need?

2. What must I have?

3. What would I like?

4. What are they giving me?

5. What will it cost?

6. How does it compare to my specs?

7. Make test runs on selected systems.

8. Who's more cost effective?

9. Make a selection.

Proposal #3

Proposal #2

Proposal #1

the XYZ needs and requirements. The three most qualified were invited to run special benchmark programs which had been included in the bid specification. These programs, prepared by the consultant, were designed to represent the typical workload which might be anticipated on the XYZ machine.

Results of these benchmark runs were to be used in the final evaluation process to determine the proposal which best fit the needs. The overall selection process is illustrated in Figure 5-6.

EXERCISE

5-4   The manager of a business approached a computer manufacturer and said, "Our present second-generation computer system is overloaded; we would like to install a third-generation computer in four months." Comment on this statement.

FINANCING COMPUTER EQUIPMENT   During the analysis and selection period, one of the many important factors facing the study team related to how the equipment should be financed. Numerous methods are commonly available. Three of them are: a rental arrangement with the computer manufacturer, a long-term lease with the manufacturer or a third-party leasing company, and outright purchase.

Rental.   Over the years, IBM has stressed the advantages of renting a computer—from IBM, of course. (During the early days of the industry, IBM machines were not for sale, only for rent.) Even today the majority of IBM machines, as well as those of many other large computer manufacturers, are rented. For a fixed monthly rate, the manufacturer provides the computer, required maintenance of the machine, certain basic software, and a limited amount of staff education and training.* The principal advantages of renting include the features that the user can avoid obsolescence, since the rental agreement can be cancelled (usually on a 60–90 day notice), the responsibility for all maintenance rests with the manufacturer, and a large capital outlay is not required. On the other hand, over a period of several years renting becomes more expensive.

Leasing.   A large variety of leasing agreements can be made with so-called *third-party* leasing companies or with the manufacturer. Typically, a leasing company will arrange to purchase the computer desired by a user, then lease it to the user for an extended period of time, usually ranging between three and five years. A disadvantage of this type of agreement is that it tends to lock a user into a given system for a set period of time, although this is usually not a problem with careful planning. The primary advantage is cost savings, which can be significant over a long period of time. Many installations find it to their advantage to lease from a third-party leasing company. Far too often, the decision is made to stay with a manufacturer rental arrangement because of the "parent company security blanket" psychology.

---

*Prior to 1970, the cost of extensive system support and all software was included, or "bundled," into a single price. The effect of this was to retard the growth of independent service and software firms. With pressure from the Justice Department and pending antitrust lawsuits from other companies, IBM "unbundled." The prices for IBM and most other equipment, software, and services are now separated.

Purchase.   Although computer rental is the most common procedure, more and more companies are purchasing computers. A number of reasons account for this fact. First, computers now being manufactured are far more reliable and have a significantly longer useful life than those of ten years ago. Second, the cost of a computer with a given computational power has declined rapidly with the evolution of the modern computer. And third, a large number of small companies have emerged in the minicomputer field, making available small but powerful computers. In many cases, their capital base is insufficient to support large-scale rentals, so their machines are available only through purchase. The principal advantage of purchase relates to the cost savings over a long period of time. Figure 5-7 illustrates typical costs for these three methods for a computer with a purchase price of $200,000. The ongoing cost associated with purchase reflects maintenance charges which will typically be $10,000–$15,000 per year for a $200,000 computer. Not illustrated by the graph is that the user owns the computer in the purchase arrangement. With modern computing equipment this can be an important economic factor.

The primary advantages and disadvantages of these three basic methods for financing are summarized in Figure 5-8. In addition to the methods described, there are numerous other variations. One of them is the lease-purchase arrangement which combines the advantages of leasing and purchasing. An average consumer would think of it as merely a time-payment purchase (similar to what most of us do when purchasing an automobile). However, the ownership of the computer and the debt obligation remain with the leasing company until the end of the lease period. Then ownership transfers to the user—sometimes with a relatively small buy-out fee. The advantage to the computer user is that it does not affect the "borrowing power" of the company.

EXERCISE

5.5   Describe the commonly used methods for financing computers.

Figure 5-7 Comparative computer costs for rental, lease, and purchase.

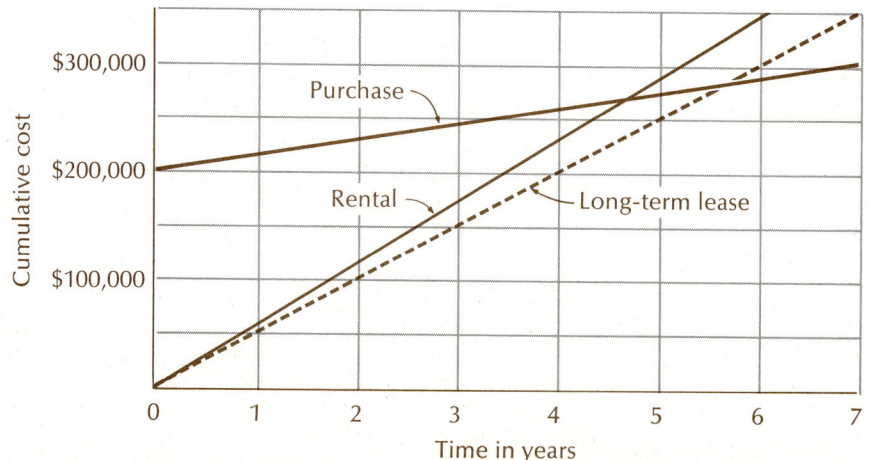

Advantages	Disadvantages
Rental	
1. Danger of obsolescence reduced	1. Most expensive in long run
2. No large capital outlay required	2. Rental costs may increase periodically
3. All responsibility rests with the manufacturer (a single contact)	
Lease	
1. Significant cost savings over rental	1. User is committed for a long time period which reduces flexibility
2. No large capital outlay required	
3. Lease costs remain fixed over life of contract	
Purchase	
1. For the long range, generally the least expensive method	1. Large capital outlay required
2. Tax advantages can be accrued by the owner	2. Less flexibility to meet changing needs
	3. Danger of obsolescence

**Figure 5-8
Comparison of
computer acquisition
methods.**

**STAFFING
THE DATA
PROCESSING
DEPARTMENT**

One of the most common pitfalls encountered by many businesses when installing or expanding a computer center is to underestimate the staff required. Computers do not perform all of the wonders we have studied without the aid of people. (We have already learned that programming can be a slow and painstaking task.) Typically, between one-half and two-thirds of the total cost of operating a computer center will be for staffing (salaries), with the remainder being the cost of the computer. In fact, the preliminary study finding of XYZ and Associates cautioned that computer costs would increase with the acquisition of a computer system. This predicted increase was due in part to increased staffing requirements.

The staffing recommendation of the XYZ study team included the following five positions.

1. *Data processing supervisor.* Shall be responsible for supervision of the computer center. Will coordinate and schedule computer activities and job assignments for the programming staff. In view of the relatively small size of the department, will perform system studies for all new applications.

2. *Programmer, business.* Shall report to the supervisor and be responsible for all business data processing programming required. Shall function as a liaison to software companies performing contract programming for XYZ.
3. *Programmer, general.* Shall report to the supervisor and be responsible for all programming not of a business data processing nature. Shall provide assistance to engineering department as well as act as a liaison to software companies performing contract programming for XYZ.
4. *Computer operator.* Shall be responsible for operation of the computer system, including loading of programs, monitoring results, dispatching reports to appropriate departments, and maintaining system libraries.
5. *Data entry clerk.* Shall enter source data and programs into the system via key-driven data entry devices.

The existing computer and data processing operation at XYZ included a programmer-coordinator assisted by a data clerk. As noted earlier in this section, the programmer-coordinator reported to the business manager (Figure 5-3), which created somewhat of a problem within XYZ. That is, the business manager had his own area of responsibility and was not always completely objective about the relative importance of various computing needs within the entire company. In fact, the engineering manager felt that the business manager "didn't give a damn" about anything but the accounting functions. The point was argued that the computer and data processing operation services all areas of the company and should not be under control of one of the users of those services.

Recognizing this as an extremely important point, the consultant pointed out to the president that companies with the more successful computer installations were marked by the following qualities:

1. An aggressive and alert management totally committed to the use of data processing.
2. The computer manager reporting directly to the chief executive of the business.
3. Clearly defined lines of authority and resonsibility relating to all aspects of the computer operation.
4. Constant coordination and communication between the data processing center and the users.

In fact, in perusing a management magazine, the president took special note of a survey of computer installations (Figure 5-9) which illustrated the importance of having the computer manager reporting directly to the chief executive.

Another sobering fact was that only 34 percent of the companies surveyed termed their data processing operation successful, that is, as actually

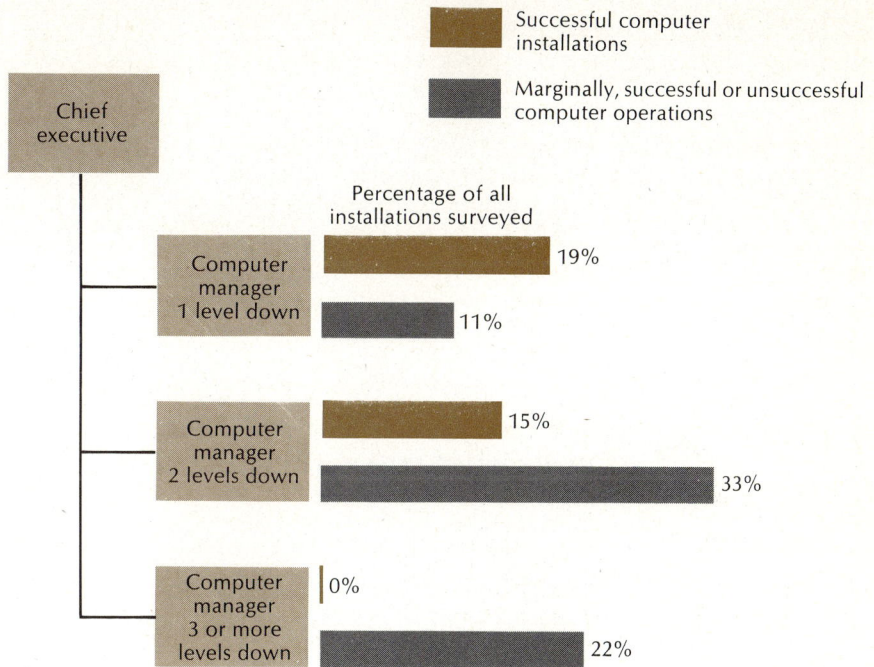

Figure 5-9
Organization level of
the computer manager.

justifying its cost (many experts term this figure closer to 15–20 percent). Determined to have the most effective and efficient operation possible, the president placed the data processing department directly under his office as illustrated by the organizational chart of Figure 5-10.

EXERCISES

5.6 Assume that you are the manager of a business which is in serious need of upgrading its data processing operation. Your data processing manager approaches you with the proposal: "We can upgrade our operation by replacing our existing Model X computer costing $60,000/year with a new Model Z computer costing $80,000/year. The increased cost for upgrading our system would only be $29,000/year." What would your reaction be?

5.7 The president established the data processing supervisor position as reporting directly to him rather than to a subordinate office. Discuss this action relative to the previous XYZ system.

Figure 5-10
Organization structure
of XYZ and
Associates.

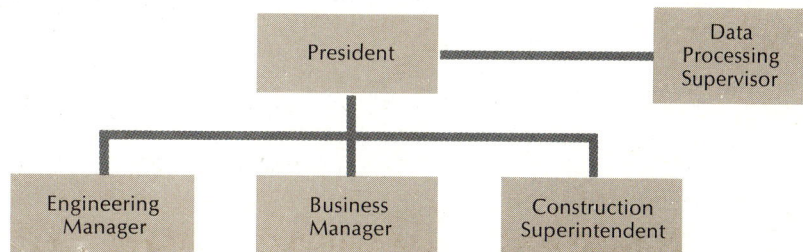

The Conversion Process

SYSTEMS DEFINITION AND ANALYSIS

At this point, we have seen the word *system* used in a number of ways: a computer system (hardware), an operating system (software), and a data processing system (procedures). In planning for the new computer, the XYZ management was very much aware of the importance of thoroughly analyzing all aspects of their systems and procedures. The overall processing systems had, to a large extent, simply evolved with the growth of the company; very little long-range planning had ever taken place in any of the accounting areas. For instance, when the need for an improved payroll system arose, a brief evaluation was made, resulting in the use of a service bureau. Little attention was given to how the payroll system was to interface with other accounting systems in the company; also, modifications to the XYZ clerical procedures were kept to a minimum in order to simplify the conversion. Generally speaking, most organizations see the growth of their data processing systems lagging behind the corresponding growth of the organization. Reorganization of an existing data processing system rarely occurs until serious problems come to the attention of management.

Unfortunately, a common solution is to "beef up" the existing system (which itself may be inadequate) with more hardware and/or personnel. The management of XYZ and their consultant recognized the importance of starting from scratch. The setting up of a new system meant far more than writing a series of programs and getting a new computer. The systems analysis must go back to the basic processing functions performed, including: (a) what accounting methods are used, (b) what types of files are maintained, and (c) what type of reports are generated. Internal procedures designed for a manual record-keeping system or a semiautomated one will probably be poorly suited to an automated one. The goal of the study team must be to evaluate all aspects of the company, beginning with management goals and methods of accomplishment. The end result must be a detailed plan for implementing the changes and modifications necessary to fill the needs of the organization. In the case of a total system, the implications can be quite significant from a number of points of view, including cost and disruption of ongoing activities. Normally, the plan involves a building block approach in which the basis for the system is laid and components are implemented piece by piece over a period of time.

This was the avenue taken by XYZ: to adjust their basic accounting and clerical methods toward a database management system. Then the first systems to be brought online were to be payroll, accounts payable, and accounts receivable. Once the computer was installed and these applications were up, work on a series of other applications (beginning with an online inventory control system) was to commence. Thus, transition to a modern computerized information system could proceed with a minimum interruption of ongoing activities.

STAFFING TRAINING AND ORIENTATION People, like objects, seem to suffer from the physical phenomenon called *inertia*. With people, changes tend to bring on stress, especially when the changes might be interpreted as threatening job security. For instance, the accounting clerk might find that many of the tasks required of his/her position will be done by the new computer—alas, no more job. However, on closer consideration, the clerk, rather than being replaced by a machine, will find that much of the dull, boring work is to be eliminated and replaced with more challenging tasks using the clerk's accounting expertise. It is vitally necessary to orient each employee to his or her place in the new system and how it will influence the job requirements. For some employees who have a minimum interface with data processing, a brief orientation session will be adequate. For others whose jobs will be substantially changed or even eliminated, a considerable amount of company-sponsored training and/or retraining might be required.

To insure that the new data processing operation is recognized as a tool to provide better services and not as a device to put people out of work, the DP supervisor implemented a series of "training and exposure" classes for XYZ employees. Two sections of three two-hour training sessions were held describing the overall operation of the system, the roles played, and the services provided for each of the various departments. These sessions were eagerly attended by most of the staff, many of whom devoted several evenings to further study. In general, the overall program dispelled many false notions and dissolved a number of negative attitudes (although several employees remained highly suspicious). At the completion of the orientation, *most* members of the clerical staff were looking forward to installation of the new system with very positive attitudes regarding "being involved."

Staff training at XYZ was not limited to the non-DP employees of the company. With the exception of the computer operator (hired four months before installation of the computer), none of the programming staff had experience on the computer selected by XYZ. As do most computer manufacturers, the one selected by XYZ provided training classes at their educational facility. The following staff members were scheduled for classes at the manufacturer's site as follows:

1. Data processing supervisor
   a. Introduction to the operating system (1 week)
   b. File design and structure (1 week)
2. Programmer, Business
   a. Introduction to the operating system (1 week)
   b. File design and structure (1 week)
   c. Database considerations (3 days)
3. Programmer, General
   a. Introduction to the operating system (1 week)
   b. File design and structure (1 week)
   c. Interactive programming (1 week)

LEARNING TO COPE WITH DEFEAT IS HARDEST DP SKILL
by Miles Benson

One skill they don't teach in computing courses is how to cope with failure.

Once failure has been officially proclaimed, there's still a world out there to be dealt with . . . the people who are concerned about going down with the ship, the people who paid for the ship in the first place and the people who are still waiting for the ship to come in.

Some folks just seem to know intuitively how to do a job right. Some of the people in this story were that kind of people. When this project had fallen on its face, these people picked themselves up, dusted themselves off and began thinking about the uncomfortable tasks still ahead: getting a corporate decision on how to admit to the failure which had occurred, and carrying out that corporate decision.

To these people, there was only one way to do this particular job right.

But picture the strategy sessions leading up to that corporate decision.

Imagine the factions at work, each with its own way of decommitting the failed project.

"Let's convince them we cancelled out in their best interest," says one.

"Let's make it all seem like it wasn't important in the first place," says another.

"Let's just hit them with a snowstorm so dense they'll never realize until later what really happened," says still another.

"Why not tell the truth?" comes a voice from the back. "Why not just admit that we screwed up, that we tried to do something we didn't really know how to do and that we learned that we still don't know how?"

A gasp goes through the assembled crowd. Use honesty as a tactic? Lie down and let the users walk all over us? Our competitors will laugh us out of the marketplace. We may be sued. Can't we at least *try* to make it look like we knew what we were doing? . . .

During the scheduled classes, each employee was relieved of all job responsibilities in order to concentrate on the coursework. By spreading this training over three months, ongoing needs of the company could continue to be handled.

EXERCISE

5.8 The importance of programmer education and training when a new system is to be installed is obvious. However, why bother with classes for clerical staff who will not be directly involved in the data processing operation?

PROGRAM PREPARATION Contrary to the arguments often proposed by representatives of computer manufacturers, the experienced data processing professional will usually insist that "there is no such thing as an easy conversion." Generally speaking, this tends to be true, although the task can be considerably simplified by careful planning. In an ideal situation, all programs would be written, tested, and running prior to installation of the new computer. However, this is seldom practical. If we refer to the time schedule of Figure 5-4, we see that approximately seven months are scheduled for programming. For normal month-to-month programming needs, the programming staff of XYZ was considered adequate. However, the task of bringing in a new computer and all associated programming systems is monumental in size and one requiring several person-years of programming effort. One commonly used solution to this dilemma is the use of outside assistance; the approach to XYZ involved the following:

- The purchase from a software company of a database management system for the business data processing needs. Applications programs for payroll processing and accounts payable and receivable to be prepared by the software company through the coordination of the XYZ programming staff.
- Obtaining contract programming services to prepare a job analysis and scheduling program. This system was developed and used with three other construction companies that had the same need.
- Reprogramming by the engineering staff, assisted by one of the programmers of several basic programs used by the engineering department.

The notion of adapting prewritten software can often pay huge dividends. In many cases, the cost of "reinventing the wheel" is far more expensive (and often impractical) than simply purchasing from someone who has already completed the job. A wide variety of excellent applications packages are available from a myriad of software vendors. Similarly, the use of contract programming services can also fill an important need. Many software-oriented companies will provide contract programming in a variety of ways ranging from "a programmer by the day, week, or month" to contracting at a fixed price for systems analysis and programming a predefined application.

With the combined effort of service companies and their own programming staff, XYZ devoted the 7½-month period of January into August (Figure 5-4) for the initial programming activities. Since XYZ owned no computer, the computer manufacturer had agreed to provide XYZ extensive test time on a computer with a configuration similar to that of the one ordered by XYZ. Thus it was possible to carry on programming, debugging, and testing operations prior to installation of the new computer. By August, all of the scheduled programs were reasonably ready for operation, although some compromises were necessary due to the tight time schedule.

EXERCISE

5.9 What is "test time," and what is its importance in a system conversion?

INSTALLATION AND TESTING

Installing a computing system is somewhat more complex than installing a television, which merely requires plugging it in. Actually, the installation process must begin with site preparation months before actual delivery. It is the responsibility of the vendor to advise the customer of the power and air-conditioning requirements and other environmental conditions. From information such as this, necessary electrical circuits and air conditioning can be planned and installed. Site preparation always takes longer than expected and should not be ignored until the last minute. There is nothing quite as embarrassing and frustrating as no place to plug in a newly arrived computer. If teleprocessing is to be involved, then delivery of equipment from other vendors must be carefully coordinated. Even the simple matter of telephone lines requires planning ahead, since installation of special telephone circuits can require up to a month.

Prior to delivery of the computer, the customer will have supplied the vendor with a room configuration plan. With delivery of the hardware, the vendor can proceed to install the system. Since most computer systems are delivered as several components (with the exception of small units) a considerable amount of interconnection and testing is usually necessary. When all connections have been complete, the service engineer will run special diagnostic routines to ensure that all connections have been properly made and that all components are functioning properly. At this point, a vendor's systems specialist will generate an operating system (this process is called a *sys-gen*) which is tailored to the particular installation. The entire process of installation through generation will require a week or more on a small system. In many cases, the customer will require that the benchmark programs or other typical workload conditions be run prior to acceptance of the computer. In some cases, formal acceptance (and thus payment) are postponed until the computer has operated in a normal environment for a set period of time (often 30 days) with a failure rate and downtime not to exceed precisely defined limits.

If everything has gone according to plan, the applications programs should be ready to be put on the new computer when control is passed from the vendor to the customer. This begins the long and arduous task of fully integrating the computer into the overall workings of the company.

The important stages of a computer system life cycle are summarized in the amusing poem on the opposite page.

In Retrospect

The life cycle of a business system involves the following important steps.

- feasibility study
- detailed study and analysis
- development
- installation
- operation

THE INFORMATION SYSTEM*
Marilyn Driscoll

[Canto the first: Proposal]
"An information system," said the president, J. B.,
"Is what this company sorely needs, or so it seems to me:
An automated, integrated system that embraces
All the proper people, in all the proper places,
So that the proper people, by communications linked,
Can manage by exception, instead of by instinct."

[Canto the second: Feasibility study]
They called in the consultants then, to see what they
    could see.
And to tell them how to optimize their use of EDP.
The consultants studied hard and long (their fee for this
    was sizable)
And concluded that an information system was quite fea-
    sible.
"Such a system," they reported. "will not only give you
    speed.
It will give you whole new kinds of information that you
    need."

[Canto the third: Installation]
So an information system was developed and installed
And all the proper people were properly enthralled.
They thought of all the many kinds of facts it could
    transmit
And predicted higher profits would indeed result from it;
They agreed the information that it would communicate
Would never be too little, and would never be too late.

[Canto the last: Output]
Yet when the system went on line, there was no great
    hurrah.
For it soon became apparent that it had one fatal flaw:
Though the system functioned perfectly, it couldn't quite atone
For the information it revealed—which was better left un-
    known.

*Marilyn Driscoll, from The Arthur Young Journal, copyright 1968
 by Arthur Young & Company.

Careful attention to each of these steps is important to installing an efficient, well-conceived system.

During the feasibility study, problems are identified (rather than solutions), and information is gathered to determine whether or not to continue.

Once the "proceed" decision has been made, attention must be focused on a detailed study and analysis. At this time, decisions are made regarding data handling procedures, personnel needs, and hardware and software required to do the job. At this time solutions to problems identified during the feasibility study are worked out.

As the detailed study progresses, system and program development can begin. Once the general system design is set forth, work can begin on detailed components. This includes activities such as definition of reports to be generated, processing needs, and file methods to be used.

When the basic complement of programs is ready, the system is installed. Frequently a new computer system will be operated in parallel with the old one as components of the software system are brought online. At some point, full operation is transferred to the new system which is then considered operational.

However, upon completion of installation, system development and implementation does not simply end. To the contrary, the needs of a modern business continually both change and grow. If the data processing system is to serve the business, it must change and grow also.

ANSWERS TO PRECEDING EXERCISES

5.1 Cost. If a relatively low level of service is required, then a service bureau will probably be most economical. However, as data processing needs increase, it becomes more economical at some point to provide the needed capabilities in-house.

5.2 A carefully selected committee can serve a valuable function in improving data processing services. Through the committee, each user can explain his needs and gain an understanding of and appreciation for those of other users. However, care must be taken to avoid petty arguing within the committee, thus reducing it to a "debating society." Furthermore, the committee's role must be recognized as advisory, with final decisions made by the data processing director or company president.

5.3 a. Is the required input data available? b. Will the output be used? c. Is it economical? d. Is it practical?

5.4 The process of ordering a new computer and performing a conversion cannot be handled in the same manner as buying a new car. Feasibility studies, often requiring several weeks of effort, should be made even before a computer selection, system design, program conversion and preparation, and system installation and testing will require from 12 to 30 months, depending upon the system's complexity.

5.5 The three commonly used means for financing computers are: renting from the manufacturer, leasing from a third-party leasing company, and purchase (including lease-purchase). For advantages of each, see descriptions preceding this exercise.

5.6 The cost of the computer itself would be increased by $29,000 per year, but we must recall that computer costs generally average about 30–50 percent of the total data processing costs. Thus, to fully utilize the new system, some increase in personnel and other costs should be anticipated.
pated.

5.7 In most installations, the data processing operation serves a wide variety of users and affects virtually all areas of a business. Thus, it is generally unrealistic to have the department administered by one of the users, as was the case at XYZ. It is necessary that top-level direction and coordination be provided for the data processing operation to serve all users in the best way. As we recall, the engineering manager complained that his work was not adequately handled. It is this situation which the president wished to avoid.

5.8 Although members of the clerical staff are not directly involved in the data processing operation, they form an integral and important portion of the overall data gathering, processing, and using network. As such, they can more efficiently perform their functions within the company if they have a basic knowledge of the data processing system. Furthermore, employees are less prone to feel "threatened" by the computer if they are aware of how it is to be used.

5.9 When a computer is ordered, the manufacturer usually provides "test time" on a comparable computer system which the user can utilize to prepare and test programs for conversion to the new system. Thus, a major portion of the programming conversion and testing can take place prior to delivery of the new computer.

ADDITIONAL EXERCISES

5.10 Name and describe the stages of the life cycle of a data processing system.

5.11 What is a data processing service bureau?

5.12 Why is it important to give all employees some orientation regarding the implications of a new computer system?

5.13 What is a bid specification and what is its purpose?

5.14 When a new computer system is installed, there is often a need for new software or reprogramming old software. Describe three methods for handling this.

5.15 **Matching**   Items a, b, and c are three methods for financing computers and 1, through 7 are significant points relating to financing. Match each method to the description which best fits.

      a. rent from manufacturer
      b. lease
      c. purchase

  1. Requires large capital outlay
  2. Responsibility for equipment maintenance rests with manufacturer
  3. More expensive than other methods over a long time period
  4. Can show significant savings over a long time period as compared to other methods
  5. Requires no capital outlay and provides significant cost saving over a period of two or more years
  6. Usually involves a penalty if contract is terminated early

Glossary of Terms

Following each term below is a page number to which the reader can refer.

Acoustic coupler   113
A communications device which allows an ordinary telephone to be used with a computer device for data transmission.

ANSI   78
An acronym for American National Standards Institute, an organization that establishes standards for U.S. business and industry.

Arithmetic unit   27
The unit of a computing system that contains the circuits that perform arithmetic operations. It is one of the components of the central processing unit (CPU) of the computer.

ASCII   33
An acronym for American Standard Code for Information Interchange, one of two widely used methods for coding data.

Assemble   81
To convert or translate a computer program from a symbolic language to a machine language.

Assembler   81
A computer program which performs the task of assembling a symbolic program to machine language.

Auxiliary storage   38
A storage that supplements the main storage of a computer. Magnetic disk and tape are commonly encountered auxiliary storage media.

Background processing   106
The automatic execution of lower priority computer programs when higher priority programs are not using the system resources. Contrast with foreground processing.

Backup file   128

A copy of a file that is set aside for reference in case the original file is destroyed.

Basic   109

Beginner's All-purpose Symbolic Instruction Code, a widely used interactive programming language.

Batch processing   41

A technique in which information items to be processed are collected and processed in groups (batches) for efficient operation. Magnetic-tape processing usually involves batching.

BCD   33

See Binary-coded decimal notation.

Binary   32

Pertaining to a characteristic or property involving a choice or condition in which there are two possibilities. Pertains specifically to the number representation system with a base of 2, using the digits 0 and 1.

Binary-coded decimal notation (BCD)   33

Positional notation in which the individual decimal digits expressing a number in decimal notation are each represented by a binary numeral; for example, the number 23 is represented by 0010 0011 in the 8, 4, 2, 1 type of binary-coded decimal notation.

Binary digit   33

In binary notation, either of the digits 0 and 1.

Bit   33

A binary digit.

Bubble memory   37

An internal memory device capable of storing large quantitites of information in a small space.

Bug   85

A mistake or malfunction in a program or a computer system.

Byte   33

A sequence of adjacent binary digits operated upon as a unit and usually shorter than a computer word. As used with the IBM 360/370, a byte consists of 8 bits.

Central processing unit (CPU)   26
A unit of a computer that includes the main storage and the circuits controlling interpretation and execution of instructions.

Cobol (Common Business Oriented Language)   79
A business data processing language.

COM (Computer Output Microfilm)   57
An output technique by which computer/output is recorded on microfilm.

Compile   81
To convert or translate a program from a procedure- or problem-oriented language (for example, Fortran, Cobol, or RPG) to an absolute or machine language form.

Compiler   81
A computer program that performs the compiling operation.

Conversational computing   109
See Interactive computing.

CPU   26
See Central processing unit.

CRT (cathode-ray tube)   59
In the computing field, associated with a terminal which displays output on a TV-type screen.

Data   3
A representation of facts or concepts in a formalized manner suitable for communication, interpretation, or processing by humans or by automatic means.

Data communication   111
The transmission over the telephone network of computer data, without change or processing.

Database   119
A collection of data files integrated and organized into a single comprehensive file system. The data is arranged to minimize duplication and to provide convenient access to information within that system to satisfy a wide variety of user needs.

Database management system (DBMS)　119
The software used for the management and retrieval of the data stored in a database.

Data rate　41
The speed at which data is transmitted from one device to another.

Debug　85
To detect, locate, and remove mistakes from a program or malfunctions from a computer.

Density　41
The number of useful storage positions per unit of length or area; for example, a common recording density for magnetic tape is 800 frames per inch of tape.

Detail file　12
See Transaction file.

Diagnostic　82
A statement printed by an assembler or compiler indicating errors detected in the source program.

Direct access　43
Pertaining to a storage device in which the time required to obtain data is independent of the location of the data. Synonymous with random access.

Disk　43
See Magnetic disk.

Diskette　66
A thin, flexible magnetic disk storage device.

Distributed data processing　122
The decentralization of a computer system through the use of multiple computers interconnected by a communications network.

Document　2
A data record which is intended for human use, such as a report sheet, a book; any record that has permanence and that can be read by humans or by machine.

Documentation　84
The process of preparing descriptions concerning the preparation, use, and general description of a computer program, procedure, or system.

EBCDIC   33
An 8-bit code used for data representation in the IBM 360/370 and several other commonly used computers.

Electronic funds transfer (EFT)   126
A computer network which facilitates the movement of funds by electronic means.

Field   8
In a record, a specified area used for a particular category of data; for example, a group positions used to represent a student file number.

File   9
A collection of related records treated as a unit. For example, the entire set of student master data records make up the Student Master File.

Flowchart   93
A graphical representation for the definition, analysis, or solution of a problem, in which symbols are used to represent operations, data, flow, equipment, and so on.

Flowchart symbol   94
A symbol used to represent operations, data, flow, or equipment on a flowchart.

Flowline   94
On a flowchart, a line representing a connecting path between flowchart symbols.

Foreground processing   107
Automatic execution of the computer programs that have been designed to preempt the use of the computing facilities. Contrast with background processing.

Format
The arrangement of data in a record.

Fortran (FORmula TRANslating system)   78
A language primarily used to express computer programs by arithmetic formulas.

Hard copy   59
Printed output from a computer device (as opposed to soft copy).

High-level language   77
A programming language whose structure is application oriented and is independent of the structure of the computer; for example, Fortran and Cobol.

Hollerith   49
Pertaining to a particular type of code or punched card utilizing 12 rows per column and usually 80 columns per card.

Indexed file   117
A file that includes an index directory to facilitate random processing.

Input   26
The source data entered into a data processing system.

Input area
An area of storage reserved for input.

Input device   46
A device used to bring information into a computer or other data processing devices; for instance, the card reader.

Input/output (I/O)   26
Pertaining to either input or output, or both.

Integrated circuit   36
Refers to miniaturization of electronic circuits such that thousands of components are formed on a small chip of silicon.

Interactive computing   109
A programming method by which a programmer can "converse" with a computer through a typewriterlike terminal.

Interblock gap   41
See Interrecord gap.

Internal storage   38
Addressable storage directly controlled by the central processing unit of a digital computer.

Interrecord gap   41
A blank space between records (blocks) on a magnetic tape; same as interblock gap.

I/O   26
See Input/output.

Job   107
A specified group of tasks prescribed as a unit of work for a computer.

K   34
When referring to storage capacity, 2 to the 10th power; 1024 in decimal notation.

Key   114
A field within a data record to identify the record or to control its use.

Library   74
A collection of files or programs.

Library routine   74
A proven routine that is maintained in a program library.

Line printer   56
A device that prints all characters of a line as a unit.

Loop   95
A sequence of instructions that is executed repeatedly until a terminal condition occurs.

Machine language   75
A language that is used directly by a machine, thus requiring no translation.

Macro instruction
An instruction in a source language that is equivalent to a specified sequence of machine instructions.

Magnetic core   36
A small donut-shaped piece of magnetic material capable of storing one binary digit.

Magnetic disk   43
A flat, circular plate with a magnetic surface on which data can be stored by magnetization of portions of the flat surface.

Magnetic tape   40
A tape with a magnetic surface on which data can be stored by magnetization of portions of the surface.

Management Information System (MIS)   120
An all-inclusive system designed to provide instant information to all levels of management for effective decision making.

Mass storage device   43
A device having a large storage capacity; for example, magnetic disk, magnetic drum.

Master file   8, 41
A file that is either relatively permanent or that is treated as an authority in a particular job, for instance, the employee master file. Contrast with transaction file.

Master-detail processing   41
The periodic processing of records in a transaction (detail) file against corresponding records in a master file to bring the master file information up to date.

Memory   32
Some as storage.

Merge   11
To combine items from two or more similarly ordered sets into one set that is arranged in the same order.

Microprocessor   64
A microminiature version of a computer central processing unit etched into a single integrated-circuit chip.

Microcomputer   64
A small computer (often little larger than a typewriter) which, in its basic form, commonly sells for $2000 or less.

Microfilm   57
See COM.

Microsecond
One millionth (0.000001 or 10^{-6}) of a second.

Millisecond   45
One thousandth (0.001 or 10^{-3}) of a second; commonly abbreviated ms or msec.

Minicomputer   62
A relatively small size computer which exhibits most of the features of a large-scale system but on a limited basis. Generally the cost for a basic system is under $100,000.

MIS   120
See Management information system.

Modem   112
A device that allows computer information to be transmitted over communications circuits.

Monitor   74
See Supervisor.

Multiprogramming   106
Pertaining to the concurrent execution of two or more programs by a computer.

Nanosecond
One billionth (0.000000001 or 10^{-9}) of a second; commonly abbreviated ns or nsec.

Network   126
In data processing, usually refers to an arrangement of two or more computers interconnected by a communication system.

Object program   82
A fully compiled or assembled program that is ready to be loaded into the computer.

Offline storage   14
Storage not under control of the central processing unit.

Online   46
Pertaining to equipment or devices under control of the central processing unit. Also pertaining to a user's ability to interact with the computer.

Online storage   14
Storage under control of the central processing unit. Usually pertains to mass storage devices such as magnetic disk.

Operating system   74
Software that controls the execution of computer programs and that may provide scheduling, data management, and related services.

Output   2
The finished results of processing by a system.

Overhead   107
"Nonproductive" time required by the operating system in managing the computer resources.

Parity check   33
A check that tests whether the number of 1s (or 0s) in an array of binary digits is odd or even.

Pascal   93
A high-level structured programming language.

Password   131
A code or name by which a user gains access to a timesharing computer.

Problem-oriented language   78
A programming language designed for the convenient expression of a given class of problems; for example, RPG.

Procedure-oriented language   78
A programming language designed for the convenient expression of procedures used in the solution of a wide class of problems; for example, Fortran and Cobol.

Pseudocode   96
An "English" version of actual programming statements used as an aid in program preparation.

Queue   107
An ordered "waiting line" of tasks or jobs to be handled by a computer.

RAM (Random Access Memory)   36
Computer memory which is capable of direct access of stored data.

Random access   43
Same as direct access.

Random processing   46
Processing in which records of a file are processed in random sequence (contrast with sequential processing).

Read-only memory   36
See ROM.

Realtime   14
Pertaining to the performance of a computation during the actual time that the related physical process takes place, so that results of the computation can be used in guiding the physical process.

Record   8
A collection of related fields of data, treated as a unit; for example, the customer master-balance record. A complete set of such records forms a file.

Remote job entry   122
See RJE.

Response time   43
With an online system, the time delay between a request to the computer for information and the return of that information from the computer.

RJE (Remote Job Entry)   122
Submission of batch processing jobs through an input device which has access to a computer through a communication system.

ROM (Read-Only Memory)   36
Prewritten computer memory whose values cannot be changed.

Semiconductor   36
A material that can be made to conduct or not conduct electricity. Semiconductors form the basis of microminiature computer technology.

Sequential   40
Pertaining to the occurrence of events in time sequence (one after the other), with little or no overlap of events.

Sequential processing   40
Processing in which records are processed beginning with the first and continuing through the last (records processed sequentially).

Serial   56
Pertaining to the sequential or consecutive occurrence of two or more related activities in a single device.

Serial access   40
Pertaining to the process of obtaining data from or placing data into storage, where the access time is dependent upon the location of the data most recently obtained or placed in storage. Magnetic tape is a typical serial access medium.

Soft copy   59
Computer output which is displayed on the screen of a terminal and provides no permanent copy (as opposed to hard copy).

Software   74
A set of computer programs, procedures, and possibly associated documentation concerned with the operation of a data processing system; for example, compilers, library routines, manuals, circuit diagrams. Contrast with hardware.

Sort   11
To arrange records into a predetermined sequence.

Source document
The original document (usually manually prepared) from which information is entered into a system.

Source language   82
The language from which a statement is translated; for example, assembly language or Cobol.

Source program   82
A computer program written in a source language such as assembly language or Cobol. Contrasts with object program.

Storage   26
Pertaining to a device into which data can be entered, in which it can be held, and from which it can be retrieved at a later time; loosely, any device that can store data. Synonymous with memory.

Stored program computer   26
A computer controlled by internally stored instructions which can store, and in some cases alter, instructions as though they were data and which can subsequently execute these instructions.

Structured programming   93
An organized approach to programming involving the use of three basic control structures. Characterized by minimizing or eliminating the need for branching instructions.

Summarize   11
To condense a set of data into a more concise form through simple arithmetic operations.

Supervisor   74
A program, resident in the computer, which maintains overall control of the computer.

System   6
A collection of methods, procedures, or techniques united by regulated

interaction to form an organized whole. An organized collection of people, machines, and/or methods required to accomplish a set of specific functions.

Telecommunications   111
Pertaining to the transmission of data over long distances through telephone facilities.

Terminal   59
A device which allows a user to communicate directly with a computer.

Throughout   100
The total amount of useful processing carried out by a data processing system in a given time; effectively, an indication of the system efficiency.

Timeshare   109
The use of a device for two or more interleaved purposes; for example, the use of one computer by two or more users through terminals.

Top-down design   88
An approach to solving large programming problems by breaking the problem into smaller components which in turn are broken into still smaller components. The end result is a series of related modules, each of a manageable size.

Transaction file   8
A file containing relatively transient data to be processed in combination with a master file. For example, in a payroll application a transaction file indicating hours worked might be processed with a master file containing employee name and rate of pay. Synonymous with detail file.

Turnkey system   67
A computer system which is furnished complete with all hardware, applications software and documentation in a "ready to use" form for the purchaser.

Universal Product Code (UPC)   13
A standardized code adopted by the grocery industry for use with computerized check out systems.

Index